Perceptions of quality in higher education, rankings and benchmarking

Leif M. Hokstad and Fabio Bento (Eds.)

Perceptions of quality in higher education, rankings and benchmarking

Proceedings of Uniqual 2009
The 6th International Conference on
Universities Quality

ᘎtapir academic press

© Tapir Academic Press, Trondheim 2011

ISBN 978-82-519-2714-7

This publication may not be reproduced, stored in a retrieval system or transmitted in any form or by any means; electronic, electrostatic, magnetic tape, mechanical, photocopying, recording or otherwise, without permission.

Layout: Type-it AS, Trondheim
Cover Layout: Mari Røstvold, Tapir Academic Press
Printed and binded by: AIT Oslo AS

This book has been published with funding from Norwegian University of Science and Technology (NTNU).

Tapir Academic Press publishes textbooks and academic literature for universities and university colleges, as well as for vocational and professional education. We also publish high quality literature of a more general nature. Our main product lines are:

- *Textbooks for higher education*
- *Research and reference literature*
- *Non-fiction*

We only use environmentally certified printing houses.

Tapir Academic Press
NO–7005 Trondheim, Norway
Tel.: + 47 73 59 32 10
Email: post@tapirforlag.no
www.tapirforlag.no

Publishing Editor: may.solberg@tapirforlag.no

Preface

The sixth International Conference on Universities' Quality Development Under Globalisation, UNIQUAL, was organised at the Norwegian University of Science and Technology (NTNU) from July 14 to 16, 2009. The present publication contains the diverse contributions made to the conference by colleagues from nine countries in three different continents.

As editors of the report we would like to thank our department head Per Ramberg and our section coordinator Marte Johansen for all their support and conscious advice throughout the preparation process of this conference. We also wish to express our gratitude to Kirsti Ramberg and Ole Kristen Solbjørg from NTNU's Education and Quality of Learning Unit for taking part in all aspects of the planning and implementation of the conference in a friendly and imaginative manner. Our section's administration officer Grethe Aune deserves thanks for her professional and attentive role in the planning of the conference.

We would also like to thank our international colleagues for attending the conference in Trondheim, some of whom travelled long distances to enthusiastically share their research interests with us and bring new perspectives. Special thanks go to colleagues from Kaunas University of Technology and Xiamen University for such an enriching academic cooperation.

Trondheim, October 2010
Fabio Bento   Leif Martin Hokstad

Contents

Preface	5
Opening Speech UNIQUAL 2009	11
Julie Feilberg	
Introduction: an international perspective to quality in higher education	15
Fabio Bento and Leif Martin Hokstad	
On the Phenomenon of Competition Between Two Rival Universities in the University Ranking Era	23
Liu Haifeng	
Fostering awareness and self-assessment to achieve intended learning outcomes: A case study	31
Vidar Gynnild	
Multiple Scholarship Fostered Staff Development Toward Enhancing University Quality	51
Fan Yihong	
Implementation of an International Master's Degree Programme in Educational Leadership in a Learning Environment of Care and Challenge	69
Lea Sandholm	
The Relativity of Academic Assessments: How to compare apples with oranges	81
Boaz Shulruf	
Quality in university teaching: Learners' perceptions in foreign language education	95
Janete Zygmantas	

Contents

What makes the high-quality research experience of research postgraduates? Implications from Mainland Chinese research students' experiences at the University of Hong Kong 113
Zeng Min

On the "Evaluation of undergraduate teaching work" in Chinese universities 127
Xie Surong

From Principles to Practice – or vice versa? The Value of Studying Consensus about Scholarship 137
Marit Allern & Lillian Vederhus

Impacts of Rankings on Internationalization of Higher Education Institutions in Hong Kong 147
Kwang Heung Lam

Quality development through the graduates' perceptions and experiences 173
Ana Paula Cabral

What is in between from teacher-centred to student-centred teaching? A comparison of Western European and Chinese research-intensive university teachers' beliefs 187
Wu Wei

Participants

Names and affiliations (2009)

Julie Feilberg
Pro-Rector for Education
Norwegian University of Science and Technology

Fabio Bento and Leif Martin Hokstad
Programme for Teacher Education
Norwegian University of Science and Technology

Liu Haifeng
Institute of Education
Xiamen University

Vidar Gynnild
Programme for Teacher Education
Norwegian University of Science and Technology

Fan Yihong
Institute of Education
Xiamen University

Lea Sandholm
Institute of Educational Leadership
University of Jyväskylä

Boaz Shulruf
Faculty of Medical and Health Sciences
University of Auckland

Janete Zygmantas
Department of Educalogy
Vilnius University

Zeng Min
Centre for Enhancement of Teaching and Learning
University of Hong Kong

Xie Surong
Institute of Education
Xiamen University

Marit Allern and Lillian Vederhus
Department of Education – Department of Psychology
University of Tromsø

Lam Kwan Heung Queenie
International Center for Higher Education Research, Kassel, Germany

Ana Paula Cabral
Sciences of Education Department
University of Aveiro

Wu Wei
Institute of Education
Xiamen University,
Graduate School of Teaching
Leiden University

Opening Speech UNIQUAL 2009

Julie Feilberg

Dear eminent guests,

It is a great pleasure to welcome you to Trondheim, the Norwegian University of Science and Technology (NTNU as we call it), and of course to UNIQUAL 2009.

I am the Prorector of this university with special responsibility for education and quality of learning. Thus, the theme of this conference is something very dear to my professional heart.

The role of universities in the knowledge system is undergoing important changes, and universities are now dependent and will become even more dependent upon their reputation understood and perceived quality, influence and trustworthiness. In this context, it is necessary to rethink the way that academicians in universities evaluate our activities and the quality of such activities.

Some of you possibly consider *quality* to be a worn-out buzzword or a term used only in speeches without being clearly defined. Quality could be likened to a wet bar of soap that slips between our fingers when we attempt to grasp it. And this idea of quality is partly true. It *is* difficult to define quality in education and teaching. A number of questions linked to such terms soon emerge: What is quality education composed of? This question assumes that it has a clearly definable size.

Is there any worldwide consensus on what quality education is? How can we identify it? Or quantify it, if this is at all possible. How can we measure quality in a way that the measuring tools both capture and can help to promote quality?

What, for example, is the most important aspect of student evaluation if the object of the exercise is to describe and increase quality, not just to measure how students are or find their expectations. And last, but not least, what does the creation of quality education involve?

NTNU's current strategy, international ranking systems and the problems with rankings:

Our vision is that by 2020 NTNU should be internationally recognised as an outstanding university. By means of generally accepted criteria and evaluation systems, NTNU has set the following goals for 2020:

- To be among the international leaders in selected strong focus areas
- To be among the ten leading technological and scientific universities in Europe
- To be among the top 1 per cent of comprehensive universities in the world

The process of developing NTNU's strategy has been important in order to define the distinct profile and identity of NTNU both internally and externally. However, the process has also revealed certain weaknesses of operationalising societal responsibility and academic ambitions in terms of ranking.

Two facts are clear with regard to rankings. First, existing international rankings place NTNU within a global context. We are competing in the global arena for students, staff and funding. Second, ranking systems are here to stay because global university rankings have an increasingly strong impact on student and staff recruitment, on public opinion, and on important stakeholders. We therefore have to take them seriously into consideration.

However, we should also acknowledge the fact that university ranking systems must be developed further, and their quality should be improved.

The complexity of universities, their institutional organisation and their role requires more sophisticated instruments of assessment than those currently provided by existing university rankings. For this reason, NTNU has put a great deal of effort into a complementary approach, the European Classification System, which has the potential to enhance the value of rankings if it is employed before rankings are determined.

Although there have been some improvements in quality of the various ranking systems, few resources seem to be invested in the quality assurance of the data these rankings are based on. We have discovered inconsistencies and imprecise definitions in the various reports from ranking compilers, decreasing the rankings' reliability. Some rankings change their indicators from year to year, making the ranking less suited for benchmarking a university's performance over a period of time. The leading league tables also seem to have a bias in favour of the natural sciences, technology and medicine and for publications in English. Furthermore, some give a lot of weight to an institution's reputation, while the same institution's contribution to society is given little or no weight at all.

Providing an opportunity to be compared with other universities

There is an ongoing debate concerning whether competition between universities enhances academic quality or is instead a threat to academic endeavour, to creativity and boldness in developing universities as institutions. I will not go into this debate here, because both views can be used as arguments for establishing means of comparing universities. The household word for this is *benchmarking*. There are plenty of benchmarking tools, but most are based on commercial thinking and are not best suited to universities. We want to measure quality because we want to improve our academic performance. For this we need relevant instruments. We need to cooperate to establish standards that fit the need to classify institutions prior to any measurement of academic quality. We need relevant standards that will be acceptable to the academic community. This is an important consideration as acceptance from academic staff is vital to the success of the benchmarking.

Challenges and central issues

A conference such as UNIQUAL 2009 is both important and timely as it enables us to address the above issues in an international context. It is generally acknowledged that as there are numerous aspects of quality in education and teaching they are difficult terms to pin down. A second challenge is addressing the issue of university rankings.

I am confident that during the conference we will identify the challenges and issues where we can work together towards finding solutions. We can use this opportunity to learn from each other and pool our collective experience and thoughts on these issues.

There is no single answer to a multi-faceted issue such as quality education. It is impossible to address everything at once. However, UNIQUAL 2009 has compiled a programme that will address the challenges I have mentioned. It will spark discussion and generate reflective thought. By bringing voices form around the world together, UNIQUAL 2009 is a unique opportunity for us all.

I close as I began by welcoming all our eminent guests to NTNU, and I declare UNIQUAL 2009 open. Thank you very much for your attention.

Introduction: an international perspective to quality in higher education

Fabio Bento and Leif Martin Hokstad

UNIQUAL 2009 was the sixth event of a series of international conferences on university quality development organized by the Norwegian University of Science and Technology (NTNU), Kaunas University of Technology (KTU), and Xiamen University. The cooperation among higher education researchers in these universities was initiated in the early 2000s and derived from the intellectual interest in better understanding what was identified as common challenges facing higher education in the three countries. At that time, Norwegian higher education was undergoing a programme of system-level reforms that aimed at following international developments in higher education policy by restructuring the degree system, promoting internationalization and increasing commercialization of knowledge and, more important, by transforming universities' relation with the society and with the state.

Higher education policy reform then sought to provide institutions with greater autonomy from the state and to increase accountability to the stakeholders and to the society in general (KUF-NOU 2000). These reforms were known as the Quality Reform. However, the very concept of quality is a disputed one in higher education. As the number and interests of stakeholders have diversified, the concept of "quality" in higher education has become a contested matter with meanings linked to different streams of demands and to a variety of understandings of what the mission of higher education should be. But rather than being an exclusively Norwegian phenomenon, changing definitions of quality in education constitute a controversial topic that cannot be understood disassociated from relatively complex power struggles among national states, professors and the market (Morley, 2003). In this context of increasing competition among higher education institutions, university rankings and benchmarking have been presented as sets of ideas of what was regarded as indicators of quality and evidence of standards. Thus, our conference discussed perceptions of quality, university rankings and benchmarking with a special focus on teaching and learning in higher education institutions. We are proud to have received participants from various parts of the world who contributed to an extremely enriching academic environment that addressed questions such as the following:

- What are benchmarking procedures really measuring?
- What is the contribution of university rankings?
- In what respects do they differ, and what do they present in common?
- What do we understand by "quality teaching/learning", and what steps are to be taken to maintain high standards?
- What are good indicators of quality in higher education?
- Through an international comparative perspective, to what extent and how perceptions of quality differ worldwide?

Although quality has become a buzzword for higher education since the early 1980s, it would be a misconception to regard the search for quality as a new phenomenon. For centuries, quality assessment mechanisms have always been part of the university's existence in Europe (Neave 1994:116, Green 1994). What is new here is the difference between traditional quality control and new approaches to quality assessment. According to van Vught (1996:186), there is a whole chain of factors that explain the recent increase in attention to quality in higher education. The new feature here is that the "extrinsic values" of higher education have become more important since the 1980s. Such extrinsic values are related to services that higher education institutions are expected to provide to the society. The extrinsic values can be distinguished from the intrinsic values of higher education, which are found in the ideals of the search for truth and the pursuit of knowledge. Van Vught (1996) lists the following factors that led to the rise of the debate about quality in higher education:

- *Increase in public expenditure in general*: questions have been raised about the priority of higher education within the list of other socially desirable activities. Financial constraints in many countries have led to the relative quality of the activities that are being financed by public means.
- *Expansion of the Western European higher education system*: the rapid growth of the student-body has intensified the societal discussions about the amount and direction of public expenditure in higher education.
- *Increased openness*: it is related not only to improved communication facilities, both nationally and internationally, but also to the general concern for accountability in various sectors.
- *Increased international mobility of students, teachers and researchers:* linked with the internationalization of the European labour market, increased mobility led

to a growing need to understand the equivalence of qualifications, standards and credits in the various European higher education systems and thus to more attention towards quality assessment systems.

Universities are extremely complex organizations, each one with its own special characteristics and programmes, strengths and weaknesses. No single measure could ever accurately reflect the quality or character of a university, where hundreds of professors and lecturers teach a broad array of courses across disciplines as varied as medicine, law, engineering and music, where students come from diverse backgrounds, and where research and outreach may have different purposes and be targeted to answer different demands. Thus, success in higher education is hard to define and even more difficult to measure. However, the growth of the higher education sector was accompanied by the rise of an evaluation culture, which by claiming accountability, demanded evidence of quality and efficiency. This development together with an increasing competition for financial resources constituted the context in which the number of university rankings increased and in which they gained space in the media. More than ever, universities are referred to in TV and newspapers worldwide in relation to their positions in those rankings. Assumptions about quality in higher education which led to the choice of methodology in which different rankings are constructed are certainly linked with different perceptions of universities' role in society. Another topic of debate is the impact of these rankings in higher education institutions themselves. Our own university has demonstrated concern with international competitiveness as expressed on *NTNU's Strategic Plan* (NTNU 2007). According to this document, NTNU's main strategic goal is to be internationally known as a world-class university by consolidating a position among the 1 per cent top universities in the world and among the top ten technological universities in Europe by 2020. At the time when this chapter was being written, the four main higher education institutions in Norway (NTNU, the University of Oslo, the University of Bergen and the University of Tromsø) received with enthusiasm the results of the 2008 edition of *The Times Higher Education Supplement World University Ranking (THES)*, which is the most known comparison of indicators of quality among higher education institutions worldwide. However, the *THES* ranking is not free from controversies as its methodology has been strongly criticized in the following terms:

* The ranking methodology is dominated by a peer review survey, where a sample of academics are asked for their opinion on the quality of other universities. Such criterion seems to be based on the assumption that there is frequently good communication among researchers worldwide and that they know where quality research is being conducted. However, there is no evidence that this is always the case.
* The methodology is based on a "weight and add" approach – scores in individual categories are multiplied by the weight for that category and added up to give a total score. The choice of weights is essentially arbitrary.

> * A comparison of the 2007 and 2008 rankings shows that some institutions went up or down about seventy positions. Large research-intense universities are complex and multifaceted institutions where changes usually happen at a slow pace. Therefore, it is not likely that the "quality" of a university would change so much in a period of just one year. Significant contradictions between the two rankings might indicate inaccuracies regarding the data used.

However, more than methodological criticism, there are conflicting interpretations of the role of university rankings and what contribution these might bring to the sector. Stensaker and Kehm (2009) identify five different interpretations of university rankings in terms of potential and threats.

Rankings as Market Regulation: those interpreting university rankings argue that national states do not have anymore a key role as regulator of higher education, and governance in the sector has assumed a hybrid shape. The role of rankings here is that of an *instrument of regulation* in a global market.

Rankings as Globalization: although most rankings focus on institutions in one country, international rankings are the ones that receive more attention. According to this perspective, the rankings play a role in *providing consumer information* to buyers and sellers of higher education services worldwide.

Rankings as the Rise of the Audit Society: in this perspective, rankings are regarded as *accountability mechanisms* developed due to the perception that previous mechanisms were insufficient in providing satisfactory information to external stakeholders. This perspective regards that rankings play an important democratic role as a transparent source of information.

Rankings as Institutional Identity Creation: this perspective shifts the level of analysis from a macro to the institutional level. It assumes that ranking positions help to determine the prestige of an institution in a hierarchy. From this perspective, rankings play the role of a *fashion arena* through which each university compares itself with others and negotiates its own identity.

Rankings as a Symptom of the Knowledge Society: the focus here is on universities' role as providers of new ideas and theories relevant to different intentions and on qualitative changes in the production and dissemination of knowledge. Innovation is a key concept here. In this perspective, university rankings have the function of *structuring devices of knowledge*.

Federkeil (2009) raises an interesting argument regarding the weight of reputation in relation to indicators of performance in university rankings. Indicators of reputation at present are used in most rankings although varying in weight and type of reputation (among scholars and/or among employers). For example, in the *THES* Ranking, reputation among scholars and among employers constitutes 50 per cent of the university's total score. Federkeil uses Luhman's (1992, p. 7) conceptualization of reputation as a "selective code" in the dynamics of a social system. In complex systems where an overflow of information might constitute a challenge, symbols like reputation simplify or reduce the complexity of information. However, if we understand reputation as a general estimation or the attribution of a general characteristic of a person or an institution, then reputation cannot be regarded as an indicator of performance. In this sense, reputation plays more the role of social capital that can be transformed in economic capital than of an indicator of performance (Federkeil 2009, p. 32). It creates a paradoxical situation where reputation becomes both one of the sources of orientation on which rankings are based and at the same time rankings might influence reputational hierarchies.

Also at the time when UNIQUAL 2009 was being planned, NTNU was witnessing an internal discussion regarding benchmarking and indicators of quality of its own learning environment. This internal debate was motivated by the recognition that although NTNU's main strategic documents emphasized the necessity to compete with other institutions, there was no agreement regarding what sort of indicators would be taken into account in order to assess the quality of our own activities. This discussion that involved the participation of some members of the Section for Higher Education certainly inspired the formulation of the theme of our conference. The definition of benchmarking presented by Jackson and Lund (2000, p. 2) is helpful here: "benchmarking is, first and foremost, a learning process structured so as to enable those engaging in the process to compare their services/activities/products in order to identify their comparative strengths and weaknesses as a basis for self-improvement and/or self-regulation". Although benchmarking in higher education has encountered resistance based on arguments emphasising the danger of standardization of practices, which would hinder innovation and change, most higher education systems and institutions have sought to establish benchmarking mechanisms. In the particular case of teaching and leaning in higher education, it is interesting to follow the implementation of the European Qualification Framework (EQF). The 2006 EQF recommendation defines the framework as "an instrument for the classification of qualifications according to a set of criteria for specified levels of learning achieved. It aims at integration and coordination of national qualifications subsystems and the improvement of transparency, access, progression and quality of qualification in relation to the labour market and civil society" (European Commission, 2006). This development cannot be understood disassociated from the shift towards the learning outcomes approach. EQF has been presented as an instrument for change in which the main expectation is that it will constitute a mechanism for different stakeholders as a common ground and a benchmarking for assessing student achievements and qualification levels (Bjørnåvold & Coles 2007).

All these developments shaped the formulation of the theme of our conference. In this report, we present contributions from different parts of the world, and the sharing of knowledge production has demonstrated once again that although the problems faced by different countries may differ in scope and proportion, there is a lot in common in terms of dilemmas and ideological tensions.

Keynote Speakers:

Liu Haifeng discusses how university rankings impact the competition between traditional rival institutions in the same country or even in the same city. He highlights that competition and cooperation have historically co-existed and that although international rankings might reinforce the latter in negative ways, they have a strong potential in creating a frame of reference that motivates improvement.

Vidar Gynild discusses a shift in the search for evidences of improvement in student learning in higher education from student evaluations of teachings towards student self-assessment. The article provides empirical evidence of the positive impact of self-assessment in learning and discusses how self-assessment skills may be developed. It suggests that there is a need to make students familiar with the philosophy of self-regulated learning.

Peer-reviewed articles:

In her paper ***Fan Yihong*** departs from a discussion of limitations of university rankings and benchmarking to discuss the concept of multiple scholarship and its contribution to the design of staff development programmes. It is argued that this holistic approach to professional development, which has influenced practices in Western universities, could pave the way to changes in staff development programmes in China. This perspective aims at overcoming the tension between teaching and research by focusing on the full scope of academic work.

Lea Sandholm describes an innovative master degree programme in educational leadership offered since 2007 by the University of Jyväskylä in Finland. The implementation of this programme reflects the long-term development of the Institute of Educational Leadership, which has been characterized by a shared cumulative leadership practice.

Based on quantitative data from large polytechnic institutions in New Zealand, ***Boaz Shulruf*** presents an alternative method to assess student achievements across programmes and institutions. This new method focuses on qualification rather than course completion. He suggests that the current practice of using linear models for entire populations of students marked by diversity presents several limitations. Thus, it is necessary to look at different student trajectories within and across different groups.

In her paper, ***Janete Zygmantas*** highlights the importance of analysing learners' perceptions from a critical perspective when assessing the quality of teaching and learning. Her study, which is based on the experience of students of Lithuanian as a foreign language, demonstrates that this theoretical and methodological approach can shed light on preliminary indicators of quality in learning and teaching processes.

Also discussing students' perceptions of quality, **Zeng Min** presents what thirty postgraduate mainland China students at the University of Hong Kong identified as major elements contributing to the quality of their research training. Factors such as good supervision, peer support, infrastructure and research environment were identified as decisive. She argues that surveys on student experience may be more effective means for quality assurance than league tables as these can provide administrators with information regarding learning processes.

Xie Surong discusses governmental efforts to evaluate teaching at the undergraduate level in the context of expansion of access to higher education in China. The implementation of external evaluation initiatives has been a controversial issue in Chinese higher education as misunderstanding and conflict between internal and external values emerge. The study presents different aspects of evaluation programmes and suggests further improvements.

Not peer reviewed:

Kwang Heung Lam's paper employs a qualitative research strategy including discourse and textual analysis to discuss the impact of university rankings in higher education in Hong Kong, in the context of the implementation of policies aiming at consolidating its position as a hub of higher education excellence in Asia. Here, university rankings have played a crucial role both as the objective and the means of internationalization strategies. This has posed different challenges and provided opportunities to both old and new institutions.

Ana Paula Cabral presents the case of a Portuguese private polytechnic higher education institution where the assessment of graduates' perceptions of quality highlighted the importance of fully integrating three aspects: defining and reviewing programmes in order to incorporate graduates' expertise; practical work during studies and strengthening ties with the outside world.

Wu Wei presents in her article an international comparison of university teachers' educational beliefs based on qualitative interviews. Her study contributes to the discussion regarding shifts in educational perspectives from a teaching- to a learning-centred paradigm. As a result of her exploratory study, she presents a model where it is possible to locate different categories of university teachers' beliefs.

The project presented by *Marit Allern & Lillian Vederhus* investigates the impact of the implementation of a new curriculum at the Fculty of Medicine at the University of Tromsø. Their project based on small-scale gathering statements about the scholarship in this departments discusses how new principles embedded into this new curriculum plan impact the roles of teachers and students.

References

Bjørnåvold, J., & Coles, M. (2007). Governing education and training; the case of the qualifications framework. *European Journal of Vocational Training, 42.*

European Commission (2006). *Implementing the community Lisbon programme: proposal for a recommendation of the European Parliament and of the Council on the establishment of the European qualifications framework for lifelong learning.* Luxembourg: Official Publications of the European Communities.

Federkiel, G. (2009). Reputation Indicators in Rankings of Higher Education Institutions. In B. Stensaker & B. Kehm (eds.), *University Rankings, Diversity and the New Landscape oh Higher Education.* Rotterdam: Sense Publications.

Green, D. (1994). What is Quality in Higher Education? Concepts, Policy and Practice. In Diana Green (ed.), *What is Quality in Higher Education?* Berkshire: Open University Press & Society for Research into Higher Education.

Jackson, N., & Lund, H. (eds.) (2000). *Benchmarking for Higher Education.* Buckingham: SRHE/Open University Press.

KUF-NOU (2000). *NOU 2000:14: Om høgre utdanning og forskning i Norge (Mjøs-utvalget) avgitt til KUF 08.05.00.* Oslo: Elanders Publishing AS.

Morley, L. (2003). *Quality and Power in Higher Education.* Berkshire: SRHE/Open University Press.

Neave, G. (1994). *Models of Quality Assessment in Europe.* London: CNAA.

NTNUs strategiplan (2007). Retrieved from www.ntnu.no on January 15th 2007.

Stensaker, B., & Kehm, B. (eds.) (2009). *University Rankings, Diversity and the New Landscape oh Higher Education.* Rotterdam: Sense Publications.

van Vught, F. (1996). The Humboldtian University under Pressure. New Forms of Quality Review in Western European Higher Education. In P. Maassen & F. van Vught (eds.), *Inside Academia. New Challenges for the Academic Profession.* Utrecht: De Tijdstroom.

On the Phenomenon of Competition Between Two Rival Universities in the University Ranking Era

Liu Haifeng

Abstract

"The phenomenon of competition between two universities" refers to the situation in which two universities or colleges that are comparable in strength and stature compete against each other. This is a universal phenomenon among higher education institutions, especially among research universities. Different from the situation in countries or cities that have only one reputed research university, there is fierce competition between two leading research universities in some countries or cities. The competition between Oxford University and Cambridge University in the United Kingdom, Harvard University and Yale University in the United States, Tokyo University and Kyoto University in Japan and Beijing University and Tsinghua University in China are typical examples of this phenomenon. Entering the era of university rankings, the competitors now have quantified indicators for comparison, and the competition is becoming more and more widespread. Universities have their own characteristics and strengths however, they might be ranked at different levels in different world university ranking lists. Therefore, universities only emphasize and advertise their positive aspects. In reality, competitive research universities are not only competitors but also friends. Competition and cooperation often co-exist. Despite some negative impacts from such competition, research universities gain the advantage of having a competitive frame of reference and also the pressure and power for competition. They are encouraged to develop and create a win-win situation. In the process of competition, competing universities advance their educational standards and reputation and promote their academic status to some extent.

Keywords: phenomenon of competition, research universities, rival universities, university ranking

The phenomenon of competition between two universities

Although cooperation between universities is one of the important factors that promote their development, competition has also proved to be the most significant impetus to propel them toward a higher status.

University competitions include those between different universities in the same country and nation-to-nation university competition. However, among such competitions the most intriguing type is the competition between two research universities of comparable status in one country.

The two-university competition refers to the competition between two universities with relatively close strengths and levels, which commonly exists among higher education institutions, especially research universities. Standard higher education institutions or even key middle schools sometimes compete in pairs, but as comparison is among a group of schools with similar characteristics or levels, this kind of competition is not as obvious as that between two research universities. Due to the small number of universities and the fame of these research universities, when they are compared, people can instantly understand which two universities are rivals. Therefore, this sort of competition has become quite obvious. Due to the similarity in their strengths and levels, people tend to debate their advantages and disadvantages.

In some countries, there is only one or a few research universities of repute that flourish. However, in some other countries or cities where there are many research universities of established fame, competition occurs frequently between two rivaling universities. The most well-known examples of this phenomenon are the competition between Yale and Harvard Universities in the United States and that between Oxford and Cambridge Universities in the United Kingdom. Harvard and Yale compete against each other not only for higher academic prestige and university ranking but also, as the two have similar school mottos, they rival for the recognition as to who was the first to use their mottos. In addition, University of California, Berkley (UC Berkley) and University of California, Los Angeles (UCLA) in the United States and Tokyo and Kyoto Universities in Japan are also competing rivals.

Competition Between Oxford and Cambridge

Competition between Oxford and Cambridge is a typical example for university competition in pairs. Both universities are top universities of equal stature among the higher education institutions in United Kingdom, and for a long period of time they have been indulging in competition for a better reputation, in areas ranging from academic achievements to physical education. Back in 1993, I asked an Oxford graduate whether he was familiar with Cambridge, and his response was "For the Oxford fellows, it doesn't matter at all whether one is familiar with Cambridge or not." In other words, it was sufficient to be familiar only with Oxford. Such competition has lasted for a long time, and at a time when relationships were rather tense between the two institutions, they regarded each other as enemies, avoiding mentioning the names of each other. If they had to, they would refer to each other as "other place", meaning "the other place". At that time, people from Oxford and Cambridge understood the special meaning of "other place".

Nevertheless, the two universities share quite a few similarities and a lot of common language. They both respect traditions and strive for perfection, regarding history and traditions as part of the school's dignity. The employment from each other's faculties has far outnumbered the graduates from other universities. In terms of scholar robes at academic dinner parties, there remains a distinction between those graduating from Oxford and Cambridge and those from other universities. As a result, even though the two universities have been competing with each other, the relationship between them has been one of being "in the same boat", competing to promote mutual prosperity.

The rival complex: since heaven has given birth to Yu, why should it also allow Liang to come into being?[1]

In many places in China, we can see two famous universities launching fierce "battles" against each other. In Beijing, Tsinghua is battling with Peking University; in Shanghai, Fudan is battling with Shanghai Jiao tong University; in Tianjin, Nankai with Tianjin University; in Nanjing, Nanjing University with Southeast University; in Wuhan, Wuhan University with Huazhong Science and Engineering University; In Hong Kong, HK University with HK Mandarin University. "Why does Heaven make our rival exist to prevent us from getting to the top?" The rival universities compete for funds, excellent students and professors, and higher ranking positions. The tense and sensitive relationship produces a "rival complex" or "Yu and Liang Complex" among some research universities.

The counterparts also care about who goes first when their names are referred together in public talks. If Oxford and Cambridge are put together, will they be referred to as "Oxbridge" or "Camford"? For an outsider it makes no difference, but for someone from Oxford or Cambridge, it makes a world of difference. People from Oxford tend to refer to the two universities as "Oxbridge", while Cambridge people deliberately choose "Camford", afraid of being the lesser one. In the same vein, when the Chinese refer to the two best universities together, will it be "Beida, Tsinghua" or "Tsinghua, Beida"? People from Beijing University would settle for the former, while

---

[1] Yu and Liang were generals during the Three Kingdom Period in ancient times in China, fighting fiercely against each other by employing cunning military strategies.

those from Tsinghua would tend to use the latter. In the past people were accustomed to using the former; nowadays many people use the latter.

University Ranking Era

Since in 1983 "US News and World Report" issued "American's Best Colleges, more and more countries have witnessed the occurrence of university ranking lists. In 1993, in UK *The Times* started to release "the Good University Guide"; in 1991, "Maclean's University Ranking" appeared in Canada; in 1998, in Germany the Center for Higher Education Development worked with *Stars Weekly* to issue "CHE University Ranking"; in 1991, in Australia Hobson's began to publish "Good University Guides". All the above are well-known university rankings. In China, at present, there are about ten university ranking lists. What is worth mentioning is that after "Academic ranking of World Universities" by the Higher Education Research Institute of Shanghai Jiao tong University in 2003, followed by "World University Rankings" released by *The Times Higher Education Supplement* in 2005 and the successive regional rankings of universities, university ranking has ushered in a globalization era. Now, there are more than 60 university ranking lists in terms of the university types in different countries; therefore, we can say that we are gradually entering a university ranking era.

In the past, comparison of universities was conducted in a general and obscure sense. However, with the coming of the university ranking era, the comparison among universities has been quantified to include detailed figures and ranking positions. Therefore, competition between rival universities has become more prominent, featuring hand-in-hand combat.

Two competing universities in university rankings

Let's view the ranking of rival universities in US, UK, Japan and the Netherlands from the "Academic Ranking of World Universities" and "World University Rankings" by Shanghai Jiao tong University and *The Times Higher Education Supplement*, respectively.

Academic Ranking of World Universities (Shanghai Jiao Tong University)[2]

Institution	2003	2004	2005	2006	2007	2008
Harvard Univ	1	1	1	1	1	1
Yale Univ	8	11	11	11	11	9
Univ Cambridge	5	3	2	2	4	4
Univ Oxford	9	8	10	10	10	10
Tokyo Univ	19	14	20	19	20	19
Kyoto Univ	30	21	22	22	22	23
Univ Utrecht	40	39	41	40	42	47
Univ Leiden	78	63	72	72	71	76

World University Rankings (*The Times Higher Education Supplement*)[3]

Institution	2005	2006	2007	2008
Harvard Univ	1	1	1	1
Yale Univ	7	4	2	2
Univ Cambridge	3	2	2	3
Univ Oxford	4	3	2	4
Tokyo Univ	16	19	17	19
Kyoto Univ	31	29	25	25
Univ Utrecht	120	95	89	67
Univ Leiden	138	90	84	64

---

[2] http://www.arwu.org/rank2008/EN2008.htm
[3] http://www.topuniversities.com/worlduniversityrankings

Let's take a look at the rankings of the three groups of university "rivals" in China:

Academic Ranking of World Universities (Shanghai Jiao Tong University)[4]

Institution	2003	2004	2005	2006	2007	2008
Peking Univ	251-300	202-301	203-300	201-300	203-304	201-302
Tsinghua Univ	201-250	202-301	153-202	151-200	151-202	201-302
Fudan Univ	301-350	302-403	301-400	301-400	305-402	303-401
Shanghai Jiao Tong Univ	401-450	404-502	301-400	201-300	203-304	201-302
Chinese Univ Hong Kong	301-350	202-301	203-300	201-300	203-304	201-302
Univ Hong Kong	251-300	202-301	203-300	151-200	203-304	201-302

World University Rankings (*The Times Higher Education Supplement*)[5]

Institution	2005	2006	2007	2008
Peking Univ	15	14	36	50
Tsinghua Univ	62	28	40	56
Chinese Univ Hong Kong	51	50	38	42
Univ Hong Kong	41	33	18	26
Fudan Univ	72	116	85	113
Shanghai Jiao Tong Univ	169	179	163	144

Widening of the gap between two famous universities

University rankings have widened the gap between universities which at previous times were regarded as close counterparts by the public. Even if a survey of academic prestige is conducted right now, chances are that the gap between the best universities is narrow. As some university rankings stress on scientific research, especially the research production volumes of natural sciences, the rankings put those universities that make strong appeals in science and engineering fields at superior positions. For

---

[4] http://www.arwu.org/rank2008/EN2008.htm
[5] http://www.topuniversities.com/worlduniversityrankings

instance, "Academic Ranking of World Universities" by Shanghai Jiao tong University gives 20% weighting for the volume of publications by *Nature* and *Science*, the two top world journals; the number of Nobel prize and Fields Medal winners constitutes another 30% statistical weight. Economy apart, all the indexes of prize winning fall into the category of natural science. On the other hand, the fostering of top national officials by a university has not made less impact than that of winning a prize in natural science or that of publications by *Nature* and *Science*. To illustrate this point, Oxford cannot compete against Cambridge in the number of Nobel Prize winners, but it is well known for being a cradle of a great number of political leaders. Among Oxford alumni, there have been 5 kings, 25 prime ministers as well as a large number of other top national leaders. However, the prime ministers cultivated in Cambridge only numbered 7. If the factor of excellent graduates is added, the gap between the two universities would be much narrower. This accounts for the much narrower gap between the two universities in the ranking by *the Times Higher Education Supplement* than that by Shanghai Jiao tong University. In the university ranking in China, the gap between Peking University and Tsinghua University has also been affected by the hard indexes in favour of natural science and engineering.

Binary stars among universities

The competition between rival universities among world famous universities has existed for a long time and has now become more and more prominent and fierce, due to the ushering in of the university rank era. As the same university has been ranked quite differently on different ranking lists, and each university has its own characteristics and strengths, usually they emphasize and advertise their positive aspects and favour the rankings stressing their advantages. In fact, each university has its own distinct strengths just like flowers blooming at different seasons with their unique fragrance and beauty. The competition may bring about some negative effects, but not completely negative, for the competition will also promote university development and create a win-win situation. In the course of competition, these research universities are both rivals as well as friends. Competition usually co-exists with cooperation. In the framework of competition, both universities can get the impetus and stimulation for greater progress. As long as the competitions are held within appropriate limits, they will provide pressure and impetus, and to a certain extent, mutually promote each other's better performance and prestige. Just as the Binary Stars existing in the natural world, in the ecological world of universities, where a large number of good universities mushroom, the competition between rivalling universities is a phenomenon with a high probability, or it may be something inevitable.

Fostering awareness and self-assessment to achieve intended learning outcomes: A case study

Vidar Gynnild

Abstract

Evidence of significant improvements in student learning is scarce, although student evaluations of teaching have been widespread and widely accepted as a major quality enhancement measure in tertiary education. Recent research takes a different view suggesting that students themselves should take more responsibility for their progression. Self-assessment enables students to get a sense of the level of their learning and to set the direction for future efforts. In this study, student self-assessment was encouraged by introducing clear and concise learning objectives, a weekly worksheet to raise students' awareness of learning, and a self-assessment instrument based on learning objectives. For high achievers, professional standards were already internalized to the extent that extra support seemed superfluous, while low achievers largely ignored the new measures. As a step forward, a more comprehensive introduction of the philosophy and relevance of self-assessment is suggested as is the provision of training sessions requiring self-assessment skills. Re-designing the course would entail student self-assessment to become a key component in teaching as well as in exercises, assignments, and exam questions.

Introduction

By the mid 1990s, engineering faculties at the Norwegian University of Science and Technology (NTNU) had mandated a campus-wide system for semester-end instructional evaluation by students. The overall purpose was to improve the quality of teaching; however, the measure soon became controversial among academic staff. Some even neglected the responsibilities imposed by the new rules. The system was under attack for lack of methodological rigour, and academic staff disagreed on the extent to which collected data would serve significant educational purposes. The expressed concerns correspond well with those presented in articles published by members of the international research community (Sainsbury & Walker, 2008).

A dissertation addressing follow-up procedures of student evaluation of teaching confirmed minor changes in teaching; however, there was no noticeable impact on approaches to learning (Gynnild, 2001). Of far greater significance to learning was the timing and content of exams. Students seem to pick up cues about learning as they participate in a learning culture with structuring features that extend beyond the content of lectures. Such influential variables have captured the attention of researchers and have come to be labelled the "hidden curriculum" (Sambell & McDowell, 1998; Snyder, 1973). Assessment of student performance is widely acknowledged to greatly influence student priorities (Rust, O'Donovan & Price, 2005). Brown and Knight indicated the centrality of student assessment when they claimed that it is at the "heart of the student experience" (Brown & Knight, 1994).

While summative assessment involves issues of certification and ranking of students, the purpose of formative assessment is concerned with learning and growth, and feedback is a key concept in the process of improved student performance. In everyday usage feedback is commonly understood to mean information about the success of something, but as Sadler comments, there is more to the notion (Sadler, 1989): "Few physical, intellectual or social skills can be acquired satisfactorily simply through being told about them" (p. 120). Evaluative knowledge from instructors is often tacit, which inhibits student understanding of evaluative feedback (Sadler, 1989). From a learning perspective, it would be better if students could get a handle on assessment criteria in order to be able to self-assess and self-improve their own learning.

This study seeks to enhance student self-evaluative skills to enable students to become part of the assessment "guild," the goal of which is a realistic picture of their own learning. To improve learning, students need a sense of their achievement relative to a required standard or agreed learning outcome. Helping students to become more self-driven requires a transfer of power from instructors to students, but we believe this path can be justified by students' potentially greater acquisition of life-long learning skills.

The following argument builds on several conceptual distinctions already established in the research literature (Andrade & Du, 2007):

Self-*reflection* takes a global view of learning in terms of one's own general qualities, attitudes and dispositions.

Self-*evaluation* involves students in making summative judgments of their work that result in a final grade or mark.

Self-*assessment* is a process of formative assessment during which students reflect on and evaluate the quality of their work and their learning, judge the degree to which they reflect explicitly stated goals or criteria, identify strengths and weaknesses in their work, and revise accordingly.

In educational situations feedback is commonly understood to mean some kind of knowledge transfer from an expert to a learner. By contrast, self-assessment requires the student to manage the entire assessment process; it can be regarded as feedback from oneself to oneself.

Setting and background

Our study was carried out in the context of an optional module (TMR 4230 Oceanography) within the Master of Science programme at NTNU in two cycles, the first in 2007 and the second in 2009. Since the number of students enrolled in the module was only 19, the course offered an ideal setting for the exploratory nature of our in-depth research into learning within a single course. The teaching team consisted of a professor and a student tutor; course content featured three major areas: wind, waves, and currents. Learning resources included a course book and three weekly lectures plus optional tutoring sessions. The weekly workload was six hours, but several students "crammed" their study in the days ahead of two sets of oral exams rather than spreading it more evenly throughout the semester. The purpose of the mid-term exam, counting for 30% of the final grade, was to give students a feel for the kinds of skills and knowledge required in the course so they could better prepare for the final exam counting for 70%.

The course, TMR 4230 Oceanography, is theoretical, requiring students to be familiar with basic concepts and to understand relationships between physical phenomena and their mathematical counterparts in terms of formulae and equations. Pure recall of facts and procedures would not suffice. These learning objectives created an ideal situation for the researcher to observe student performance at the two oral exams. In particular, we wanted to observe the level of understanding of basic phenomena and the extent to which each student was able to express phenomena both by reasoning and mathematically.

Research questions and method

In the first cycle, we explored learning behaviours among 19 students in Oceanography in the spring term of 2007. By observing student performance in two sets of exams with subsequent one-on-one interviews, we were looking for characteristic patterns of study behaviour. Based on the analysis of data obtained from this first study, we set up a follow-up study in the same course in spring 2009 to further examine issues of learning and self-assessment.

Our research draws on methods associated with action learning. Zuber-Skerritt (2002) proposed a common understanding of the term: "Action learning involves learning about learning, and using this to learn" (Zuber-Skerritt, 2002). The main characteristics of our research are elements such as reflecting on practice and learning about learning. Action learning encourages self-exploration of curricular issues to figure out solutions. The author formed a research team with the course instructor and the teaching assistant. As a group, we enjoyed a sense of joint "ownership" of the project, which clearly motivated all of us to examine the effects of measures that had been implemented. The author assumed that simply offering external advice to the instructors would have been less authentic to the context and most certainly would have generated less learning.

Our action learning approach was also guided by Kolb's famous concept of the learning circle (Kolb, 1984). The cycle concept is useful in the sense that it can begin at any of the following points: concrete experience (1); observation and reflection (2); forming abstract concepts (3); and testing in new situations (4). A key challenge is to be able to move from observation of concrete cases to abstract concepts and generalizations. In the first cycle, concepts may be tentative, but they may be refined or changed when applied to different circumstances in subsequent cycles. Checking the validity of concepts may require the observation of a range of cases to gain extended experience and suggest a general principle. Such general principles explain a class of something: "One way that theories explain is by providing a sense of process or mechanism for how one thing is related to another (http://www.analytictech.com/mb870/handouts/theorizing.htm, 27.03.09). As discussed below, the quality of our analysis fully relies on our ability to theorize or explain how variables are connected, and only valid interpretations may help us suggest interventions that eventually may contribute to improved learning outcomes.

Because our study aimed at both research and development, the professor (P) attended and actively participated in the interview sessions along with the graduate teaching assistant (TA) and the researcher (R) in the first cycle in 2007. While the professor's attendance may have distorted the opinion of some students, many clearly appreciated his presence because it provided an opportunity to debrief and discuss issues of learning and achievement. In the interviews, students spoke openly and provided numerous suggestions for improvements. We used qualitative techniques to discern patterns of mindset and strategy associated with high or low performance. Our semi-structured interview approach inquired into students' individual learning issues and the extent to which they were able to pursue problems in depth. The interviews were recorded and transcribed verbatim for subsequent analysis.

In 2007 learning and achievement were addressed in one-on-one interviews the day after students had received their grades. First, we explored students' approaches by asking open-ended questions such as: "How have you been studying in Oceanography this semester? What has been most important to you? Which learning challenges have you encountered in this course, and how have you been coping?" Based on the careful analysis of data from the 2007 study, new measures were implemented in 2009 with the aim of raising students' awareness and self-assessment skills. This time, we wanted to explore the extent to which these measures were used and their effects.

Observations and reflections

After careful reading and re-reading of the 19 interview transcripts, general themes emerged from the data. For example, high-achieving students typically expressed a desire to understand course content: "I am trying to acquire an understanding of course content instead of just remembering. Sometimes I am running short of time in order to achieve a complete understanding, but this is always my intention". To some extent, obtaining a decent grade was important to high-achieving students, but it was never stated as a primary concern:

> I am trying to understand. That is the most important, and in addition to get a decent grade.

Another feature of high-achieving students is their commitment and persistence:

> I stay committed till I understand.

> If it is a formula I don't understand, then I try until the last minute. Then if I really can't understand, I try just to learn by heart, but memorising is not my best ability.

When asked to justify approaches, high achievers typically stated desires to pursue deep learning:

> My understanding lasts longer. Just remembering may work out for the exam, but not for the future.

> I have to understand from the beginning.

Low achievers also expressed an intention to understand while simultaneously practicing approaches associated with shallow learning, such as memorization of facts and procedures. Their words and their actions persistently diverged, however. These students obtained correct solutions in exercises without being able to explain the underlying meaning and structure, as evidenced by the following assertion: "I have attempted to read the compendium in order to get to grips with what it is all about, but when I am doing the exercise, I'm very focussed on solving it. I am not sure that's the best way." While high achievers managed to reason and explain constructs, low achievers frequently resorted to recall strategies and the manipulation of formulae and equations: "If you do the exercises, it's a lot of calculation. You can just do them without thinking, because it's just math". The disconnection of theory and real-world phenomena is but one of a range of learning characteristics of low achievers, which also include the absence of meta-cognitive skills, as demonstrated here: "I was a little bit shocked when I realized I got so few questions about 'understanding'. It was kind of understanding based on the equations."

To promote conceptual growth, high-achieving students systematically used self-regulatory strategies to monitor their own cognitive development. The meta-cognitive skills associated with self-evaluation enabled these students to check on the quality of their own learning and to take action as appropriate to attain required standards, as shown by these two quotes:

> Basically, I know if I understand or not. I have experienced that the things I know turn out to be fairly easy to handle at exams.
>
> I don't doubt it when I understand something.

By contrast, low achievers exhibited a lack of awareness of the demands of the course and failed to implement measures to improve their own learning. When elaborating on their learning experiences, these students used words like 'feel', 'think', 'believe', 'hope', or 'guess', as demonstrated in the following interview:

> Researcher (R): To what extent were you aware of what you didn't understand?
> Student (S): Maybe not too much.
> R: But you have been aware that there are some things that you have not really understood? Or will you say you thought you understood most of it?
> S: Yes, I guess so. First, you try to understand, but if you look at the solution, everything looks so logical, so you think you understand. But maybe you don't?
> R: Were you still uncertain if you understood, or did you feel that you knew this well enough?
> S: I had the feeling that I knew it.
> R: If you think of your performance yesterday, what would be needed to improve learning?
> S: That's a good question. I don't know!

Low achievers tended to invent excuses to explain why they did not take action to improve, but it can be difficult to know whether a student is consciously inventing excuses or is exhibiting personality characteristics, such as a lack of ability to face reality. A common feature of high-achieving students is their greater ability to self-check and pursue learning tasks that they set for themselves; however, there is no "one size fits all" strategy. High-achieving students practice a range of behaviours, such as working completely on their own, working with peers when needed, attending or not attending lectures, and so on. What unites them is their ability to pursue and sustain their learning.

Theorizing observations

Self-driven students exposed an ability to self-assess and self-improve their learning. Self-assessment refers to a learner's capability of self-appraising the quality of learning and competence. Self-assessment can be a useful tool to promote meta-cognitive skills, by which one can learn about one's own learning: "By engaging in self-assessment process, the learners' thinking is made conscious and explicit, their awareness heightened, and their learning actions deliberate" (Mok, Lung, Cheng, Cheung & Ng, 2006). Some researchers (Kirby & Downs, 2007) argue that self-assessment is linked to the development of a deep approach to learning and self-regulated learning (Benett, 1993; Ramsden, 2002). Others (Cole, Ryan & Fick, 1995) argue that self-assessment is an authentic means by which students can monitor and improve learning through kinds of "self-feedback" techniques.

Becoming a self-directed learner requires a set of capacities including goal setting, self-monitoring, and self-correction, all of which call for practical intervention. For example, engaging in self-regulated learning requires the transition from "other-regulation" to "self-regulation" (Zimmerman & Schunk, 2001). Four milestones in the development of self-regulated skill have been identified: observation, emulation, self-control, and self-regulation (Zimmerman, 2002).

Research on self-regulated learning suggested that an inward focus of attention as a meta-cognitive strategy causes a person to compare his or her own behaviour to set standards in the learning context (Duval & Wicklund, 1972). Any discrepancy between the self's behaviour and the standard for the behaviour might induce action to conform more closely to the standard: "Thus, self-focus is presumed to cause a closer correspondence between ongoing behaviour and salient standards" (Scheier & Carver, 1982, p. 158). A closed feedback loop presumably enables comparison of own performance with that of a "comparator", a reference against which selves can be compared. In everyday situations or routine work, reference standards match fairly well with observed behaviour. In education, challenges may arise if a student has never experienced the satisfactions of understanding something well. If a standard, or comparator, is either non-existent or vague, a malfunction in the student's internal feedback loop may occur.

But, how do students in real-life contexts make the transition from "other regulation" to "self-regulation"? Instructors and students alike bring their cultural values and beliefs into educational settings, and entrenched notions of right and wrong do not easily change (Tan, 2004). Although focusing on learning outcomes rather than on teaching methods allows all parties to direct attention to shared targets, the design of an appropriate learning environment still renders a challenge in the sense that frame factors, such as teaching, assignments, and tutoring sessions, need to be aligned to promote specified learning outcomes. Arguably, awareness and self-assessment are just means towards ends; greater student independence or shifts in student–instructor power relations do not by themselves bring about automatic transitions to deep and self-driven learning.

Practical implications

Investigation of student learning in Oceanography in 2007 revealed two distinct patterns of behaviour: (a) students practicing self-assessment, self-monitoring, and self-regulatory skills and (b) students resorting to recall of facts and procedures rather than pursuing issues in depth. The latter students were typically striving to comply with formal course requirements or achieve a passing grade. In contrast, self-regulated learners in the course typically paid heed to the inner satisfaction of learning as a driving force. We do not believe these skills are hereditary; rather, we believe they come into being and grow in favourable learning environments. Thus, our approach relies on a theoretical model featuring three components: frame factors, processes, and learning outcomes (Dahllöf, 1967; Lundgren, 1985). In this study, we use the aforementioned model to establish a relationship between factors in the learning environment, learning processes, and learning outcomes. Wise manipulation of course design can improve learning and competency acquisition; however, the complexity of this endeavour calls for the involvement of the student to make sense of interventions: "Meaning is constituted through an internal relationship between the individual and the world" (Prosser & Trigwell, 1999, p. 12).

In the 2007 interview sessions, several students argued that some exam questions were either unexpected or too detailed and believed this contributed to their lower-than-expected grade. Yet, only one learning objective had been stated in the course materials: "The emphasis will be on the physical understanding of phenomena contributing to the interaction between the atmosphere and ocean, and which also contribute to the motions in the ocean" (http://www.ntnu.no/sa/sfs/studsys/emner/, 30.03.09). This broad objective was presented along with the following list featuring major topics in the course:

> Properties of seawater. Conservation equations. Equations of motion. Coriolos effect. Geostrophic current. Inertial current. Planetary boundary layer flow. Wind-induced current. Bottom currents. Circulation. Tides.

Global and local wind description. Mean wind. Wind gust. Wave forecast. Surface waves. Wave refraction. Non-linear waves. Breaking waves. Wave-current interaction. (http://www.ntnu.no/sa/sfs/studsys/emner/, 30.03.09)

The quoted objective indicates an essential feature of the course by stating that "physical understanding of phenomena" will be emphasized but provides no detailed information on what exactly will be required. By contrast, recent literature on "learning outcomes" suggests the efficacy of a higher level of specificity, especially in course modules: "The classic learning outcome describes what the student should be able to do to complete a course of study" (Baume, 2009). Based on results from the 2007 study, the professor wrote general objectives for the three major sections of the course and specific objectives (outcomes) for each (Wind: 7; Waves: 4; and Current: 6). In the spring term of 2009, learning objectives were presented to students in a chart, as exhibited in Table 1. Column 3 refers to frame factors intended to help students achieve learning outcomes.

1. **General objectives** within the course description.	2. **Specific objectives** (**outcomes**) in terms of student learning.	3. **Learning activities** or **assignments** to achieve the specific objectives
This course aims to support students' physical understanding of phenomena contributing to global and local wind conditions.	a) At the mid-term exam, you should be able to explain the meaning of the geostrophic balance, Coriolis force, as well as in terms of the relevant formulas.	The objectives specified in the column to the left can be achieved by attending the lectures, reading Compendium Part I (Wind, pp. 4-47) and by working on Exercise 1.

Table 1. Chart displaying the setup of learning objectives and learning activities

Learning objectives do exist in all courses, yet in many instances they remain unarticulated. By closely attending to lectures and assignments, students will be able to abstract fundamental issues of "the hidden curriculum". The instructor's effort in making learning outcomes explicit was guided by the belief that the greater transparency of expectations would encourage and enable self-assessment and self-improvement. The instructor also ensured that learning objectives were aligned with other resources such as lectures, exercises, and former exam questions. Some learning objectives were adopted more or less directly from previous exam questions.

Contradictions between intention and strategy were evident in low-achieving students; self-awareness may play a role in this discrepancy. A student cannot change something of which he or she is unaware: "A conception cannot be fruitful without being plausible, and cannot be plausible without being intelligible" (Hewson, 1981, p. 389). One might ask whether the learning context can be crafted to overcome tacit, counterproductive didactics. Hewson (1981, p. 385) suggests that learning in science represents an interaction between "existing knowledge and new ideas or information" and claims that the fundamental challenge of learning is one of conceptual change. Initial meanings may be limited or distorted; however, humans possess the capacity to change when these meanings are challenged by new ideas (Dee Fink, 2003, p. 117), such as:

- What was the muddiest point in today's lecture?
- What was the most important idea you encountered in class this week?
- **In your own words, how would you describe the relationship between topic X and Y?**
- What important questions remain unanswered for you?

The third bullet point was tailored to key topics presented in individual lectures:

- In your own words, how would you describe the relationship between topic X=geostrophic balance and Y=estimation of wind speed from a weather map? (13.01.09).
- In your own words, how would you describe the relationship between topic X= local wind conditions, i.e. mean wind speed profile plus wind gust, and Y= information required for complete description of X (20.01.09).
- In your own words, how would you describe the relationship between topic X =phase function, and Y= wave number, wave ray, and wave frequency (27.01.09), etc.

Finally, our last intervention was the self-assessment instrument presented in Table 2. While learning objectives were introduced during the first week of the semester, students received the self-assessment instrument approximately one week ahead of the mid-term exam, in February 2009. The purpose of it was explicated in the lecture theatre, and students were assured that systematically covering all learning objectives would be to their own benefit if they wanted to address learning deficiencies ahead of the mid-term exam. The implicit purpose of interrogations about learning was to raise awareness of the gap between what was required and current level of performance (see Table 2). In the third column of Table 2, the student works out precisely how to respond to the challenge.

Specific Objectives (Learning Outcomes)	Please indicate your level of mastery of each of the stated objectives in column 1. Put a circle around only one of the five alternatives (A-E) for each of the stated objectives in column 1.	If your response is "C" or "D", please indicate what you are going to do (if anything) to achieve the specified objective presented in column 1. If your response is "E", how do you know?
a. At the mid-term exam, you should be able to explain the meaning of the geostrophic balance, Coriolis force, as well as in terms of the relevant formulas.	A. I **hope** that I am able to …. B. I **think** that I am able to …. C. I **seriously doubt** that I **am able** to … D. I **know for sure** that I am **not** able to .. E. I **know for sure** that I am able to …	

Table 2. Chart displaying self-assessment instrument in Oceanography

The exact wording of statements of mastery, as seen in Table 2, was inspired by student responses in the first research cycle, in 2007. The researchers hoped that this exposure to a range of options would raise students' awareness of learning and motivate due action.

Preliminary results, 2009

Due to the submission deadline, data associated with the final exam in 2009 are missing, but they will be included in a later publication. The oral mid-term examination accounting for 30% of the final grade was conducted on February 25–26. Well ahead of the examination, students were invited to contribute in one-on-one interviews, which were, with a few exceptions, conducted on February 27. First, students were urged to fill in a mini-survey featuring ten items related to the student's use of learning objectives, a weekly worksheet, and a self-assessment instrument. Each item was a statement that students were urged to evaluate on a nine-ordered response line. The criteria were subjective: respondents indicated level of disagreement or agreement (see Appendix). The questionnaire also helped to structure the interviews and to ease the categorization of data from 13 responding students (61.9 %). On completion of the questionnaire, each student was asked to elaborate on any item to provide additional information for a more complete picture.

Figure 1 portrays a telling image of respondents in interviews (13) and non-respondents (7) in terms of percentage scores at the mid-term exam. The 13 students obviously represent a distorted sample in terms of scores at the exam. Generally, with only two to three exceptions, non-respondents were low-achieving students compared to those who did respond. Not only did our respondents perform better at the mid-term, they also uniformly articulated a learning-oriented approach aiming for deep understanding of phenomena (see Q7 in Table 3), as expressed by this student, "I have been fully committed to in-depth understanding, maybe because I am not good at recall. It is always more fun if I am able to figure things out for myself" (Anna). Responses to Q8 confirm that these students aimed for good grades (see Table 3) yet still assigning poorer grades to themselves than would have been the case based on scores at the mid-term exam (see Q9): A=4 (2); B=8(7); C=1(4); D=1(0) (grade distribution converted from percentage scores; self-grading in parenthesis). The examination scores for the interviewees were for the most part in the upper range of the percentage point scale (11 out of 13 received scores in the range of 80-100 percentage points). They largely assumed their exam performance reflected their competencies in Oceanography pretty accurately (see Q10) and made no complaints regarding practical arrangements, questions asked, or grades assigned. Students responded on a nine-ordered scale (Table 3), but because of the small number of respondents, item responses are summed to create an aggregate score for three groups of items (1-3; 4-6; 7-9).

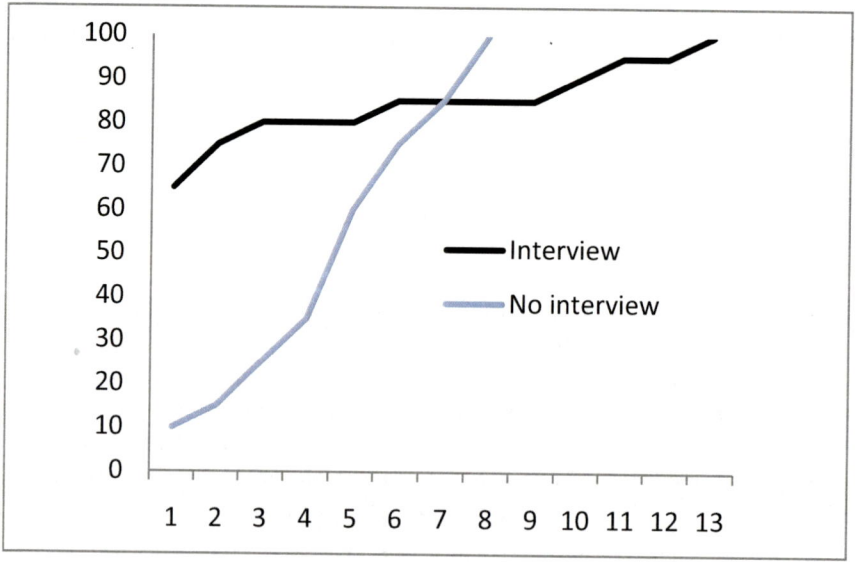

Figure 1. Scores (y-axis) at exam for 13 interviewees versus 7 non-interviewees

We also wished to investigate the use of objectives, worksheets, and self-assessment instruments. Table 3 documents some use of learning objectives (see Q1); however, responses to the next question (Q2) indicate that three other learning resources (compendium, lectures, and exercises) were of greater significance to direct students' learning efforts in Oceanography.

Q1: To what extent did you make use of the specified learning objectives in Oceanography?				
Scoring groups	(1, 2, 3)	(4, 5, 6)	(7, 8, 9)	
Never	2	6	5	Every week

Q2: Please rank the significance of the stated items in terms of what to learn in Oceanogr.				
Exercises	Compendium	Learning obj.	Lectures	Tutoring sessions
3	1	4	2	5

Q3: To what extent did you make use of worksheets distributed by the professor each week?				
Scoring groups	(1, 2, 3)	(4, 5, 6)	(7, 8, 9)	Every week
Never	5	4	4	

Q4: Were the worksheets helpful for your learning? (Please respond only if you used them).				
Scoring groups	(1, 2, 3)	(4, 5, 6)	(7, 8, 9)	
Not at all	5	2	5	Very much so

Q5: Was the Self-Assessment Instrument helpful in raising awareness of strengths and weaknesses in your own learning?				
Scoring groups	(1, 2, 3)	(4, 5, 6)	(7, 8, 9)	
Not at all	3	4	6	Very much so

Q6: Were learning deficiencies addressed due to the use of the Self-assessment instrument?				
Scoring groups	Yes	No		
	4	9		

Q7: What have you been aiming for in terms of learning in Oceanography this semester?				
Scoring groups	(1, 2, 3)	(4, 5, 6)	(7, 8, 9)	
Mostly recall of facts and procedures			9	Mostly deep understanding of phenomena

Q8: What are you aiming for in terms of final grade in Oceanography?				
Grades (A-F)	A	B	C	D
	4	8	1	

Q9: What would you consider an appropriate grade based on your mid-term performance?				
Grades (A-F)	A	B	C	D
	2	7	4	

Q10: Did the exam accurately reflect your knowledge and skills in Oceanography?				
Scoring groups	(1, 2, 3)	(4, 5, 6)	(7, 8, 9)	
Not at all	0	5	8	Very much so

Table 3. Display of scores for selected items in the questionnaire

Our students took part in a learning culture in which the application of learning objectives is marginal or non-existent. Students are accustomed to attending to cues in the curriculum, exercises, or lectures to direct efforts, "I make use of the exercises because they normally deal with the most important issues" (Anna). Still, comments on objectives were positive:

> I checked if I could explain each learning outcome, and for obscure parts I returned to the compendium. It was a very useful tool for me. The first time I did it I realized I had to study much deeper" (Larissa).

> I am very positive; learning objectives gave me a better overview and facilitated self-check of progression: Does my learning match standards and expectations?" (Anna).

The poor rating of the teaching assistant's tutorials can be explained primarily by low attendance, as on average, only 1–3 students took advantage of the tutorials on a weekly basis. A greater commitment by students could potentially have resulted in a higher rating, as more of them would have enjoyed the benefits and personal satisfaction of improved learning. The same logic applies to questions three and four. Less frequent use of worksheets corresponded to poorer ratings, and vice versa. There is nothing inherent in terms of content or design to explain the poorer ratings. I believe this resource became useless primarily because students did not use it.

The same logic applies to results presented to Q3 and Q4 in Table 3. Those respondents who deemed the weekly worksheets unhelpful were the ones who never used them (although students were advised not to respond to Q4 if they had not used this tool). Here, like in any trade, practitioners seem to need extensive training and tutoring to become proficient in their work.

The self-assessment instrument received a mixed reception. Although this initiative does not conform to the current philosophy of teaching and learning at NTNU, some students apparently made use of it as an awareness-raising tool (see Q5). Four students claimed that they addressed learning deficiencies by applying the self-assessment instrument (Q6); however, our respondents turned out to be largely self-driven learners already practicing self-assessment skills, as exhibited in this quote: "To me, it was kind of humiliating. I always paid attention to learning objectives to make sure my learning was up to standards, so it turned out to be kind of superfluous to me (Anna). The students potentially most in need of the self-assessment instrument did not participate in our interviews. Our suspicion is that few, if any, of those students tried any of the self-assessment tools. Such a result further underscores that engaging in self-assessment to inform individual development does not occur by itself. Rather, this mode of assessment requires sustained effort, perseverance, and professional support.

Discussion

In this study, we imposed carefully selected instruments to attempt to promote students' ability to judge the degree to which their learning met explicit objectives (outcomes) in one specific course. We sought to extend a growing body of research that indicates that many students are in fact able to take responsibility for their own learning (Kirby & Downs, 2007). Our data bolster the significance of specified learning objectives; interviewed students spoke highly of this measure. Paradoxically, the volunteering sample of students was already highly motivated and at least to some degree exhibited capabilities of self-assessment. The better performing students may simply be willing to exert more effort, which would also explain why they would take time to go to the interviews. These students had internalized performance standards to the extent that interventions to self-check knowledge and skills seemed superfluous. Before we embark on serious challenges associated with self-assessment, we dwell briefly on three theoretical approaches in order to expand the understanding of self-driven learning.

According to the cognitive developmental model, learning may occur when existing structures are challenged by new information, and the learner is able to regain a new equilibrium by sustained effort (Piaget, 1975). Examples of statements fitting into this line of thought are readily available in our data, as seen in the following interview excerpt:

> R: If you do not understand, how is that for you?
> S: I get frustrated, and it increases my commitment to pursue the task. I simply have to figure it out. My approach has its pros and cons because I am having a hard time putting my work aside, even though this might have been to my benefit. I need to figure it out. (Anna)

In research based on a socio-cultural approach, the concept of "internalization" takes on a different meaning requiring the adoption of conceptual and pedagogical tools based on values and beliefs held by experienced academic staff (Andrade & Du, 2007). In this study, the novel instruments primarily attracted the interest of students familiar with internalized procedures of self-control and self-assessment. Although we cannot be sure, the absence of low-achieving students in interviews indicates a lower level of interest and ability to use the tools: "If a teacher's expectations are especially demanding or novel, students may experience incongruence, struggle longer, and suffer more 'pain' in order to effectively appropriate those expectations" (Andrade & Du, 2007).

From the perspective of self-regulated learning, the key issue is the transitioning from "other regulation" to "self-regulation". Although all learners are assumed to practice self-regulatory skills to some extent, the key distinguishing feature is the greater ability to do this on a systematic basis (Zimmermann, 1990). A self-oriented feedback loop enables students to advance successfully even with little or no external support; their will and skill are integrated components, and the attractiveness of the learning becomes a major motivator. In contrast to operant theorists' emphasis on external rewards such as grades, phenomenological researchers point to the importance of immaterial rewards, for example self-actualization and self-esteem. Our high-achieving students agree with this assumption; the real reward is associated with personal mastery of learning issues.

Researchers have argued that the level of self-regulatory skills may affect ways in which students respond to an instructor's expectations as articulated in the learning objectives (outcomes) (Andrade & Du, 2007). These researchers speculate that students with better self-regulatory skills may more easily detect any discrepancy or incongruence between required standards and one's own learning. Awareness of this "gap" is a necessary condition for gap closure. In a very practical sense, there are similarities between Piaget's cognitive approach and the perspective known as "self-regulated learning". Our students practiced self-regulatory skills to varying degrees; some used learning objectives and the self-assessment instrument inconsistently or not at all.

A tentative conclusion of our study is that self-assessment of achievement is feasible and likely to be beneficial for those making the effort to review learning with an eye to improvement. Our data suggest that the biggest challenge is for students to become more proficient users of skills associated with self-regulated learning. These observations suggest an urgent need to introduce students to the philosophy of self-regulated learning, its purpose, and its main features as well as how the various components of course design endorse the underlying pedagogical philosophy. This could entail training students in self- and peer assessment and providing them with opportunities to practice self-assessment skills in exercises. Our study and the course offered no additional exercise addressing issues of self-assessment, so students were never given the opportunity to develop these skills over a sustained period. Furthermore, we know that our interventions did not fit well with the culture of learning to which students were accustomed.

Even though there is increased recognition of the need for measures aimed at improved learning at our university, evidence of the outcomes of such endeavours is still scarce. One way to proceed in our case would be to give increased attention to learning objectives and self-assessment as part of lectures and exercises. If a student's sense of achievement is vague and required standards in terms of learning outcome remain unfocused, chances of improved learning are minimal. Tasks aimed at meta-cognition and self-assessment could increase the acquisition of skills and bring the notion of self-assessment into the core of the learning experience.

Concluding remarks

The purpose of this study has been to examine the effects of specific measures aimed at fostering awareness and self-assessment to endorse the pursuit of learning outcomes. Our study confirms that high-achieving students did perform better than low achievers partly because of their greater ability to practice self-assessment skills. Our qualitative data also indicate that high achievers stayed committed and exerted sustained effort to pursue tasks in-depth. Although this study confirms benefits of self-assessment skills in learning, it renders less of evidence of ways in which such capabilities may be developed. We do know that learning cultures exert impacts on students in terms of cues and expectations, and we speculate that challenges may be solved by re-designing the entire curriculum rather than imposing random instruments as part of a research project. In order to proceed, a more comprehensive introduction of the philosophy and relevance of self-assessment is suggested as is the provision of training sessions requiring self-assessment skills. Re-designing the course would also entail student self-assessment to become a core component in teaching and tutoring as well as in types of exercises and exam settings.

Appendix (Survey Items)

1. To what extent did you make use of the specified learning objectives in Oceanography?
   Never   1   2   3   4   5   6   7   8   9   Every week

   If you have been using the stated learning objectives, please explain when and how.

2. Please rank the significance of the stated items in terms of what to learn in Oceanography.

   Exercises [ ]; Kompendium [ ]; Learning objectives [ ]; Lectures [ ]; Tutoring sessions [ ]

3. To what extent did you make use of worksheets distributed by the professor each week?
   Never   1   2   3   4   5   6   7   8   9   Every week

4. Were the worksheets helpful for your learning? (Please respond only if you used them.)
   Not at all   1   2   3   4   5   6   7   8   9   Very much so

5. Was the "Self-Assessment Instrument" helpful in raising awareness of strengths and weaknesses in your own learning? (Please respond only if you filled in the form).
   Not at all   1   2   3   4   5   6   7   8   9   Very much so

6. Were learning deficiencies addressed due to the use of the "Self-Assessment Instrument"?
   Yes [ ]   No [ ]   If yes, what?

7. What have you been aiming for in terms of learning in Oceanography this semester?
   Mostly recall of facts and procedures   Mostly deep understanding of phenomena

                    1   2   3   4   5   6   7   8   9

8. **What are you aiming for in terms of final grade in Oceanography this semester?**

    A   B   C   D   E   F

9. **What would you consider an appropriate grade based on your mid-term performance?**

    A   B   C   D   E   F

10. **Did the mid-term exam accurately reflect your knowledge and skills in Oceanography?**

Not at all   1   2   3   4   5   6   7   8   9   Very much so

Acknowledgement: The author wishes to thank Professor Dag Myrhaug, Department of Marine Technology, NTNU, who generously gave permission for the data collection for this article.

References

Andrade, H., & Du, Y. (2007). Student responses to criteria-referenced self-assessment. *Assessment & Evaluation in Higher Education, 32*(2), 159-181.

Baume, D. (2009). Writing and using good learning outcomes. Available from www.leedsmet.ac.uk

Benett, Y. (1993). The validity and reliability of assessments and self-assessment of work-based learning. *Assessment & Evaluation in Higher Education, 18*(2), 83-94.

Brown, S., & Knight, P. (1994). *Assessing learners in higher education.* London: Kogan Page.

Cole, D., Ryan, C., & Fick, F. (1995). The road to authentic assessment and portfolios. In D. Cole, C. Ryan & F. Fick (eds.), *Portfolios across the curriculum and beyond.* Thousand Oaks, CA: Corwin Press.

Dahllöf, U. (1967). *Skoldifferentiering och undervisningsförlopp.* Stockholm: Almqvist & Wiksell.

Dee Fink, L. (2003). *Creating significant learning experiences.* San Francisco: Jossey Bass.

Duval, S., & Wicklund, R. A. (1972). *A theory of objective self-awareness.* New York: Academic Press.

Gynnild, V. (2001). *Læringsorientert eller eksamensfokusert? Nærstudier av pedagogisk utviklingsarbeid i sivilingeniørstudiet.* Trondheim: Fakultet for samfunnsvitenskap og teknologiledelse, Pedagogisk institutt, Norges teknisk-naturvitenskapelige universitet.

Hewson, P. W. (1981). A conceptual change approach to learning science. *European Journal of Science Education, 3*(3), 383-396.

Kirby, N. F., & Downs, C. T. (2007). Self-assessment and the disadvantaged student: potential for encouraging self-regulated learning? *Assessment & Evaluation in Higher Education, 32*(4), 475-494.

Kolb, D. A. (1984). *Experiential learning: experience as the source of learning and development.* Englewood Cliffs, N.J.: Prentice-Hall.

Lundgren, U. P. (1985). Frame factors and the teaching process. In T. Husén & N. Postlethwaith (eds.), *The international encyclypedia of education. Research and studies* (Vol. 4). Oxford: Pergamon Press.

Mok, M. M. C., Lung, C. L., Cheng, D. P. W., Cheung, R. H. P., & Ng, M. L. (2006). Self-assessment in higher education: experience in using a metacognitive approach in five case studies. *Assessment & Evaluation in Higher Education, 31*(4), 415-433.

Piaget, J. (ed.). (1975). *The equilibration of cognitive structures: the central problem of intellectual development in school.* Chicago, IL: The University of Chicago Press.

Prosser, M., & Trigwell, K. (1999). *Understanding learning and teaching: The expereince in higher education.* Buckingham: Open University Press.

Ramsden, P. (2002). *Learning to teach in higher education.* London: Routledge.

Rust, C., O'Donovan, B., & Price, M. (2005). A social constructivist assessment process model: how the research literature shows us this could be best practice. *Assessment & Evaluation in Higher Education, 30*(3), 231-240.

Sadler, D. R. (1989). Formative Assessment and the Design of Instructional Systems. *Instructional Science, 18*(2), 119-144.

Sainsbury, E. J., & Walker, R. A. (2008). Assessment as a vehicle for learning: extending collaboration into testing. *Assessment & Evaluation in Higher Education, 33*(2), 103-117.

Sambell, K., & McDowell, L. (1998). The Construction of the Hidden Curriculum: messages and meanings in the assessment of student learning. *Assessment & Evaluation in Higher Education, 23*(4), 391-402.

Scheier, M. F., & Carver, C. S. (1982). Cognition, affect, and self-regulation. In M. S. Clark & S. T. Fiske (eds.), *Affect and cognition* (pp. 157-183). Hillsdale, NJ: Lawrence Erlbaum Associates.

Snyder, B. R. (1973). *The hidden curriculum.* Cambridge, Mass.: MIT Press.

Tan, K. H. K. (2004). Does student self-assessment empower or discipline students? *Assessment & Evaluation in Higher Education, 29*(6), 651-662.

Zimmerman, B. J. (2002). Achieving self-regulation: the trial and triumpf of adolescence. In F. Pajares & T. Urdan (eds.), *Academic motivation of adolescents.* Greenich, CT: Information age Publishing.

Zimmerman, B. J., & Schunk, D. H. (2001). *Self-regulated learning and academic achievement: theoretical perspectives* (2nd ed.). Mahwah, NJ: Lawrence Erlbaum.

Zimmermann, B. J. (1990). Self-regulated learning and academic achievement: An overview. *Educational Psychologist, 25*(1), 3-17.

Zuber-Skerritt, O. (2002). The concept of action learning. *The Learning Organization, 9*(3), 114-124.

The paper has been reviewed by external referees.

Multiple Scholarship Fostered Staff Development Toward Enhancing University Quality[1]

Fan Yihong[2]

Abstract

Higher education today is facing multiple challenges and demands and is under tremendous pressure to develop, maintain, and enhance its qualities, at the same time. University ranking and benchmarking is drawing increasing attention, both internally and externally, of the higher education world. It offers a vehicle for universities to respond to accountability and for a larger audience to learn what is generally going on in universities. However, university ranking and benchmarking, no matter how well designed, will not be enough in and of itself to develop and enhance university quality. Developing and enhancing university quality needs more in-depth effort and initiatives to address the developmental and growth needs of the staff/faculty[3] members who are working in this environment and contributing not only to research but also to teaching and learning as well as to cultural and intellectual development of the society. Thus, it needs a perspective of multiple scholarship to design and develop staff development programs that foster staff to develop and grow in a holistic way. Nearly 20

---

[1] This research is one of the outcomes of the research project on Comparative Study of Staff/Faculty Development between Chinese and European countries sponsored by MoE Research Base of Social Science and Humanities.
[2] Fan Yihong, professor of higher education, the Research Center for Higher Education Development, Institute of Education, Xiamen University, P.R.China. Email: fanyihong@yahoo.cn.
[3] In North America, "faculty development" is used for tertiary teacher development, while in European countries, the most used term is "staff development". Since this paper investigates in the context of both the European and North American universities, we use both terms interchangeably.

years have passed since Ernest Boyer proposed the conception of multiple scholarship (Boyer, 1990). This paper sets out to explore how this multiple scholarship view has affected the university staff development policies and practices in universities both in U.S. and European countries to shed light on constructing and designing the next phase of staff development policies and programs in China.

Keywords: Multiple scholarship; staff/faculty development; university quality

Introduction

This study constitutes the literature review of the theoretical underpinning of a Ministry of Education funded research project on *Comparative Study of Staff/Faculty Development between Chinese and European Universities*. We choose Ernest Boyer's multiple scholarship (Boyer, 1990) as the theoretical underpinning of our research since it offers a more holistic view to study staff development than the current practice of tertiary teacher training in China. First, the paper lays out the context of the challenges Chinese higher education is facing and the need for carrying out this study. Next, the study goes on to give a brief overview of how Boyer's multiple scholarship impacted the direction and evolution of faculty development at universities in both North American and European countries over the past 20 years. Then, the paper analyses the implications of applying multiple scholarship for staff development in China. Finally, this study proposes recommendations on developing multiple scholarship fostered staff development in China.

Context and Preamble of the Study

Higher education in China has witnessed dramatic changes and tremendous development in the past two decades. The following section gives a brief overview of the various major changes that have taken place in China in recent years.

Restructuring of Chinese Higher Education

In the 1990s, higher education in China experienced major system and structural changes, ranging from consolidation to decentralization nationwide. In the consolidation phase since 1993, a considerable number of universities merged to boost comprehensiveness and competitiveness of the universities. This restructuring and consolidation reform involved a total of 31 provinces, municipalities, autonomous regions and 60 sub-sectors of the State Council (Zhao, 2005).[4] By the year 2000, 612

---

[4] Notes taken from a PPT presentation on website in 2005. Did not store more detailed information.

universities and colleges were consolidated into 250 as a result of the restructuring and consolidation (Postiglione, 2001).

In addition to consolidation, another governmental policy was to decentralize the universities, which means that the central government ministries that used to have the upper hand over hundreds of universities let go of their governance of most of their universities. From 1999, about 360 formerly ministry-run universities were shifted to the governance of provincial or municipal governments. Only the Ministry of Education still governs 70 key state universities, while other Ministries retained only a total of 25 universities under their governance. As of 2007, there are 95 ministry-run universities in China.[5]

These changes of restructuring and decentralizing of Chinese higher education resulted in the expanded capacity of universities to share resources and in enlarged autonomy of the universities to plan their own strategic moves. At the same time, some of the universities have been shifted under the governance of provincial and municipal government, which makes universities more able to engage in local community development endeavors.

China entering mass higher education

The year 1999 brought another dramatic change in Chinese higher education. In June 1999, the central government in China made a decision to expand higher education, which brought unprecedented increase in enrolment in higher education in China. The gross enrolment rate (GER) of the age-cohort (18-22 years) increased from 6.8% in 1998 to 17% in 2003, demonstrating that China has entered the stage of mass higher education, according to Martin Trow's theory (Trow, 1984). In 2007, the GER further increased to 23%, almost about four times that of 1998. Student numbers in Chinese HEIs increased from 6.43 million in 1998 to 27 million in 2007. Staff and teacher numbers increased from 1.02 million in 1998 to 1.945 million in 2007.[6]

New demands for university teachers and staff development

The statistics above demonstrates that over the past decade the student number in higher education in China quadrupled while the number of university teachers almost doubled. We can see immediately that university teachers are facing tremendous demands for teaching, research and service, not to mention new challenges placed on them from globalization, internationalization, information technology revolution, etc. Without questioning, there are inevitably increasing needs for staff/faculty development at universities.

---

[5] http://www.dachuanmei.com/news.asp?39. Retrieved 26 July, 2008.
[6] Data consolidated from 1998-2007 Annual Statistic Review of Development of Chinese Education.

In China, the tertiary teacher training system was established in mid-1980s, containing a three-tier faculty training scheme, mainly focused on entry training for the young staff, and implemented by two state tertiary teacher training centres, six regional tertiary teacher training centres and about three scores of provincial or municipal tertiary teacher training centres, each responsible for a number of universities in the region without considering the developmental needs of each specific university. The philosophical underpinning, the content and the methods of the programs, as well as the organizational structure remained unchanged since their inception. In addition, the publication-oriented tertiary teacher evaluation system and staff development work faces very serious challenges. Undoubtedly, the tertiary teacher training system in China needs some considerable changes facing the new demands from the external world and the new needs from the internal world specifically.

The need for exploring staff/faculty development in the international arena

How to design and plan the new phase of staff/faculty development system and programs in China? Under the above-mentioned circumstances, it is imperative to learn more about staff development programs in North America and in European universities. Ernest Boyer's multiple dimensions of scholarship, namely scholarship of discovery, scholarship of integration, scholarship of application, and scholarship of teaching (Boyer, 1990), will certainly shed light on how to develop the next phase of the staff development system in China.

This study holds the view that developing and enhancing university quality needs more in-depth effort and initiatives to address the developmental and growth needs of the staff members who are working in this environment and contributing not only to research but also to teaching and learning as well as cultural and intellectual development of the society. Thus, it needs a perspective of multiple scholarship to design and develop staff development programs that foster staff to develop and grow in a holistic way.

The following section gives a brief review of how the conception of multiple scholarship has been evolving and developing over the past two decades and how this updated notion of scholarship influenced faculty development in North American and European universities.

Multiple Scholarship as Conceptual Framework for Staff/Faculty Development

Nearly 20 years have passed since Ernest Boyer proposed the concept of multiple scholarship (Boyer, 1990). This section sets out to explore how this multiple scholarship view has affected the university staff development policies and practices in universities both in U.S. and European countries to shed light on constructing and designing next phase of staff development policies and programs in China.

In 1990, Ernest Boyer, the president of Carnegie Foundation for the Advancement of Teaching, published his special report on *Scholarship Reconsidered: Priorities of the Professoriate* (1990), in which he proposed the concept of multiple scholarship, the scholarship of *discovery*, the scholarship of *integration*, the scholarship of *application* and the scholarship of *teaching* (p. 16). His purpose for proposing this concept was to step out of the trap of "research vs. teaching" debate to give "scholarship" "a broader, more capacious meaning, one that brings legitimacy to the full scope of academic work (p. 16)." He then offered more detailed explanation about the functions of multiple scholarship (For detailed explanation please see: pp. 16-25). The following subsections give a brief summary of the four-faceted scholarship.

The scholarship of discovery

In Boyer's original report (Boyer, 1990), he first mentioned *the scholarship of discovery*, which means adding to the stock of human knowledge, the concept that closely related to *research* as we are used to hearing. However, Boyer gave it a more in-depth view compared to the conventional ideas of research, saying, "Not just the outcomes, but the process, and especially the passion, give meaning to the effort" need to be legitimized (p. 17). From Boyer's view we know clearly that if faculty's attention were only directed to the number of published articles, it goes contrary to Boyer's notion of scholarship of discovery.

The scholarship of integration

When proposing *the scholarship of integration*, Boyer wanted faculty to pay attention to *interdisciplinary* connections that lead to new understandings, to be *interpretive* of one's own research in relation with others' research and to fit into a larger view or broader patterns, as well as getting used to *integrative* ways of thinking (Boyer, 1990, pp. 18-21). He reminded us that "Today, more than at any time in recent memory, researchers feel the need to move beyond the traditional discipline boundaries, communicate with colleagues in other fields, and discover patterns that connect" (p. 20). When we look at the academic reality in China, we realize how important it is to promote this notion of scholarship of integration.

The scholarship of application

The scholarship of application means putting knowledge into use by addressing real-world problems. Boyer alerted us that discovery and application is not a one-way street, discovery can be the result of application, or vice versa. He opined that "a view of scholarly service—one that both applies and contributes to human knowledge—is particularly needed in a world in which huge, almost intractable problems call for the skills and insights only the academy can provide" (p. 23). In the past 20 years the conception of scholarship of application has evolved and developed to be *the scholarship of professional service* (Lynton, 1995), and *the scholarship of professional service and outreach* (Driscoll & Lynton, 1999), which recognize the faculty's scholarly work engaged in application of knowledge and community service. Further on the notion developed to be *the scholarship of engagement* (Driscoll, 2005; Harkavy, 2006; Rice, 2002; Schon, 1995, and Walshok, 1995)). Rice (2002) elaborated on the components of the scholarship of engagement as three fold, including engaged pedagogy, community-based research, and collaborative practice (pp. 14-16). From these development features, we can sense how much emphasis has been placed on serving the community with interactive and collaborative endeavours for the broader purpose of academic, research and intellectual work.

The scholarship of teaching

When defining the *scholarship of teaching*, Boyer used the terms "dynamic", "trans forming" and "extending" to distinguish from only transmitting knowledge and understanding by teaching, thus giving an extended view of scholarly teaching (pp. 23-24). The concept of the scholarship of *teaching* also developed over the past 20 years to be shifted to the scholarship of teaching and *learning* (Hutchings, 2000; Huber & Morreale, 2002; Lyons, Hyland, & Ryan, 2002).

In summarizing his four categories of scholarship, Boyer alerted us that "What we urgently need today is a more inclusive view of what it means to be a scholar—a recognition that knowledge is acquired through research, through synthesis, through practice, and through teaching" (p. 24).

Eugene Rice (2007), when attending the UNIQUAL 2006 conference at Xiamen University, reported that National Science Foundation (NSF) recently funded a Center for the Integration of Research, Teaching and Learning (CIRTL) for preparing graduate students for their future career "in sciences, engineering and mathematics across the several sectors in higher education" (p. 27).

All these stated initiatives aim at fostering a new and more encompassing concept of scholarship that stresses not only research but also teaching and learning, community engagement as well as integrating knowledge and practice from different disciplines and fields of studies. From the following section we could see how these initiatives bare fruits.

The Impact of Multiple Scholarship on Faculty Work and Faculty Reward

In reviewing the impact of Boyer's 1990 report, and how Boyer's multiple scholarship influenced the evolution of the faculty development both in and out of North America, Eugene Rice described it as a "tipping point" that critically changed the fundamental value and reward system for scholarly work over the past decade (Rice, 2002). Rice's review pays special attention to the development of the scholarship of teaching and the scholarship of engagement, which evolved from the original concept of scholarship of application. The following section will give a brief overview about how the conception of all four dimensions of multiple scholarship evolved and developed over the past two decades.

According to Rice (2002), Boyer's report came at the right time and "struck a responsive chord" since the academic world had been bored by the dichotomous view of research vs. teaching. There was already a readiness in accepting a more encompassing and fuller view toward a broader sense of scholarship. Also because of Boyer's leadership and advocates, there followed a movement toward giving legitimacy to a broad notion of scholarship and advocacy in changing significantly the faculty reward system (p. 9).

Associations' joint effort in advocating multiple scholarship

Other organizational initiatives also supported the movement of promoting the scholarship of teaching. Among them American Association for Higher Education (AAHE) immediately established AAHE's Forum on Faculty Role and Rewards, taking on the regular task of promoting the new notion of scholarship and advocating change in the faculty reward system (Rice, 2002). This was followed by the efforts of various professional and disciplinary associations that were heavily involved in the reconsideration of scholarship, trying to develop guidelines for evaluating and rewarding a broader notion of scholarship. For learning the disciplinary development of the new concept of scholarship, Rice recommended Robert Diamond and Bronwyn Adam's two edited books of 1995 and 2000: *Disciplines Speak: Rewarding the Scholarly, Professional and Creative Work of Faculty* (Diamond and Adam, 1995, 2000).

In 1997, Charles Glassick, Mary Taylor Huber, and Gene Maeroff published the Carnegie Foundations' follow-up publication *Scholarship Assessed: Evaluation of the Professoriate*, with Boyer stating in the prologue that the aim of the publication is for colleges and universities in the nation to truly "embrace the full scope of the scholarship" and for the "full range of intellectual life" to gain "new dignity and new status" (Glassick, Huber and Maeroff, 1997). In this study they surveyed chief academic officers (CAOs) at four-year colleges and universities in 1994 and found that 80 per cent of the institutions had recently re-examined or planned to examine their workloads (p. 12); more than two-thirds of the campuses reported providing funds for teaching improvement, sabbatical leave for teaching improvement (74 per cent), and grants for curriculum or course development (68 per cent) (p. 16).

In 1998, under the leadership of Lee Shulman, another major initiative was launched at the Carnegie Foundation for the Advancement of Teaching, the establishment of Carnegie Academy for the Scholarship of Teaching and Learning (CASTL). With this initiative, the scholarship of teaching gained an extended meaning and focus, not only on teaching but also on learning. CASTLE's work includes 1) *Scholarly and Professional Societies Program*, which rallied support from more than 30 professional and disciplinary associations to support the scholarship of teaching and learning and/or working directly with the Carnegie Academy for the Scholarship of Teaching and Learning; 2) *Carnegie Scholar Program* from 1998 to 2005 that offered support for about 140 scholars to take a one-year residency at the Carnegie Foundation to produce scholarship of teaching and learning; 3) *Campus Program*, engaging more than 240 universities and colleges for fostering the campus movement in promoting the scholarship of teaching and learning; 4) *CASTL Institutional Leadership and the CASTL Affiliates Program* to "facilitate collaboration among institutions with demonstrated commitment to and capacity for action, inquiry and innovation in the scholarship of teaching and learning".[7]

Higher education institutions joint force in promoting multiple scholarship

Collaboratively the clusters of American higher education institutions have been working on a dozen related themes of promoting scholarship of teaching and learning, ranging from "Building Scholarship of Teaching and Learning Communities", "Building Scholarship of Teaching and Learning System-wide", to "Mentoring Scholarship of Teaching and Learning" (Ibid). All the collective efforts together brought the significant paradigm shift in the American higher education institutions, influencing not only faculty development developers but also administrators, policy makers, professional and disciplinary associations, and key players in each of the higher education institutions that committed to bringing needed changes in the policy and practice, evaluation and reward system, tenure and promotion scheme for faculty work that encompasses a broader and fuller understanding of scholarship and more legitimate recognition of multiple scholarship.

Kerry Ann O'Meara and R. Eugene Rice, in their effort to trace the impact and initiatives in promoting multiple scholarship across the American universities and colleges, published a book on *Faculty Priorities Reconsidered: Rewarding Multiple Forms of Scholarship* (O'Meara & Rice, 2005). This book sets out to assess how the universities and colleges redefined faculty roles and restructured their reward systems

---

[7] For more details see: http://www.carnegiefoundation.org/programs/index.asp?key=21, retrieved 15-04-2009.

to facilitate the realignment of the American professoriate with the essential missions of the nations' universities and colleges. After giving an overview of the development of the multiple scholarship, this book presents nine case studies of diverse universities and colleges to portray the continuous struggle and efforts in redefining the faculty roles and restructuring the faculty reward system based on the new concept of multiple scholarship on various campuses as well as the policy and practice issues at hand.

Dissemination of multiple scholarship via professional conferences and journals

In 2001, Indiana University started an on-line journal *The Journal of the Scholarship of Teaching and Learning (JoSoTL)*. In 2004, the International Society for the Scholarship of Teaching & Learning (IS-SoTL) was founded by a committee of 67 scholars from several countries, and they started to organize annual conferences with the first year conference in 2004 set in Bloomington, Indiana. After having been held in different places and countries (2005 in Canada; 2006 in Washington DC; 2007 in Australia; 2008 in Canada), IS-SoTL Conference 2009 was back in Bloomington, Indiana, in October 2009.

In 2007, the *International Journal for the Scholarship of Teaching & Learning* (IJSoTL) was launched by the Center for Excellence in Teaching at Georgia Southern University to be an international vehicle for articles on the study of multiple scholarship in general and the scholarship of teaching and learning in particular. It is an open, peer-reviewed, international electronic journal published twice a year, generating essays and discussions about the scholarship of teaching and learning (SoTL) and its applications in higher education today. By now, it has more than 4500 readers from 114 countries.[8] On the Scholarship of Teaching and Learning (SoTL) website, about 20 associations in North America and Europe and a similar number of publications focused on the scholarship of teaching and learning are listed.[9]

Multiple scholarship in practice in Nordic universities: the case of NTNU

When we look at the staff development programs' role in university quality, we see a rather different approach. Take Norwegian University of Science and Technology (NTNU), for example; they did not use much of the terms of promoting multiple scholarship. However, they embedded the concept of multiple scholarship in all their staff development design and implementation. The NTNU's entry staff training

---

[8] For more details, see IJSoTL website: http://academics.georgiasouthern.edu/ijsotl/, retrieved 26 April, 2009.
[9] For more details see SoRL website: http://www.issotl.org/SOTL.html, retrieved 26 April, 2009.

program places new teachers in multi-disciplinary peer groups both for participating in training programs and for peer observing each others' teaching. There are also organized social activities for them. Therefore, in the first two years of their career the new teachers are continuously immersed in an interdisciplinary environment and multi-disciplinary teamwork. Thus, they learn to look at things in a more broad perspective, and in turn, gain the scholarship of teaching and scholarship of integration. They also have courses introducing them to pedagogical issues for teaching large classes, for evaluating students' progress, for facilitating problem-based learning, project-oriented learning, team building and so on. In this way, they learn the scholarship of teaching and learning (Engvik and Halland, 2006).

For scholarship of application, there are various programs that fully engage teaching and learning with real world needs and community demands. Take NTNU's successful project "Expert-in-Team" as an example; the project offered all fourth-year students with interdisciplinary teamwork projects working on real problems coming either from the company or from the professors. At the end of the course, the solution will emerge as collaborative efforts of the teachers and students in the study group (Sortland, 2006). NTNU sets apart one day for all students and teachers of this program to mingle together from various fields of study to work on solving real world problems. All these programs start with staff development sessions that are offered in the previous semester so that the teachers and graduate learning assistants learn the appropriate approach to facilitate these new programs. From their practice, we can see clearly that multiple scholarship, namely, scholarship of discovery, scholarship of teaching and learning, scholarship of application, and scholarship of integration, is at work (Fan et al., 2006).

Extending the influence of multiple scholarship to graduate programs

Carolin Kreber, working both in North American settings and later in European settings, advocates promoting multiple scholarship in faculty development and graduate education, (Kreber, 2001). She offers five specific suggestions, 1) faculty developers and professors engaging in collaborative action research exploring teaching and learning in the discipline department wide; 2) Allow dissertation to focus on pedagogy in the discipline; 3) Guide and mentor graduate students' teaching with the practice of scholarship of teaching; 4) Offer more workshops and seminars based on educational theory and research; 5) Identify professors who can act as mentors to graduate students, *as well as new faculty members* (italics added by the author) (pp. 81-82).

The continuous evolution and development processes of promoting multiple scholarship in North America and Europe in the past 20 years can shed light on designing and developing faculty development programs in China.

Multiple Scholarship and its implication for staff development in China

Higher education in China today is facing multiple challenges and demands and is under tremendous pressures to develop, maintain, and enhance its qualities, at the same time. University ranking and benchmarking is drawing increasing attention both internally and externally of the higher education world. It offers a vehicle for universities to respond to accountability and for a larger audience to learn what is generally going on in universities. However, university ranking and benchmarking, no matter how well designed, will not be enough, in and of itself, to develop and enhance university quality.

Developing and enhancing university quality needs more in-depth effort and initiatives to address the developmental and growth needs of the staff/faculty members who are working in this environment and contributing not only to research but also to teaching and learning as well as cultural and intellectual development of the society. Thus, it needs a perspective of multiple scholarship to design and develop staff development programs that foster staff to develop and grow in a holistic way.

After reviewing the literature on how Boyer's advocate of multiple scholarship has affected the university staff development policies and practices in universities both in U.S. and European countries, we have gained a full awareness that we need the framework of multiple scholarship for constructing and designing the next phase of staff development policies and programs in China.

In China, a three-tier faculty training system has been developed since the mid-1980s, which consists of 2 national centres, 6 regional centres, and about 70 provincial and municipal centres. This system served the centralized higher education quite well in the first 15–20 years, but recently, facing the convergent forces of decentralization of higher education, mass higher education, globalization of higher education, and the different ways of learning caused by the rapid development of ICT, the centralized faculty training system is not able to deal with all these challenges. Thus, a new system and new model are needed in the changing context to meet with the real needs of improving university quality through faculty development.

Looking back at the Chinese faculty training system, though it offers various training programs, the most regular and the one that faces more teachers is the entry training program in which four books are taught via lecture mode, *Higher Education Pedagogy*, *Educational Law and Regulations*, *Higher Education Psychology*, and *Working Ethics for Tertiary Teachers*. These four courses are taught in two weeks before the new teachers enter their job and by traditional lecturing method. In the end, the new teachers take some examinations, and if they pass they will be given the teaching certificate that verifies the teachers' ability to teach.

The problem of this approach is that most of the new teachers have not had a chance to experience teaching when they are studying these books. So they have no anticipation of what would be problems in their real work, not to mention how to develop adequate strategies to deal with the problems. When they actually do encounter real problems with their teaching and their more general work in the academic world, there is no support system for them, except in a few universities that have recently started a Teaching Support Centre or a Teaching and Learning Support Centre.

Another problem arises from university ranking and benchmarking, which resulted in more demands for teachers to publish. Most universities are accelerating their requirement on how many articles teachers need to publish in a year in their teacher evaluation system. This diverts the teachers' attention largely from teaching to research.

One more serious problem is that as the result of mass higher education, there are more university graduates than the job market can absorb. At the same time, there are certain jobs the university graduates do not have the right skills and competence to fill. Thus, there is a need for more work-oriented, and more practical-oriented talent, which places a demand on universities to develop more practical and competence-driven courses and programs.

All the above challenges call for re-evaluating and reconsidering the academic and scholarship role of tertiary teachers. Only focusing on academic publication will not solve all the problems facing the higher education arena in China. We need to seriously consider establishing the framework of multiple scholarship, in which all dimensions of scholarship, namely, discovery of knowledge, application of knowledge, integration of knowledge, and teaching and learning new knowledge (Boyer, 1990), are given the same value and recognition, and teachers' efforts in various activities, as long as they are related to multiple scholarship, will be recognized and rewarded.

Toward a Multiple Scholarship Fostered Staff Development in China

In China, the three-tier faculty training system carries out centrally planned training programs, which does not leave much room for universities and colleges to care about the real needs of their university teachers to serve the strategic goals of their own university. What is more, at present, there are many different types and different tiers of universities in China, each having different needs for institutional development. Thus, the centrally focused tertiary teacher training system is not able to meet the needs of different kinds of universities. The different and new ways of learning caused by the rapid development of ICT call for a new kind of teacher development programs. Globalization and multi-cultural development of the world also call for international-oriented teacher development programs. More expectations from community development call for university teachers to be able to work together with people from other sectors for developing the local community. Thus, a new system is needed in the changing context to meet the real needs of improving university quality through faculty development. The following section envisions a Multiple Scholarship Fostered Staff Development system in China.

Multiple Scholarship as Conceptual Framework for Staff Development in China

Tertiary teachers in China are currently facing contradictory forces, consuming their energy and time in an unbalanced way. Because of university ranking and benchmarking, there is more and more pressure from the universities on teachers to pursue the numbers of publication. At the same time, mass higher education places more load on teaching. The changing societal needs call for different modes of teaching, from more knowledge driven to more competence driven methods. Instead of looking at research and teaching as dichotomous and competing pulls, there is a need to see the connections between teaching and research. In the international world, more researchers and practitioners are calling for looking at the relationship between research and teaching as a nexus (Brew, 2003, 2006; Hughes, 2005; Neumann, 1992; Trowler & Wareham, 2007) and for strengthening their connections. Though researchers have not entirely agreed upon the definitions and impacts of teaching and research nexus (TRN), the investigations along the line serve the purpose to promote integrating research and teaching and recognizing the value of different modes of teaching that connect learning with research, such as inquiry-based learning, problem-based learning, flexible learning, and community-based learning. In both UK and Australia, there are nationally supported projects on initiatives along this line (Baldwin, 2005; Trowler & Wareham, 2007).

When we look at the literature related to the scholarship of teaching and learning, there are only a few articles in the higher education arena in China, which give an introductory account on the movement in the United States on promoting scholarship of teaching (Wang, 2005; 2006). There is scarcely any literature on the whole profile of multiple scholarship and its implication to staff development in China.

In Scotland, the Scotland Higher Education Enhancement Committee (SHEEC) has identified the Quality Assurance Framework theme: Research-teaching linkages: Enhancing Graduate Attributes, and joint effort with different higher education sectors (SHEEC, 2008) to promote enhancement led, learner-centred higher education.

> The Enhancement Theme adopted a broad, inclusive definition of research to embrace practice/consultancy-led research; research of local economic significance; contributions to the work of associated research institutes or other universities; and various types of practice-based and applied research including performances, creative works and industrial or professional secondments (Ibid).

From the above short explanation of Enhancement Theme of SHEEC, we could see that it encompasses the full range of multiple scholarship, which not only cares about research and teaching but also about application/practice and integration. SHEEC sets a fine example of how higher education can make considerable change toward enhancing quality. It should start from a more broad and inclusive definition of research and should have a cadre of academic staff who are able to bring the teaching research linkage into their academic work and teaching and service practice. In the staff development initiative, it is high time for us to introduce multiple scholarship as the conceptual framework for program designing and implementation.

Paradigm shift and conceptual changes from staff training to faculty development

The following are the features of the tertiary teacher training system in China:

- Structurally and organizationally—centralized;
- Program wise—pre-planned about 20 years ago;
- Methods and approaches—lecturing and reading books;
- Evaluation and assessment—examination;
- Outcome—certificate of tertiary teaching;
- Philosophical underpinning—teachers are administrated and managed;
- Scope of the program—single dimension of scholarship;
- Significance of the program—only benefit to the individual for short term.

Envisioning a future search framework shifting from tertiary teacher training to university staff development system in China:

- Establish university-based staff development centre—regional centres shift their roles to consultancy and work on developing staff developers;
- Updating programs designed and guided by multiple scholarship;
- Starting from employing broad definition of research;
- Promoting teaching–research nexus and offering different opportunities;
- Teachers should be stimulated and nurtured rather than only managed;
- More flexible and diverse methods and approaches for carrying programs;
- More process-oriented and generative evaluation and assessment;
- Making the connection between personal and institutional development.

Overall, there should be established realization that if the universities would like to ensure their quality they need to start with enhancing their teachers' quality. There are a multitude demands on the development of staff in the context of mass higher education, globalization, decentralization, and ICT-influenced higher education. Only stressing on the numbers of publication will not build up the all-round quality of university teachers, which is badly needed in university development and quality moves. We should learn from Bringle's model in designing the implementation of multiple scholarship for community engagement and civic service. Only when the value of multiple scholarship is recognized and rewarded can the teachers engage themselves in new ways of teaching and research. In turn, the teachers will be ready to lead the students in the effort of integrating learning, research, and application of knowledge in a more meaningful way.

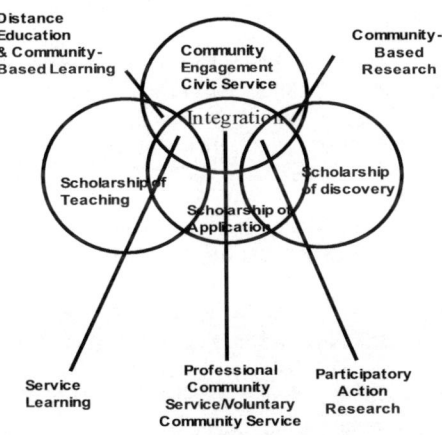

Multiple Scholarship and New Ways of Learning and Research
Source: Modified from Robert G. Bringle's PPT presentation on *Strengthening Institutional Support for Service Learning and Civic Engagement.*

By studying the experiences and processes of promoting multiple scholarship in the United States, Canada, Australia, and European countries, we learned that we need convergent efforts from higher education professional associations, higher education institutions, researchers, policy makers, staff development developers, teachers and students dedicated to this cause for working toward conceptual changes, policy changes and organizational and institutional changes in China from tertiary teacher training to staff/development in Chinese higher education guided by multiple scholarship as conceptual framework. This literature review is only a moderate start for the intended series of meaningful efforts. I hope through the UNIQUAL 2009 conference we will learn more theoretical ideas and practical tips for promoting the next phase of staff development in China.

References

Baldwin, G. (2005). *The Teaching-Research Nexus: How research informs and enhances learning and teaching in the University of Melbourne.* http://www.cshe.unimelb.edu.au/

Boyer, E. L. (1990). *Scholarship Reconsidered: Priorities of the Professoriate.* Princeton, NJ: The Carnegie Foundation for the Advancement of Teaching.

Brew, A. (2003). Teaching and Research: New relationships and their implications for inquiry-based teaching and learning in higher education. *Higher Education Research & Development, 22*(1), 3-18.

Brew, A. (2006). *Universities into the 21st Century: Research and Teaching beyond the Divide.* New York: Palgrave Macmillan.

Brew, A., & Sachs, J. (2007). *Transforming a University: The Scholarship of Teaching and Learning in Practice.* NSW: Sydney University Press.

Bringle, R. G. *Strengthening Institutional Support for Service Learning and Civic Engagement.* Retrieved 28 April, 2009 from the following website: http://www.indianacampuscompact.org/LinkClick.aspx?fileticket=y1pyzYvjIwc%3D&tabid=65&mid=519.

Diamond, R., & Adam, B. (eds.) (1995). *The Disciplines Speak: Rewarding the scholarly, professional, and creative work of faculty.* Washington DC: American Association of Higher Education.

Driscoll, A., & Lynton, E. (1999). *Making Outreach Visible: A guide to Documenting Professional Services and Outreach.* Washington DC: American Association of Higher Education.

Engvik, G., & Halland, G. (2006). UNIPED – A Key Player in Assuring Learning Quality. In Y. Fan & al. (eds), *Assuring University Learning Quality: Cross-Boundary Collaboration.* Trondheim: Tapir Academic Press.

Fan, Y. et al. (eds.) (2006). *Assuring University Learning Quality: Cross-Boundary Collaboration.* Trondheim: Tapir Academic Press.

Harkavy, I. (2006). The Role of Universities in Advancing Citizenship and Social Justice in the 21st Century. *Education, Citizenship and Social Justice, 1*(1), 5-37.

Huber, M. T. (2004). *Balancing Acts: the Scholarship of Teaching and Learning in academic careers.* Washington, D.C.: American Association for Higher Education, Carnegie Foundation.

Huber, M. T., & Morreale, S. P. (2002). Situating the scholarship of teaching and learning: a cross-discipline conversation. In *Disciplinary styles in the scholarship of teaching and learning: exploring common ground.* Washington DC, American Association for Higher Education & The Carnegie Foundation for the Advancement of Teaching.

Hutchings, P. (2000). *Opening Lines: Approaches to the Scholarship of Teaching and Learning.* Menlo Park, CA: The Carnegie Foundation for the Advancement of Teaching.

Jenkins, A. (2004). *A Guide to the Research Evidence on Teaching-Research Relations.* Higher Education Academy.

Kreber, C. (ed). (2001). Scholarship Revisited: Perspectives on the Scholarship of Teaching. *New Directions for Teaching and Learning, 86.* San Francisco, CA: Jossey-Bass.

Kreber, C. (ed.) (2006). Exploring Research-Based Teaching. *New Directions for Teaching and Learning, 107.* San Francisco, CA: Jossey-Bass.

Lynton, E. (1995). *Making a Case for Professional Service.* Washington DC: American Association of Higher Education.

Lyons, N., Hyland, A., & Ryan, N. (2002). *Advancing the Scholarship of Teaching and Learning Through a Reflective Portfolio Process: The University College Cork Experience.* UCC, Cork.

Neumann, R. (1992). Perceptions of the Teaching-Research Nexus: A framework for analysis. *Higher Education, 23,* 159-171.

Neumann, R. (1994). The Teaching-Research Nexus: applying a framework to university students' learning experiences. *European Journal of Education, 29*(3), 323-339.

Neumann, R. (1996). Researching the Teaching-Research Nexus: A critical review. *Australian Journal of Education, 40*(1), 5-18.

O'Meara, K. A., & Rice, R. E. (2005). *Faculty Priorities Reconsidered: Rewarding multiple forms of scholarship.* San Francisco, CA: Jossey-Bass.

Pan, M. (2007). Faculty Development in Higher Education Institutions. In M. Pan & al. (eds.), *Key to University Quality Assurance: Staff/Faculty Development in the Glodal Context.* Fuzhou: Fujian Education Press.

Postiglione, G. A. (2002). Chinese Higher Education for the Twenty-First Century: Expansion, consolidation, and globalization. In D. W. Chapman & A. E. Austin (eds.), *Higher Education in the Developing World.* Westport, CT: Greenwood Press.

Rice, R. E. (2002). Beyond Scholarship Reconsidered: Toward an enlarged vision of the scholarly work of faculty members. *New Directions for Teaching and Learning, 90,* 7-17.

Schon, D. A. (1995). Knowing in Action: The new scholarship of requires a new epistemology. *Change, 27*(6), 27-34.

SHHEC (2008). *Research-Teaching Linkages: enhancing graduate attributes.* www.enhancementthemes.ac.uk.

Shulman, L. S. (1999). *Visions of the possible: models of campus support of the scholarship of teaching and learning.* Carnegie Foundation.

Shulman, L. S. (2000). From Minsk to Pinsk: why a scholarship of teaching and learning? *Journal of Scholarship of Teaching and Learning, 1*(1), 48-53.

Sorcinelli, M. D., & al. (2006). *Creating the Future of Faculty Development: Learning from the past, Understanding the Present.* Bolton, MA: Anker Publishing Company, Inc.

Sortland, B. (2006). EiT – Interdisciplinary Teamwork: Preparing Students for Working Life. In Y. Fan & al. (eds.), *Assuring University Learning Quality: Cross-Boundary Collaboration.* Trondheim: Tapir Academic Press.

Trowler, P., & Wareham, T. (2007). Re-Conceptualising the 'Teaching-Research' Nexus. In *Enhancing Higher Education, Theory and Scholarship.* Proceedings of the 30th HERDSA Annual Conference [CD-ROM], July, Adelaide, Australia.

Walshok, M. L. (1995). *Knowledge without Boundaries: What America's research university can do for the economy, the workplace and the community.* San Francisco, CA: Jossey-Bass.

Wang, Y. (2005). On the Movement of Scholarship of Teaching and Learning. *Studies in Foreign Education, 32*(12), 24-29.

The paper has been reviewed by external referees.

Implementation of an International Master's Degree Programme in Educational Leadership in a Learning Environment of Care and Challenge

Lea Sandholm

Introduction

The culture of assessing the student and taking him/her into consideration as a distinguished client and a unique human being with a remarkable potential in the international Master's Degree Programme in Educational Leadership (MPEL) is parallel to the client culture developed and cherished in the Finnish programmes of the Institute of Educational Leadership (IEL) at the University of Jyväskylä, Finland, through qualification programmes to advanced studies and Ph D programmes. The student body being international from all corners of the world, an additional approach of care and caring has been developed in the programme (Starratt 2003, 2005, Noddings 1992, 2005) to ensure meeting the students' needs expeditiously and to secure a steady progress in studies.

The international Master's Degree Programme in Educational Leadership (MPEL) was launched in 2007 at a stage when through the consistent development work the strategic framework of the institute had materialized and bore fruit in the form of a learning environment where customer needs were the focus of delivery, and where a web of campus faculty, alumni, home university and international partners, and practitioners in the field had grown to trust and feel pride over the programmes, having contributed and committed to their immersion. It is a culture of cumulative leadership. (Alava 2006, 9-10). Simultaneously, internationalization has become one of the strategic focuses of Finnish higher education.

Quality is not accidental, and it emerges and sustains itself in conditions of long-term strategic development and a culture of shared, cumulative leadership (Alava, 2006). Alava, the director of the IEL, bases this claim on analysing the development of the IEL, relating quality issues to the paradigms of school leadership training, of cohorts, of learning communities, and shared, distributed and teacher leadership. Further, he analyses the institute's development through Maula's (2006) strategic component framework for living organizations, consisting of *1. identity, 2. perception of the environment, 3. strategy, 4. knowledge (distinctions), 5. boundary elements, 6. interactive process, 7. triggers, 8. experimentation, 9. internal standards, processes and communication, 10. information and communication* (Alava 2006, 1).

This paper shares the concept that quality higher education emerges and sustains itself in conditions based on long-term development and a culture of cumulative leadership. Thus, action implementing the curricula is based on a shared insight into the roots of the programme and the learners as customers, shared leadership in the development and delivery of the programmes, respectful interaction between instructors and students, commitment and trust.

This paper argues that it is in the aforementioned preconditions that responsiveness to learners' needs can become the core of programme implementation. The concept introduced is responsible leadership with care and caring. (Starratt, 2003, 2005; Noddings, 1984, 2005). The concept of responding to the learners' needs as advocated by Noddings (1984, 2005) is very close to the concept of servant leadership advocated by Greenleaf (2002).

The observations of the paper are based on an ethnographic research conducted about the MPEL since its launch in autumn 2007 by the writer.

Critical mass of educational expertise in the university as basis for provision of a quality programme

The University of Jyväskylä, celebrating its [75]th anniversary in 2009, is the home of the most remarkable concentration in educational sciences, teacher training, educational research, evaluation, open university and continuing education in Finland. The university houses the Faculty of Education divided into the Department of Educational Sciences and Teacher Training College, the Finnish Institute for Educational Research, the Finnish Education Evaluation Secretariat, an Open University with the University of the Third Age and the Centre for Continuing Education.

This state of affairs contributes to the culture of the Jyväskylä university, where the value of the existence of the long roots of the field of education is highly appreciated and acknowledged as one of the cornerstones of the Jyväskylä academia, the background of the university, which now houses seven faculties, in the teacher training seminar established in the 1860s. Additionally, the image of the Jyväskylä city is accentuated as a city of students and of learning.

Based on the accumulated critical mass of provisions in the field of education on the campus, both in terms of instruction and research, a new Master's Degree Programme can rely on the availability and stability of the best teaching resources in the most varied areas of education. Additionally, the Faculty of Economics with its Management and Leadership Department is a further provider of expertise in leadership and management studies within the home university. The exchange of teaching resources also accounts for an increase in each party familiarizing with the other one's discipline, research, pedagogy, and methodology, thus contributing to the creation of new knowledge and new efforts. This interaction is also important in increasing trust between the interacting institutions.

Yet the provision of instruction by local and national resources has not been deemed sufficient by the Institute of Educational Leadership, when launching the programme in question. As Alava (2006, 2-3) states, it has been the aim and strategy of the institute to perceive its environment triggering needs to reform educational leadership programmes and to respond to the customer needs and also to attend to the University of Jyväskylä and national higher education strategies. One of these core strategies is internationalization. Consequently, from the very beginning of the programme, expert professors in international comparative education and in educational leadership and management, well networked with the institute, have been involved in teaching in the programme.

Developing an Institute of Educational Leadership at the University of Jyväskylä

Sensitivity to customer needs, which can also be approached from the angle of a university's societal responsibility, was the incentive in launching a principals' qualifications programme of 25 ECTS at the University of Jyväskylä in 1996 as the first one in Finland. The changing environment of educational administration since the 1980s called for a new kind of leadership skills (Hirvi 1996). The programme is aimed at persons aspiring for leadership positions in educational organizations. In 1999 the Institute of Educational Leadership was founded by University President Aino Sallinen, which was an acknowledgement of the need to professionalize leadership positions in the field of education, deserving a solid professional preparation combining theory and practice of the field. In 2001 an advanced programme in educational leadership studies was launched for principals and in 2008 for superintendents and chief educational officers. The first doctoral programme commenced in 2002, followed by the second cohort in 2004. The third cohort, an international Ph D programme, was launched in 2010.

The international master's degree programme in Educational Leadership commenced in 2007, after it had been acknowledged by the Act of Master's Degrees issued by the Ministry of Education in 2006. It is the first programme in the Institute and in Finland awarding a degree in education, with a specification in educational leadership. The roots of the programme are in the Bologna process of 1999, in the long traditions of education and teacher training in the University of Jyväskylä and Finland. Finland's success in the PISA studies of 2000, 2003 and 2006 has ignited a worldwide interest in the effectiveness of the Finnish educational policy implementation, which also reflects as an interest in higher education provision. Consequently, there arose a demand for international master's programmes alongside with the strategic focus of higher education to go international (Välijärvi, Linnakylä, Kupari, Reinikainen, Arffman 2000; OECD 2001-2008).

As yet, ca. 600 learners have studied the qualification programmes in the IEL, ca. 160 the advanced programmes, four PhD theses from the first cohort have been defended, with another five by late 2010, to be succeeded by those from the second cohort. The 28 students enrolled in the two international master's degree programmes currently running as from 2009 are all estimated to graduate with their degree completed. The first ones graduated in June 2009.

Foundation of the Master's Degree Programme

The Ministry of Education defines certain special characteristics in a separate master's programme. The programmes are to efficiently meet the needs of working life and research, and for that reason, they may be interdisciplinary. They have open application procedures, they fulfil the goals set for a Finnish higher education degree and the continuation of studies is secured (MPEL curriculum 2007, 5).

The curriculum promises to provide the master's degree student with a good knowledge base of the major subject, facilities to apply scientific knowledge and practice, skills in operating in working life as an expert for the development of the field, eligibility and capability to pursue scientific postgraduate education, and possibilities to develop their communication and language skills (MPEL curriculum 2007, 5).

Basis of pedagogy: Concept of man, knowledge, and learning

The roots and the basis of the programme are Finnish, but the faculty also emphasize the contribution that the cultural and ethnic diversity of the multinational learning community is to convey to the learning framework of the programme.

The methodological and pedagogical solutions applied are based on and arise from the needs of the learners, their previous learning experiences, and the objectives of the programme. Academic research-based knowledge is reflected on in the interaction of the students with varying practical professional experience and varying cultural backgrounds. This again is reflected in the interaction of the students and the instructors of the programme. E-learning facilities are used in conveying information and learning materials, offering discussion forums, assignment delivery, development and feedback opportunities, and facilitation of interaction.

In the years 2006 and 2007 when finalizing the curriculum of the programme, we formulated our conceptual approach to learning as follows:

> The guiding principle of our work and of the means by which it is implemented is the respect for the worth, integrity and equality of every human being also in their role as learners, and the conviction that learning is a mutual process. The faculties in their role as providers of education are also learners. Through shared learning we believe in our value basis deepening and radiating via the future experiences of our students.
>
> Our concept of the human being is based on the humanistic-socio-constructivist views. The humanistic perspective entails that we believe in every human's right, capability and potential to grow towards becoming themselves and we are committed to enhancing this growth. Further, we believe in the reality of the human being constructing him/herself in relation to another human being and it is our objective to enable the opportunity for this growth.
>
> Our programme has elements of the socio-constructivist perspective of knowledge building. We respect knowledge and the accumulation of it and we endeavour to create knowledge from knowledge. We believe in knowledge growth, creation and realization from the social context where it is encountered and researched.
>
> Thus, the pedagogical solutions applied are based on the needs of the learners and their previous learning experiences. The focus is on learning. Learning is constructed in the interaction and reflection of research based knowledge and learners' learning processes and learning background. One of the focuses of the programme is to build a community of learners.
>
> (MPEL curriculum, 2007, 6)

Implementing the promise made

Implementing the promise made to the customers, that is, implementing for the international students from faraway countries a quality programme with the feasible prospect of graduation in two years' time and capacities to be enrolled in a wide range of job market opportunities, begins with acknowledging the customer needs, remaining sensitive to them, and learning together in cooperation with lecturers, students, and the campus faculty to respond to them. It is a recognized truth that the culture of the organization plays a decisive role in whether the study environment is conducive to learning or not (see e.g., Dimmock, Walker, 2005).

On culture

It has become evident that the concept of organizational culture is one fundamental backbone in our approach to facilitate the success of these students. The definition relied on is the one applied by Bolman & Deal (2004), where culture is considered stable and persistent across time, defining the meaning of recent experience, thereby independently influencing fluctuations in climate. According to this view, climate fluctuates in response to immediate events, but culture is stable. Schein (1993, 17) defines culture as the basic assumptions and beliefs that are shared by members of an organization and operate unconsciously, defining an organization's view of itself and its environment. Mostly culture is defined by shared philosophies, values, beliefs, ideologies, expectations, attitudes, cultural artefacts, and ceremonies transmitting meaning (e.g. Bolman & Deal 2004).

When discussing how culture is created and sustained, the concept of leadership. emerges. Schein (1993, 1) argues: "Organizational cultures are created by leaders… In fact, there is possibility – underemphasized in leadership research – that the *only thing of real importance that leaders do is to create and manage culture …*" Schein wrote at a stage when the concept of shared or distributed leadership was not yet acknowledged. Adhering to the conclusion and concept of cumulative leadership by Alava (2006), and combining it to Schein's concept of culture, we arrive at the statement *'The only thing of real importance that leaders functioning in circumstances of cumulative leadership do is to create and manage culture, where cumulative leadership itself is a culture'*.

On the concept of learning

Teaching with the aforementioned aims is not only about having students respond to stimuli, gaining cognitive skills, enhancing growth in a human being and a professional, or constructing learning in the social and societal context. The claim here is that the behaviourist, humanistic, cognitive, and socio-constructivist theories of learning are not sufficient. The commitment to the entity of making sure of the successful path to the learner is not advocated there.

On responsibility

The relevance of this pedagogy is both parties committing to a common cause. It is about the roles of teacher and student blurring into both becoming learners towards a shared goal within the community, which is possible to create within the culture of the institute. Teaching, studying, and learning are also art and feeling, a shared experience transcending what individual learning can achieve. Hence, the culture base, the mental mode of addressing students' needs, created in the institute is an essential prerequisite for such a community of learners to emerge. It can only emerge in circumstances of trust and patience, where sincere care and willingness, with learning to solve problems together, is in place, and where the individual life story and path of the learner is recognized to be of unique importance and motivation to the learner. (Alava 2006; Sandholm 2009) This is about sensitizing the organization to hear every voice, also the silent one, whether it is silent due to the cultural background, gender, or life circumstances.

The original meaning of the word *responsible* is 'answerable to another, for something' from Latin responsus, pp. of respondere "**to respond**" (Online Etymological Dictionary). The meaning "**morally accountable for one's actions**" is attested from 1836. Starratt (2005) discusses the dimensions of responsibility required from an educational leader in today's changing and varied circumstances. The attributes he addresses are 1) a multidimensional leader who understands the various dimensions of the learning tasks the schools must cultivate, 2) a leader with a moral vision of what is required from the entire community, and 3) a leader with proactive responsibility for making this kind of learning take place. Starratt (2005, 125) also describes the five domains of responsibility central to moral educational leadership: the responsibility as a human being, a citizen and public servant, an educator, an educational administrator, and as an educational leader. It is from these angles that the IEL is consciously accessing its MPEL students: the teacher leader is a human being in every encounter; he is a model of a citizen and he is a public servant by profession; he is an educator, an administrator and an educational leader. He shall not undress any of these roles and functions from his entity but carries the responsibility.

The master's degree programmes in Finland have had an intake of hundreds of international students, yet the number of graduates is modest. Contrary to the previous situation, the graduation percentage in the MPEL programme seems to grow high.

Combining challenging goals with support to study

Challenging goals of the MPEL

The MPEL programme is a two-year programme comprising 120 ECTS, that is, a workload of 120 x 27 hours of work. It is intended for students who have acquired a bachelor's degree in education or some related field, and it leads to an officially recognized master's degree. The programme is constructed to integrate all the key elements of school administration and educational leadership, providing both theoretical knowledge and practical skills required in the complex field of education and educational leadership in different settings. The aim of the programme is to develop internationally oriented professionals and experts. Graduates of the programme can seek employment as researchers, experts, leaders, and administrators in national and international programmes in education and in educational administration and development. The programme will not by itself provide eligibility to the position of a teacher, principal, or school leader; hence, the students need to confirm the transferability of the master's studies with the educational authorities in the respective countries.

The proud and advocated objective of the institute is the implementation of the programme in such a way as to facilitate graduating in the promised two years with a 100 % graduation outcome.

The proud and advocated objective of the students is to graduate in two years and return to make a contribution as leaders of change in their respective countries. Many of the students have a substantial professional experience, consequently not being very young any more. More than 20% of the students are with a family and small children left behind for two years, a joint sacrifice made in order for the mother or father to acquire a master's degree in a field of study not available in the country of the student's origin. As a result, the motivation level at the entrance to the study programme is extremely high, clearly advocated, and also encouraged to be voiced by the institute's orientation policy.

In sum, it can be stated that the goals of the customers (students) and the organization (the institute) are uniform at the beginning. The challenge is to sustain the goals for two years and produce the intended results, the master's degrees.

Each course, after its delivery, is subjected to an assessment by the students, based on the QAF (quality assessment framework) system applied by the university. Additionally, the ethnographic research conducted about this programme brings regular feedback to enable developing the solutions needed.

Support to study

It is a known fact that in order to achieve good learning outcomes and to implement effective education, high expectations and challenging goals need to be combined with not only excellent teaching and learning facilities but also with a supportive learning environment. Besides administrative effectiveness and well-qualified faculty with remarkable teaching skills, the essential factors in building an environment conducive to learning are the organizational culture and a pedagogy responsive to customer needs, as referred to above.

On arrival each student is welcomed by a tutor allocated by the university's international office, guiding the newcomer through practical issues concerning accommodation, banks, transport, shopping, study, and so on. The semester commences with an orientation week organized in cooperation with the international office and the students' union, advising on both practical and social aspects of life in the city of Jyväskylä and at the university, ranging on how to survive through the dark and cold months to finding a host family to visit. The orientation continues inside the MPEL programme with introductions into the ICT and library facilities, with a personal study plan drafted at the beginning as well, where the pace of study and personal goal setting are elaborated on from an individual point of view.

The MPEL programme is scheduled in a school like form in the first two semesters, with regular classes to attend and regular attendance required. This is because through interactive and constructivist methodology, the concept of man, knowledge and learning advocated in the curriculum are put into practice, the hypothesis being that to build a community of learners from total strangers in a new context requires regular contacts in order for all the parties to get to know each other and accumulate trust. For that purpose, also intercultural communication studies begin in the first weeks.

After implementing the programme for two years, it is obvious that in addition to the customer-sensitive culture of the institute, two other factors have contributed to community building. One is that from the beginning of the programme, the project of producing an e-learning version of the programme was launched, and therefore, all the lectures were filmed. The personnel in charge of that effort met the students in every session, becoming friends and sharing news and feelings, gradually also meeting in their free time. They were often the first ones to receive the comments, questions, remarks, doubts, irritations, anger, joys, and so on from the student body. Also, from the beginning, an ethnographic research project was initiated on the programme's dynamics; the researcher, that is the writer of this article, observed most of the classes, field visits, events like a Christmas party, sledge riding party, end of the school year spring party, and interviewing the students. On the other hand, my role has also been that of a teacher in the programme. The result was that around the students there grew a net of regular actors with also other roles than that of a teacher, naturally transmitting information about the students' state of mind and well-being to the faculty. At this point, it became the culture of the IEL to respond to the needs of the students expeditiously, on a now come, now served basis.

Responsiveness to learners' needs

As stated earlier, sensitivity to customer needs is in the culture of the institute created in the first 10 years in the field, prior to the programme in question. When living through this programme, a new element or a shade of meaning started emerging in the regular daily contacts with the students.

Nel Noddings is a firm advocate of the concept of *caring*, used by Gilligan in the early 1980s. Instead of advocating accountability of outcomes, this approach demands for genuine responsiveness to the learners' needs. Noddings claims that genuine responsiveness is a relationship of caring between *the carer* and *the cared for*, based on listening, expressed needs, and on mutual consent and assessed by the acceptance and acknowledgement of the cared-for. The result is the absence of the well-known outcome, a deadly sickness in educational institutions: 'Nobody cares'. In contrast to caring, the traditional responsiveness of imposing the knowledge and skills prescribed to be good for the learner has resulted in discipline-centred and teacher-centred education with the non-desired outcome of 'Nobody cares'. A cure to this problem has been provided by the progressive implementation of more flexibility and child-centred pedagogy in education, yet with the non-desired outcome of 'Nobody cares' (Noddings 1984, 2005).

Caring in this sense of Noddings' is beyond what we used to call *sensitivity to customer needs*. The international students being on campus regularly, in contrast to the other programmes of the IEL, and having a different orientation and dynamics inside their group, and in view of the environment, posed a new challenge. Responding to it came naturally from the basis of the institute's culture: faculty's fluent accessibility to the students became evident, as did also readiness for interventions on an individual basis, be it in the form of finding financial resources; comforting heartbreaks, fears, and happiness when falling in love; intercultural conflicts; grief in family; learning difficulties; deficiencies in study skills, and so on.

On the other hand, when the first cohort reached their first crisis period after the honeymoon beginning, serious efforts were made to improve the group dynamics through the methodology of the then three simultaneous courses studied, and also a group discussion based on skills learned in the aforementioned interval was arranged to facilitate solving the second crisis stage in the group. We consider these approaches as responsiveness to students' needs in the sense that Noddings (1984, 2005) uses the concept of caring.

In addition to the conceptualization of Noddings, the concept of *servant leadership* by Greenleaf (2002) bears similarities to features in the implementation of the MPEL programme. Greenleaf's concept is based on the aspects of listening, empathy, healing, awareness, persuasion, conceptualization, foresight, stewardship "holding something in trust for another", commitment to the growth of people, and building community.

Greenleaf (2002, 79-82) claims that leadership needs to be both conceptual and operational, in order for the organization to perform well in a sustained manner, which is not a quick fix, but a long-term, transformational approach to life and work. He states: "*Conceptual,* (...) is not synonymous with *intellectual* or *theoretical*. Conceptualizers at their best are intensely practical. They are also effective persuaders and relationship builders (p. 79)." Further, Greenleaf connects conceptual leadership and organizational principle: "*They (some institutions) probably lost their conceptual leadership because they were not guided by an organizational principle that required it. Therefore, not knowing when they accidentally had it, they were not aware when they lost it (p. 82)*". This article claims that conceptualizing and organizational principles are clearly connected and interdependent in the practices of the IEL, corresponding to the core of Greenleaf's servant leadership.

Conclusion

In conclusion, the analysis of Alava (2006), based on the strategic framework of Maula (cf. chapter 1) stated that the long-term development of the IEL has resulted in shared leadership and beyond, which he defined as cumulative leadership and a cumulative leadership culture.

The implementation of the international MPEL programme is based on this culture and abundance of leadership. When implemented with an international cohort on campus regularly, it has developed into what has been labelled a pedagogy of caring and responsible leadership. The concepts of caring and responsible leadership are close to the concept that Greenleaf (2002) defines as servant leadership.

The commitment to facilitate student success by the afore mentioned means coincides with the high motivation and commitment of the students, and the growth in learning to solve intriguing issues together within the community seems to contribute to the fact that the graduation percentage from this programme is likely to be far higher than that in other master's degree programmes in Finland.

References

Alava, J. (2006). *Quality is not accidental. A case of cumulative leadership.* UNIQUAL Conference Proceedings. Key to University Quality Assurance: Faculty/Staff Development in the Global Context. Edited by Pan Maoyan, Fan Yihong and Zhu Yu. Xiamen, China.

Bolman, L., & Deal, T. (2004). *Reframing Organizations.* 2nd ed. San Fancisco: Jossey- Bass.

Dimmock, C., & Walker, A. (2005). *Educational Leadership. Culture and Diversity.* London: Sage.

Greenleaf, R. K. (2002). *Servant Leadership. A Journey into the Nature of Legitimate Power & Greatness.* New Jersey: Paulist Press.

Hirvi, V. (1996). *Koulutuksen rytminvaihdos: 1990-luvun koulutuspolitiikka Suomessa, toimittanut Esa Pirnes.* Helsinki: Otava.

MPEL (Master's Degree Programme in Educational Leadership) Curriculum 2007-2009. University of Jyväskylä: Faculty of Education.

Noddings, N. (1984). *Caring. A Feminine Approach to Ethics & Moral Education.* Berkeley: University of California Press.

Noddings, N. (2005). *The Challenge to Care in Schools: An Alternative Approach to Education.* 2nd ed. New York: Teachers College Press.

OECD Education at a Glance 2001-2008. http://www. oecd.org

Online Etymological Dictionary. http://www.etymonline.com

Sandholm, L. (2008). Responsible Leadership with an Ethics of Care and Caring. Lecture series given at the University of Jyväskylä, Finland.

Sandholm, L. (2009). *Research Report on the Master's Degree Programme in Educational Leadership.* University of Jyväskylä: Institute of Educational Leadership.

Schein, E. H. (1993). *Career Anchors: Discovering Your Real Values.* Rev. ed. San Francisco: Jossey-Bass Pfeiffer.

Starratt, R. J. (2003). *Building an Ethical School.* London: Routledge Falmer.

Starratt, R. J. (2005). Responsible Leadership. *The Educational Forum,* 69(2), 124-133. Retrievable at http://www.informaworld.com/smpp/content~db=all?content=10.1080/00131720508984676

Välijärvi, J., Linnakylä, P., Kupari, P., Reinikainen, P., & Arffman, I. (2000). The Finnish Success in PISA and Some Reasons behind it. Available at: http://ktl.jyu.fi/ktl/pisa/english

The paper has been reviewed by external referees.

The Relativity of Academic Assessments: How to compare apples with oranges

Boaz Shulruf

Abstract

In tertiary institutions where modular qualifications are offered, tertiary education providers tend to focus more on course than qualification completion. Consequently, qualification completion rates within education institutions are low, which then reduces the validity of completion rates as a measure for educational effectiveness. This study, focusing on polytechnic qualifications and based on data from a large NZ polytechnic, provides an alternative method to compare student achievement across programs and institutions regardless of differences in grading scales and completion rates. Furthermore, by instituting this new method it is possible to identify more precisely the groups of students who are at the greatest risk for failure while identifying programs that require further investigation regarding low achievement and/or low completion rates. Implications for educational policy makers are discussed.

Over the past two decades the tertiary education system in New Zealand has grown significantly in response to government strategy to increase the skills level of the labour market (OECD, 2004; Philips, 2003; Wagner, 1998). Much of that growth has been at the non-degree (i.e., Certificate and Diploma) levels. (Ministry of Education, 2002; NZQA, 2007; Philips, 2003). The non-degree level education in New Zealand is operated within the National Qualifications Framework (NQF), which is a modular qualification framework. The NQF was implemented to improve access to tertiary education through non-standard entry, thus encouraging flexible learning styles, and maximising opportunities for the student by allowing them to find an optimum balance of their skills and time available for study (Bell & Wade, 1993).

The main criticism of the modular education system, however, is the potential loss of continuity in the learning process, leading to the development of shorter teaching units as well as the need to meet multiple purposes, thus resulting in a less focused system than that offered in linear curricular systems (Bell & Wade, 1993). Other challenges relate to the equivalency of qualification. For example, a group of students may acquire the same qualification, yet each of them could have taken a different combination of courses, so how can their achievements be fairly compared (Yorke, 1989)?

The New Zealand tertiary education system is composed of a number of organisations which hold different responsibilities for aspects of accreditation, course approval and auditing (OECD, 2004). In New Zealand, providers of National Qualifications Framework qualifications (including polytechnics) are awarded "accreditation" by New Zealand Qualifications Authority (NZQA) to offer the components that make up a National Certificate/National Diploma (NZQA, n.d.). NZQA also approves all degrees offered outside the university sector, which include polytechnics and Wananga (Maori tertiary education institutes) (NZQA, n.d.). Non-degree qualifications awarded by universities could, but not necessarily, be part of the NQF, yet all degree qualifications awarded by the universities are approved by the New Zealand Vice-Chancellor's Committee, which is independent of the NZQA.

The National Qualifications Framework (NQF) approves all standards, programmes and qualifications within the NZQA framework. Currently there are more than 18,000 approved standards and 800 National Certificates and National Diplomas covering almost every area of work and learning in the NZQA framework. (NZQA, n.d.).

All NZQA-approved providers report their students' achievements to the NZQA, who in turn issue qualifications to students once they have met the requirements (NZQA, 2005). Hence, students acquire credits towards a range of qualifications across a number of institutions, which keep separate institutional records, yet only the NZQA holds all these data across institutions and has the authority to award the qualification. These records affect the level of funding tertiary education institutions receive from the government. Consequently, tertiary institutions are rated based on course completion (i.e., credits gained by students) rather than by qualification completion (NZQA, 2005). It is therefore possible that this is the reason for the slight increase in the number of non-degree tertiary qualification holders (from 33% to 35%) from 1994 to 2005. However, within the undergraduate education system (where tertiary institutions issue the qualifications) the number of degree holders within the same population has increased from 38% in 1991 to 50% in 2005 (Smart, 2006). Furthermore, the five-year completion rate for Certificate and Diploma level (as of 2003) was 35% compared with 46% for undergraduate level (Smyth et al., 2006).

Since the vast majority of non-degree tertiary students do not complete their studies with a formal qualification, measuring the success of any population of students, whether defined by institution, demographic characteristics or any other determinants by rate of completion, would not be appropriate. This is important within the context of any modular educational system but particularly in New Zealand. The main question derived from this structure is: how does one know who is more successful? Students who qualified with formal qualifications by meeting the minimum requirements, or students who took some courses, completed them with high grades, but have not yet acquired the total number of credits required for qualification? Moreover, given the rise in the number of part-time students (Smyth et al., 2006) it is becoming increasingly important to measure the achievements of the non-completers.

This study introduces a new standardisation method which could solve the comparability issue with implications for policy makers. The proposed standardisation method will enhance accuracy in measuring student achievement while identifying populations and programmes/ courses where students underachieve more than would normally be expected.

Methods

Student demographic and achievement data from 2002 to 2005 were provided by a large Polytechnic in New Zealand (NZP). The NZP, like all other Polytechnics in New Zealand, offers predominantly short-term, non-degree, vocationally oriented programmes and in most cases, these programmes are based on open entry admission. Only a few Polytechnics including NZP offer a limited number of degree programmes. Non-degree programmes offered in New Zealand Polytechnics comprise one or more courses. Some of these courses are NZQA accredited and some are audited by Institutes of Technology and Polytechnics Quality, which is a quality assurance authority for Polytechnics in New Zealand, separate to the NZQA (OECD, 2004). Therefore, the assessment and credit systems differ depending on the framework in which these courses are placed.

This study focuses only on students enrolled in non-degree certificates and diploma courses. Taking into account the nature of programmes offered by Polytechnics in NZ, cohorts have been identified by student programme. That is, for students enrolled in more than one programme, each enrolment was counted separately, whether the multiple enrolments occurred concurrently or sequentially, during the period covered by this study. For each student programme, the start date of the first programme and end date of the last courses taken toward fulfilling the criteria for this particular programme were identified, and variables of time T1, T2 and T3 have been devised. T1 measures the time from the data starting point (1 January 2002) to the starting date of the first course in the programme. T2 specifies the duration of the programme and it has a unique value for each individual, depending on the study load of the students in the programme. It spans from the end of T1 to the time when the student's enrolment in that particular programme ceases. T3 measures the time from the end of T2 to the end point of the data collection period, which was

December 2005. All three variables of time are measured in weeks, not taking into account holidays.

Student achievement variables were extracted from the dataset. It is noteworthy that different courses applied different assessment systems. Hence, the assessment results (i.e., grades) needed to be standardised to be comparable. Therefore, all course grades were first classified into four bands of achievements: 0-failure, 1-achieved or pass, 2-merit, and 3 for excellence. Some courses did not have the full range of achievements (e.g., did not have excellence). To complete the comparability process, all classified grades were modified into z-scores (modifying the grade so that the mean is 0 and SD is 1). Then for each student programme a Grade Point Average (GPA) was calculated by calculating the mean standardised grade weighted for the number of credits achieved per course. These GPAs were summarised for NZQA and non-NZQA programs separately. The advantage is that all courses are now on the same scale; the disadvantage is that the relative difficulty of each subject is lost as all have the same mean (see below).

As indicated above, although completion is the ultimate measure of success, measuring student success by completion alone would not be ideal since the completion rate within five years from enrolment is around 30% (Smyth et al., 2006). On the other hand, for the non-completers, comparing a students' GPA alone would also be an unfair measure since the GPA is a measure of quality only and cannot measure quantity (i.e., number of credits gained). Moreover, the data cover a period of four years and students could have enrolled in a programme or left a programme at any time, which means that a simple comparison of the total number of credits gained is also not appropriate. No data were available on previous credits acquired so some of the completions were related to previous studies, but there was no way to get that information from NZP since these records are centrally held by the NZQA and normally are not available to the tertiary institute (in this case NZP).

All these issues led to the development of a new approach for measuring success. First, a few assumptions are made: (a) the more courses a student has successfully completed, the more likely he/she is to gain a qualification; (b) the longer the time a student was enrolled, the more likely he/she is to gain a qualification (in comparison to other students in the same programme); (c) the longer the time a student had between the end of enrolment (T2) and the end of follow-up (T3), the more likely he/she is to gain qualification (based on the ability to complete unfinished tasks or re-sit exams); and (d) the higher the GPA, the more likely the student is to gain a qualification.

A logistic regression model was tested for each of these programmes using Equation 1 as a generic equation to determine the proportional effect of each of the three components on completion: time, number of credits gained and GPA. In this equation each student was compared to the mean value of the completers (within a particular programme) in terms of time and credits gained since no other benchmarks were available. The GPA was placed in the equation as z-score within the programme to allow fair comparability. Furthermore, since some programmes comprised NZQA as well as NZP courses, GPA and number of credits gained were calculated separately.

The calculated success value (SV) was the regression predictive value for each individual minus the constant (a), modified to z-scores within each programme. In this way all the SV across all programmes were comparable. The SV was then used as a dependent variable to identify factors affecting student success within the two major groups of students: the completers and non-completers. The analysis used descriptive statistics as well as linear regression models.

Study Population

The polytechnic dataset included 22,997 students of which 12,172 (53%) were female. The mean age at enrolment was 30.1 (SD = 11.0) years. The student population was ethnically diverse with 28% Pakeha (European New Zealanders), 12% Maori (Indigenous New Zealanders), 19% Pasifika (Pacific Islands people), 36% Asians and 6% other ethnicity. Eighty-four per cent of the students were domestic and 16% were overseas students. The majority of the student population were from low-income families where the mean socio-economic status score (SES) was 4.7 (socio-economic status measured by student addresses; for details see, Salmond & Crampton, 2002) (on a scale of 1-10), and 28.4% came from deciles 1-2 (low SES). About a quarter (22%) of the students had no high school qualification, whereas 45.4% held University Entrance (UE) qualifications.

Results

Out of the total sample population only 7,272 (32%) of students completed their studies with a formal qualification (issued by either NZP or NZQA). The first analysis was to verify the assumption that the Success Value (SV) was highly associated with programme completion. It was found that the SV for completers was significantly higher than that for the non-completers (.51 vs. -.24; $p<.001$), which strongly supports the initial assumptions. Since the total completion rate is low, there was a need to measure two different types of success. The first, as indicated above, was the proportion of students who completed their studies with a qualification. The second measure was the success value (SV) as described in the Methods section above.

Student success varied across gender, ethnicity and SES. The completion rate was similar across socioeconomic groupings but not across ethnicity. Pakeha, Maori and Pasifika achieved about 33% completion rate, whereas only 29% and 28% of the Asians and other ethnic groups completed their studies with qualifications. It appeared that the success value (SV) was similar across ethnic groups among the students who completed their studies (gained the qualification), but among the non-completers the non Maori-Pasifika achieved significantly higher SV than their counterparts (difference of about .25 SD) (Figure 2). On the other hand, no statistically significant difference was found in the SV across genders among the non-completers but among the completers females achieved slightly higher SV (.52 vs. .49 p=.002). The SV did not change across SES among the completers. However, among the non-completers the SV did not change across SES deciles 5-10 but gradually dropped from decile 4 to 1 (Figure 3). Student secondary school qualifications were related to the SV only among the non-completers (Figure 4). The secondary school qualification effect on SV was greater among students who studied towards a Certificate than those who studied towards Diploma level of qualification.

Further analysis was conducted for the non-completers, in order to identify the predictability of the demographic characteristics as well as previous activities and achievements on student SV. The rationale for limiting the analysis to the non-completers was that once a student receives the qualification, the level of achievement (i.e., GPA) and the number of credits gained are no longer of high importance. However, for students who have not yet gained a qualification the SV (e.g. the combination of GPA and credits gained) has a major effect on their likelihood to gain the qualification. A linear regression model was developed to identify the effects of demographic characteristics, previous activities, educational attainment and programme chosen at NZP on student SV. A three-block linear regression model was developed. The first block included all demographic variables, the second block included previous occupation and secondary school attainment (these variables were accepted into the regression if they demonstrated statistically significant variance) and the third block included type of programme identified by type of qualification (Diploma or Certificate) and field of study. This design was based on the assumption of sequential events that is demographic precedes previous educational and occupational experiences, which then precede programmes taken at NZP.

The results (Table 1) indicate that Maori and Pasifika students gain lower SV, whereas SES has positive effect on SV. The higher the school qualification, the greater the SV achieved. The table also shows that prior study at a Polytechnic before entering programmes had a positive effect on SV. The type of programme affected the SV as well. Higher SV was achieved within the Diploma programmes as well as within Languages and Accounting & Banking programmes as compared to Arts and Marketing which yielded the lowest SV. The total regression model explained 35% of the variance in SV ($R^2 = .35$).

In summary, the results suggest that student demographics and previous experiences affect students who are low achievers in terms of completion and SV. Furthermore, differences in SV across programmes were found and suggest that some features within the programmes are also related to the SV.

Discussion

This study provides an opportunity to look into an important sector of the New Zealand tertiary education system and disentangle some of its complexity, particularly in terms of defining success and analysing how a range of factors affect students' success within a modular qualification system. The non-degree programmes in New Zealand Polytechnics fall largely within the modular systems under which students can acquire credits towards qualifications over a long period of time (NZQA, 2007; Philips, 2003). This applies to both courses within and outside of the NZQA framework. Hence, despite the short-term nature of most of the programmes, measuring student success by completion over a few years might not be appropriate since students may spread their studies over many years and institutions. Furthermore, polytechnics hold only student achievement records generated within their institutions. Therefore, individual polytechnic databases cannot provide a comprehensive view of its student success as a student can enrol across many institutions. For these reasons the current study took an alternative approach, measuring student's relative success against 'average student' achievement gained in each program. By establishing the Success Value (SV), which comprises GPA, credits gained and related administrative factors affecting it (time, see Equation 1), this study measures student success within the norm-based achievement framework (Croft, 1993).

As in previous studies (Anae, Anderson, Benseman, & Coxon, 2002; Ministry of Education, 2005; Scott, 2003; Shulruf, Hattie, & Tumen, 2008; Wagner, 1998), this study found that students from Maori and Pacific ethnicities as well as from low SES achieved lower SV scores. In a similar way, this phenomenon is also observed where the SV is compared between the Diploma and Certificate levels among the non-completers (Figure 4). Diploma level studies are more intense than Certificate level studies, and it is clear that the completion of a secondary school qualification has a lesser effect on the Diploma than Certificate level students. These findings strengthen the hypothesis that the background effects are stronger at the lower end of the achievement scale. This finding is most important particularly in the light of previous studies raising the issue of inequality of achievements across groups of students defined by ethnicity and SES in New Zealand tertiary education. (Bennett, 2002; McLaughlin, 2003; Ministry of Education, 2004, 2005; Scott, 2003; Shulruf et al., 2008; Smart, 2006).

Hence, the findings of the current study clearly suggest that interventions aiming to enhance equity in non-degree programmes within the tertiary education sector should be determined primarily by student performance (i.e., GPA and intensity of study) rather than by demographic characteristics. Identifying and supporting these students will decrease the inequality across SES and ethnicities since within that particular group the proportion of students from low SES and Maori and Pacific ethnicities is relatively high. Supporting students using the criteria of SES and ethnicity may also positively affect the overall outcomes of Maori, Pacific Island and low SES groups, However, the effect will be smaller since some of the resources will be used for students who do not require support, leaving less resources for those who have the greatest need (e.g., students with other demographic characteristics who are lower achievers). Furthermore, by focusing on the issue (i.e., performance) rather than on the group, the risk of stigmatising a specific group is minimised. Since this particular study focused on the development of the methodology there was no scope for a detailed investigation of each particular group of students. Such intervention approach is also more appropriate than pointing at students as the cause of the failure and thereby essentially "blaming the victim" (as identified by ethnicity or SES) as may happen in some educational institutions (St. Denis & Hampton, 2002) It is better therefore to focus on performance and achievement including particularly providing academic support to enhance learning strategies and social support, which then improve educational programme practices (Gilbertson, 2005; Middleton, 2003; Tinto, 1999).

Further research would benefit from using the method developed in this study to look into equity in tertiary education by focusing on particular groups rather than analysing the entire population. Applying such a method is not common but appears to be necessary, particularly when using linear models for analysing data which are vulnerable to a 'range restricted' bias (Bobko, Roth, & Bobko, 2001; Mendoza & Mumford, 1987).

In summary, this study provides a unique insight into the New Zealand tertiary education system within a polytechnic context. The first part of this paper addresses one of the most challenging issues in the non-degree programs within a modular framework (i.e. NZQA): the measurement of success. The development of the Success Value (SV) in this paper appears to make a significant contribution to the literature, particularly within a New Zealand context but also worldwide, where educational programmes are modular and the qualifications are awarded by a central agency rather than by the education providers. Within such environments and where completion of a qualification can be made through the accumulation of credits from different institutions, the completion rate within a specific institution decreases. Hence, the traditional measure of completion rates is not appropriate. Using the SV as a measure to compare student achievements across programmes and possibly across institutions may provide policy makers with a useful tool for evaluating the effectiveness of tertiary education institutions within this particular environment.

Furthermore, the SV appears to be a useful measure to identify inequalities in education outcomes more accurately. Measuring the SV separately within the completers and non-completers enabled the identification of a group of students who most needed support, and by using this information tertiary education institutions can be guided in giving effective support where it is needed. Although the current study used data from New Zealand, the implications are widely generalisable. Equity in higher education is a major issue across the world (Berk, 2002). Most countries and institutions use different types of admission policies to address inequality as well as support programmes for under-achieving students (Leathwood, 2005; Shulruf, Turner, & Hattie, 2009). Equity in assessment, however, has attracted less interest

(Leathwood, 2005). Hence, implementing the Success Value concept would benefit many tertiary education institutions and students across the world, particularly where education systems are modular and assessments are not standardised across programmes and qualifications.

In conclusion, there is a broad range of methods to measure student achievement. However, identifying the most appropriate method is very important particularly when the study population is diverse. In these particular situations, using linear models for the entire population should be considered with caution. Hence, it is suggested that such studies involving diverse populations look into student pathways and factors affecting them within as well as across groups. This is particularly important where educational pathways differ across groups, and therefore treating diverse population as one homogenised group, whether identified by ethnicity, SES, gender and so on will not reveal the different dynamics within the educational pathway of each group.

References

Anae, M., Anderson, H., Benseman, J., & Coxon, E. (2002). *Pacific Peoples and Tertiary Education: Issues of Participation. Final Report.* (No. D-Anae.M0201) Wellington: Auckland Uniservices prepared for Ministry of Education.

Bell, G. H., & Wade, W. (1993). Modular Course Design in Britain: Some Problems, Issues and Opportunities. *Journal of Further and Higher Education, 17*(1), 3-12.

Bennett, S. (2002). *Cultural identity and academic achievement among Māori undergraduate university students.* Paper presented at the National Māori Graduates of Psychology Symposium, Hamilton.

Berk, D. (2002). *Tertiary Education: Lessons from a Decade of Lending, FY1990-2000.* Washington: World Bank.

Bobko, P., Roth, P., & Bobko, C. (2001). Correcting the Effect Size of d for Range Restriction and Unreliability. *Organizational Research Methods, 4*(1), 46-61.

Croft, C. (1993). *The Conflicting World of Standards-Based Assessment.* Paper presented at the National Conference of the New Zealand Association for Research in Education, Hamilton, New Zealand, December 2-5, 1993.

Gilbertson, D. (2005). *Educating for the Ideal Graduate – A Case for New Measures in Tertiary Education.* Wellington: Te Kaihau Ltd.

Leathwood, C. (2005). Assessment policy and practice in higher education: purpose, standards and equity. *Assessment & Evaluation in Higher Education, 30*(3), 307-324.

McLaughlin, M. (2003). *Tertiary Education Policy in New Zealand.* Retrieved 20 April 2006, from http://www.fulbright.org.nz/voices/axford/docs/mcLaughlin.pdf

Mendoza, J., & Mumford, M. (1987). Corrections for Attenuation and Range Restriction on the Predictor. *Journal of Educational Statistics, 12*(3), 282-293.

Middleton, S. (2003). *Connecting with community: A strategic approach to meeting the imperatives of a changing community.* Paper presented at the American Association of University Administrators National Assembly, San Francisco.

Ministry of Education. (2002). *Participation in Tertiary Education (August 2002):* Ministry of Education, New Zealand.

Ministry of Education. (2004). *Maori student retention, completion and progression in tertiary education.* Wellington: Ministry of Education, New Zealand.

Ministry of Education. (2005). *Maori in Tertiary Education: A Picture of the Trends*: Ministry of Education, New Zealand.

NZQA. (2005). Quality Assurance Standard for PTEs, GTEs and Wānanga (QA Standard One). Retrieved 10 May 2006, from http://www.nzqa.govt.nz/for-providers/aaa/docs/qastd1.pdf

NZQA. (2007). The New Zealand Qualifications Authority. From http://www.nzqa.govt.nz/

NZQA. (n.d.). New Zealand qualifications Retrieved 19 March 2009, 2009, from http://www.nzqa.govt.nz/qualifications/index.html

OECD. (2004). *The Role of National Qualifications Systems in Promoting Lifelong Learning, Background Report for New Zealand*. Paris: Organization for Economic Cooperation and Development.

Philips, D. (2003). Lessons from New Zealand's National Qualifications Framework. *Journal of Education and Work, 16*(3), 289-304.

Salmond, C., & Crampton, P. (2002). *NZDep2001 Index of Deprivation User's Manual* (User's Manual). Wellington: University of Otago, Wellington School of Medicine and Health Sciences.

Scott, D. (2003). *Participation in Tertiary Education*. Wellington: Ministry of Education.

Shulruf, B., Hattie, J., & Tumen, S. (2008). The Predictability of Enrolment and First Year University Results from Secondary School Performance. *Studies in Higher Education, 33*(6), 685-698.

Shulruf, B., Turner, R., & Hattie, J. (2009). A Dual admission model for equity in higher education: a multi-cohort longitudinal study. *Procedia – Social and Behavioral Sciences, 1*(1), 2416-2420.

Smart, W. (2006). *Outcomes of the New Zealand tertiary education system : a synthesis of the evidence*. Wellington: Ministry of Education.

Smyth, R., McClelland, J., Lister, P., Steenhart, K., Sargison, A., Westwater, K., et al. (2006). *OECD Thematic Review of Tertiary Education: New Zealand Country Background Report*. Wellington: Ministry of Education.

St. Denis, V., & Hampton, E. (2002). *Literature Review on Racism and the Effects on Aboriginal Education*. Saskatchewan, Canada: University of Saskatchewan.

Tinto, V. (1999). Taking Retention Seriously: Rethinking the First Year of College. *National Academic Advising Association Journal, 19*(2), 5-9.

Wagner, A. (1998). *From Higher to Tertiary Education: Evolving Responses in OECD Countries to Large Volume Participation*: The World Bank.

Yorke, M. (1989). Undergraduate Non-Completion in England: Some Implications for the Higher Education System and its Institutions. *Tertiary Education and Management, 4*(1), 59-70.

Tables

Table 1 Linear Regression for Success Value (All Diploma and Certificate Programs)

	B	Std. Error	Beta	t	Sig.	95% CI for B	
Constant	-0.54	0.026		-20.60	0.000	-0.59	-0.49
Maori[1]	-0.09	0.019	-0.049	-4.75	0.000	-0.13	-0.05
Pasifika[1]	-0.12	0.017	-0.080	-7.03	0.000	-0.15	-0.09
Asian[1]	0.01	0.017	0.007	0.57	0.567	-0.02	0.04
Other ethnicity[1]	-0.03	0.025	-0.012	-1.34	0.182	-0.08	0.02
Male[2]	-0.07	0.012	-0.059	-6.20	0.000	-0.10	-0.05
SES	0.01	0.002	0.037	3.68	0.000	0.00	0.01
School qualification[3]	0.05	0.005	0.094	9.20	0.000	0.04	0.06
Age at start	0.00	0.001	0.064	6.90	0.000	0.00	0.00
Unemployed or beneficiary[4]	-0.06	0.017	-0.032	-3.40	0.001	-0.09	-0.02
PTE student[4]	-0.09	0.031	-0.024	-2.81	0.005	-0.15	-0.03
Wage or salary employee[4]	0.01	0.013	0.010	0.98	0.327	-0.01	0.04
Polytechnic student[4]	0.05	0.027	0.016	1.86	0.063	0.00	0.10
Diploma[5]	0.18	0.014	0.141	13.03	0.000	0.15	0.21
Language skills[6]	0.16	0.020	0.104	8.16	0.000	0.12	0.20
Arts[6]	-0.49	0.061	-0.067	-7.98	0.000	-0.61	-0.37
Carpentry[6]	-0.26	0.036	-0.064	-7.13	0.000	-0.33	-0.19
Other programs[6]	0.20	0.036	0.048	5.54	0.000	0.13	0.27
Sports[6]	-0.30	0.050	-0.051	-5.94	0.000	-0.39	-0.20
Hospitality or tourism[6]	-0.16	0.026	-0.055	-6.02	0.000	-0.21	-0.11
Administration[6]	-0.09	0.022	-0.040	-4.23	0.000	-0.13	-0.05
Marketing[6]	-0.38	0.090	-0.035	-4.21	0.000	-0.55	-0.20
Services[6]	-0.21	0.053	-0.033	-3.89	0.000	-0.31	-0.10
Technology of Engineering[6]	0.06	0.021	0.026	2.76	0.006	0.02	0.10
R square	.35						

1 Reference: Pakeha

2 Reference: Female

3 Ordinal categories: 1=no qualification; 2=Sixth Form Certificate or equivalent; 3=UE qualification; 4=Bursary qualification or equivalent

4 Reference: secondary school student

5 Reference: Certificate

6 Reference: Accounting or Banking

Figures

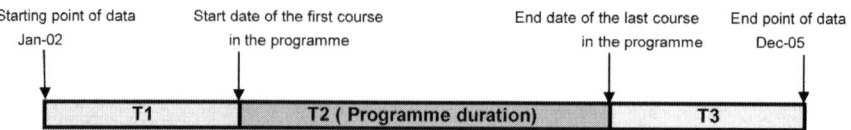

Figure 1 Variables of Time

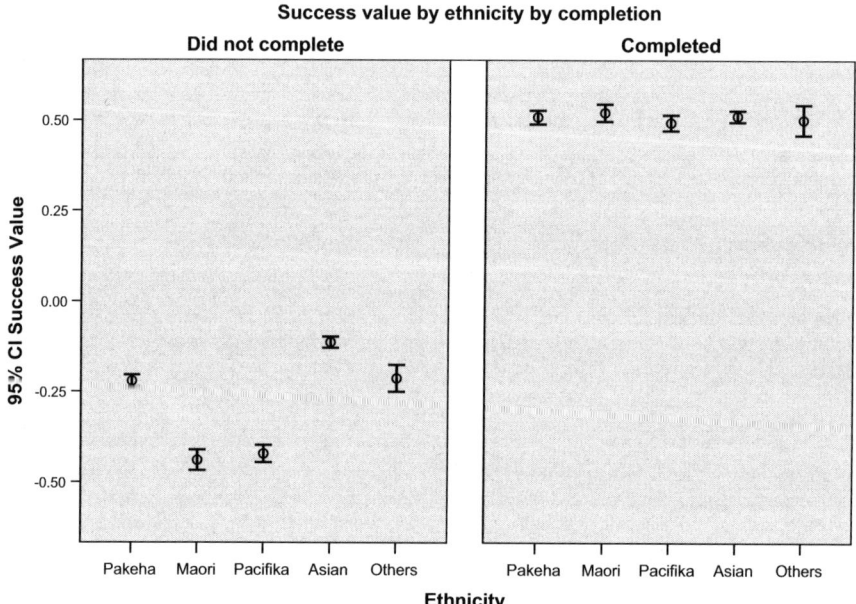

Figure 2 Success value by ethnicity by completion

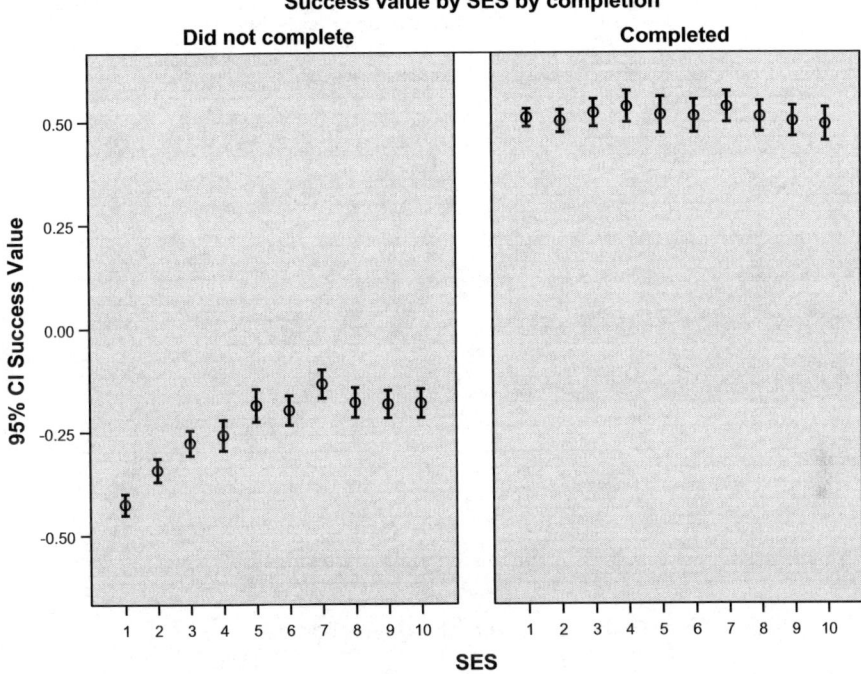

Figure 3 Success value by SES by completion

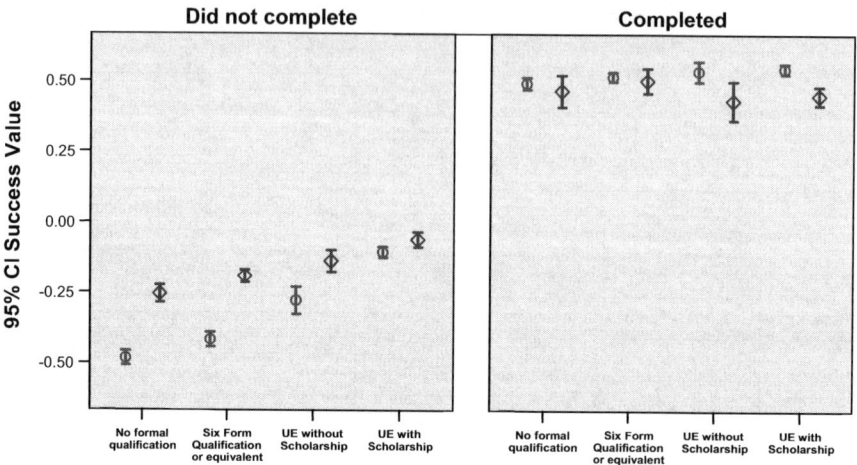

Figure 4 Success value by secondary school qualification by type of tertiary qualification by completion

Equations

$$\log\left(\frac{\theta(C)}{1-\theta(C)}\right) = \alpha + \beta_1\left(\frac{(\overline{T_{2c}}/T_{2i})}{T_{3i}}\right) + \beta_2\left(\frac{N_i}{\overline{N_c}}\right)_{NZP} + \beta_3\left(\frac{N_i}{\overline{N_c}}\right)_{NZQA} + \beta_4(GPA)_{NZP} + \beta_5(GPA)_{NZQA}$$

$\overline{T_{2c}}$ Mean enrolment time for the completers
T_{2i} Individual's enrolment time
T_{3i} Time from end of enrolment to last date of dataset
N_i No. of credits gained by an individual student
$\overline{N_c}$ Mean no. of credits gained by completers
GPA   Grade Point Average of an individual student
C   Completers

Equation 1 Logistic regression for program completion

The paper has been reviewed by external referees.

Quality in university teaching: Learners' perceptions in foreign language education

Janete Zygmantas[1]

Abstract

Social psychologists and educationalists have highlighted the important role attribution plays in education, especially when learners are given the opportunity to express the perceived causes for their successes or failures during their learning experiences. This study shows the preliminary results of the perceived difficulties attributed by forty-five students who enrolled in a language course, offered by a local university in Lithuania. The categories emerged from the data and were grouped into two main domains: 'learning-environment factors' and 'learner factors'. With regard to the latter, students attributed their difficulties mostly to internal dimensions, such as lack of ability and confidence, whereas in the former the causes were mainly attributed to lack of appropriate educational resources, lack of opportunity to practise, inappropriate instruction and course design, apart from the peculiarities of the foreign language (i.e. Lithuanian). The 'learning-environment factors' outnumbered the 'learner factors' and, considering the vital role causal attributions play in education, this paper defends the implementation of such a theoretical framework, especially at classroom levels. Finally, this study intends to show that findings such as these can be considered as a preliminary data indicator of quality in teaching and learning.

Keywords: Quality in teaching and learning, foreign language education, learner's perceptions, attribution.

---

[1] MA in Applied Linguistics from the Pontifical Catholic University in São Paulo, Brazil and, currently, a PhD student at the Department of Educational Sciences, Faculty of Philosophy, Vilnius University, Vilnius, Lithuania.

Introduction

Scholars tend to agree on the fact that learning never takes place in a vacuum and that culture – the product of all human activity – plays a vital role in the development of human beings. For instance, from an ecological perspective, studies conducted by Bronfenbrenner (1942, 1979, 2004) showed that individuals are always interacting within culturally organized settings (i.e. micro, meso, macro levels) and, consequently, have different, direct or indirect levels of participation; these interactions will in turn have a significant impact on their own development.

Likewise, while discussing the quality of learning environments, Williams and Burdens (1997) noted that educational processes are not neutral. The authors contended that each individual cannot be separated from a social system and if "something goes wrong within the system, it should not be seen as the fault of any individual, but a lack of balance in the system" (p. 190). The immediate physical environment of a classroom – which is one of the many microsystems existing within a given macrosystem – will impact learning outcomes considerably, including how one learns, for instance, a language.

Moreover, Beacco and Byram (2003) maintained that ordinary conceptions of language learning – 'language learning is difficult', 'you have to be gifted to learn languages', 'you learn languages when you are very young' – are often reinforced by schools; such representations "muddle perceptions of the nature of individual plurilingual competence and sap the motivation to learn" (p. 73).

Similarly, drawing on an ecological perspective in the sense that teachers and students are placed in interconnected social contexts, Martini and Boruchovitch (2004) noted that traditionally the whole educational system reproduces conceptions and practices that reinforce the attribution of failure to ability, which has in turn been labelled by conventional psychologists as fixed and stable. The authors added that "psychologists and educationalists cannot contribute to the formation and maintenance of such prejudices"; after all, "education is an essentially social practice and the school is a privileged space where a set of social interactions with educational aims take place" (p. 67).

Finally, in discussing the relationship between critical pedagogy and cognition, Kincheloe (2008) contended that current debates about educational reforms aiming at high-quality education should consider that "not only is cognitive ability expressed in diverse ways but that is *learnable*" (p. 163). This scholar went on to say that "individuals of various ages, backgrounds, and IQ scores can learn conceptual systems that help them make meaning, that facilitate their understanding of and ability to negotiate the world around them". Finally, he added that intelligence "can be taught in numerous places: the schools, workplaces, civic organizations, union halls, and in any other place where people interact" (p. 163-164).

It is, therefore, the aim of this paper to highlight the importance of taking into account learners' perceptions and investigating them in light of attribution theory from a critical perspective. This study intends to show that the adoption of such a theoretical/methodological approach may lead to preliminary indicators of quality in the teaching and learning process, especially when applied to microsystems such as the foreign language classroom.

1. Language learning: goals and misconceptions

Languages have always played a crucial role throughout man's existence. For instance, Jespersen (1904) viewed the act of learning foreign languages as *a tool of communication* used to exchange thoughts between different cultures, "a way of connection between souls" (p. 4). Dewey (1910) stated that language is *a tool of thinking* enabling us to train our thoughts; as "it connects and organizes meanings as well as selects and fixes them" (p. 185). Vygotsky (1930-35) considered language as *a symbolic tool that* not only *mediates human interactions* within a particular context but *also triggers the development of higher mental functions*. Freire (1970) affirmed that it is through speaking a true word that we can break from a 'culture of silence', name and transform the world; such dialogic action, according to him, is "an act of creation and re-creation" (p. 89). Similarly, Postman (1995) stressed that it is through language that we make the world and construct our realities; in other words, language is "*an act of creation*" (p. 188, emphasis added).

In view of the above, it should come as no surprise that current European Union policies prioritize foreign language education. Learning other languages helps Europe safeguard its cultural diversity and plurilingual heritage (Kelly et al., 2004); also, language learning has been a priority in the European Union for over 30 years (Eurydice in Brief, 2005). Furthermore, learning a language is for the learner: it should be based on worthwhile, realistic objectives reflecting needs, interests, motivation and abilities. It is also for intercultural communication, ensuring interaction beyond cultural boundaries. Finally, "language learning is for life: it should develop learner responsibility and the independence necessary to respond to the challenges of lifelong language learning" (Council of Europe, 2006: p. 6).

Alas, as Dornyei (2005) noted, the majority of foreign language learning experiences are not a successful endeavour. Moreover, he emphasized that "attributional processes are likely to play an important motivational role in language studies" (p. 79). Nevertheless, hitherto, little research has focused on students' attribution for their successes and failures in the area of language learning (Williams and Burdens, 1997, 1999; Williams et al., 2004).

I will now move on to describing the underlying principles in attribution theory. Next, I will provide illustrations within educational settings where such theory was applied. After discussing the preliminary results of this on-going research, I will finally emphasize the important part played by this theoretical approach in our quest for quality in education.

2. Motivation, perception and causal attributions

Motivation is one of the most powerful influences on learning. However, motivation alone does not suffice. Once an activity has started, the individual needs to sustain the effort, usually by investing time and energy into it so as to achieve their goals. Not only does this differ from individual to individual, but it is also influenced by the context and the situation where learning occurs. In this sense, "motivation is very much context bound" (Williams and Burden, 1997: p. 94).

According to Zenzen (2002), some students may have the desire to achieve and the ability to accomplish a task but for some reasons may not value or feel that doing it is worth the effort or time. Likewise, Biggs (2003) stated that learning tasks should have value to learners; moreover, they have to believe it is possible to do them, as "nobody wants to do something they see as worthless. Neither do they want to do something, however valued, if they believe they have no chance of succeeding" (p. 58).

Moreover, psychologists claim that there is a need to understand whatever is happening around us. Finding out the reasons and looking for explanations seems to be innate in humankind, as "in everyday life, it is important to understand why people do what they do" (Lippa, 1990: p. 97). Our feelings and perceptions play a vital role in our own understanding of a given cause. In this sense, Rodrigues (1996) noted that the emotions we feel are often determined by two main factors: 1) the outcome in a specific situation, and 2) the causes to which we attribute to this outcome. Franzoi (2000) defined the mechanism of attribution as "the process by which people use information to make inferences about the causes of behaviour or events" (p. 92).

Recently, psychologists and educationalists have shown the importance of analysing causal attributions in achieving failure and/or success within educational settings (Rodrigues, 1996; Williams and Burden, 1997, 1999; Bempechat, 1999; Biggs, 2003; Williams et al., 2004; Martini and Boruchovitch, 2004). The underlying principles of attribution date back to 1958 when the social psychologist Fritz Heider proposed his theory to understand how people perceive events which influence behaviour. Such theory has its focus not only on the way people think while explaining other's behaviour but also their own behaviour (Lippa, 1990). Furthermore, in applying such a theoretical construct, we are mostly interested in finding out how people perceive the causes of their failures or achievements and the further implications of this perception (Franzoi, 2000).

An important contribution in this field came from Bernard Weiner (1979, 1980, 1986) whose theoretical framework attempted to understand the reasons people attribute to "their perceived successes or failures in an academic and other achievement situations" (Williams and Burden, 1997: p. 104). Weiner focused his theory on the following dichotomy: achieving success or failure. In doing so, he identified four main factors: *ability, effort, task difficulty* and *luck*. However, Heider (1958) had noted that the most important thing in the attribution process is whether or not one decides if a given behaviour is internally or externally caused (i.e. *locus of causality*). The following table shows how people tend to explain their perceived failure or success on a particular language learning task (based on Williams and Burden, 1997: p. 104):

Table 1 – Factors contributing to perceived success or failure on a language learning task

Factors	Perceived Success	Perceived Failure
Internal		
Ability	"I am good at learning languages"	"I am not good at learning languages"
Effort	"I worked hard"	"I didn't try"
External		
Task difficulty	"The task was easy"	"It was too difficult"
Luck	"I guess I was just born lucky"	"I was out of luck"

Apart from the dimension of *locus of causality*, Weiner added the dimension of *stability* and that of *controllability*. A stable cause is permanent and enduring, such as physical characteristics and, as conventional psychologists will contend, so is the level of ability or intelligence. An unstable cause, on the other hand, is temporary, such as effort, mood and physical states (Lippa, 1990). As for *controllability*, it makes it possible to distinguish the factors which people feel are within or outside their scope of control, like the amount of effort one puts into a task (Franzoi, 2000). In addition, Williams and Burden (1997) stated that "the extent to which learners are in control of their own learning of a language will have a pronounced effect upon their motivation to be continually involved in learning that language" (p. 128).

Rodrigues (1996) and Bempechat (1999) also agreed that these dimensions play a vital role, especially within educational contexts. For instance, issues regarding one's own ability (internal dimension) are believed to be less or out of one's control, that is, we cannot exercise much control over them. Luck (external dimension) is, to a certain extent, uncontrollable. Effort (internal dimension), on the other hand, can be controllable, as learners can be advised to make more effort in order to improve their performance. As for task difficulty (external dimension), it is said to be beyond a learner's control, as teachers and/or book writers are the ones who devise the activities and tasks which are frequently used in the classroom. Moreover, in arguing that it is within instructional settings that Weiner's theory has its most successful applications, Rodrigues (1996) stated that teachers should be aware of the consequences of a student attributing his or her failure to an internal cause. For instance, when a student fails in a discipline and attributes the causes of failure to his or her lack of ability or intelligence, it is very likely that this student will carry on being unsuccessful, as this can also lead to a decrease in his or her self-esteem, not to mention contribute to solidify his or her belief that nothing else can be done. "It is the teacher's responsibility to avoid situations in which students make attributions that may lead to really unpleasant consequences in the future", said Rodrigues (p. 112).

By the same token, from a micro perspective, Williams and Burden (1997), who consider both motivation and ability as variables amenable to change, contended that teachers should enable students to make suitable decisions which might not only help them sustain the motivation to learn but also keep them interested in pursuing their initial goals.

3. Causal attributions within educational contexts

Research based on attribution theory had previously focused on the context of sport psychology (Biddle, 1993) by means of quantitative methods of data gathering or were carried out under strict laboratory conditions (Weiner, 1992). However, due to the close relation between academic performance and causal attributions, recent research has been increasingly carried out within educational settings.

According to Martini and Boruchovitch (2004), studies in Germany, in the United States and in Brazil (Barker and Graham, 1987; Weinert and Schneider, 1993; Martini and Boruchovitch, 1999; respectively) showed that children with learning difficulties tended to attribute the causes to internal factors (i.e. *ability and effort*) for their school poor performance.

In the context of language education, only few studies seem to have been conducted to date (Williams and Burdens, 1997; 1999; McQuillan, 2000; Tse, 2000; Williams et al. 2001, Williams et al., 2004). Of these, I have chosen to highlight the results obtained by Tse (2000) and Williams et al. (2004).

Tse (2000) focused on undergraduate and graduate adult learners (N=51; 37 female and 14 male), aged between 21 and 60, studying at an American university. By gathering data through the method of autobiography, the findings were compiled into three main categories: 1) opinions about teacher interactions and methodology; 2) evaluation of their own level of success; and 3) attribution for the proficiency obtained in their language studies. The results showed that students tended to attribute their failure to 1) *teaching* – the instruction focused too little on oral communication; 2) *lack of effort* – and they didn't make the appropriate effort in their studies. As a result, they "reported low estimations of their level of proficiency" (p. 69). As for perception of success, 19 out of 51 stated being successful or somewhat successful. The reasons attributed were related to *attaining the ability to communicate, gaining an understanding of the culture of the language* and *getting a good grade in their course*.

Williams et al. (2004) conducted a study with 285 students (167 girls, 118 boys) aged between 11 and 16, learning French, German and Spanish in five secondary schools in the United Kingdom. The data were collected through a questionnaire, via two questions: 1) two open-ended statements – *When I do well at learning French, the main reasons are (1) (2) (3) (4)*, and *When I don't do well at French, the main reasons are (1) (2) (3) (4)*; 2) a personal evaluation of the respondents' level of success (*I usually do well, I sometimes do well, I don't often do well,* and *I never do well*). The findings were grouped into attributions for doing well (957 occurrences: 590/internal dimension; 290/external dimension; 77/internal-external dimension) and attributions for not doing well (961 occurrences; 601/internal dimension; 241/external dimension; 119/ internal-external dimension). Among the attributions for being successful, *effort, strategy, ability, teacher* and *interest* ranked the five top positions. On the other hand, causes for not being successful were mentioned in terms of *lack of effort, lack of ability, lack of interest, misbehaviour* and *teacher* (i.e. *not liking the teacher, the teacher speaking too fast, not caring, not helping me, nagging* and *lacking control*).

According to the authors, the use of more qualitative methods to interpret and analyse data has strengthened their belief "in the value of such studies as compared with more statistically based methods"; they also contended that the use of more in-depth methods, such as interviewing, would allow for obtaining "a better understanding of the underlying reasons for learner's attributions" (p. 27). By doing so, not only will we be able to fill in the current gap in research but also provide teachers and educationalists with more information to help learners view their successes and failures as unstable and controllable, thus, becoming more autonomous and in control of their learning outcomes.

3.1 Contributions from this study

According to the literature reviewed, studies into learners' perceptions in light of causal attributions in educational contexts were mainly conducted with children and adolescents attending primary or second schools, except for the research conducted by Tse (2000) and isolated studies in Brazil, in the 1980s, as noted by Martini and Boruchovitch (2004). In this sense, we can clearly see a gap in this type of research at higher levels of education. In addition, most studies provided evidence obtained from one single method; this study, on the other hand, employed two different means of gathering data. Therefore, this study is also expected to fill in these two gaps as well as providing additional information on learners' perceptions of their academic performance.

3.1.1 Context and participants

This research, qualitative in nature, is being conducted since October 2006, at a local university in Vilnius, Lithuania[2], which offers courses of Lithuanian language[3] to

---

[2] A Post-Soviet country and a European Union Member-State since 2004.
[3] The Lithuanian language is one of the Baltic languages (currently Latvian and Lithuanian only, as noted by Schmalstieg, 1982), belonging to the Indo-European language family. It is common to find similarities between Lithuanian and Sanskrit or Latin, as the Baltic languages have undergone very few changes in phonetics and morphology. As for grammar, not only does it have both a masculine and feminine gender, plural and singular forms but also it has five noun declensions, each with seven cases. On the other hand, it has no articles, as opposed to many languages, such as the definite and indefinite articles 'the', 'a/an' in

foreigners. It is the first research of its kind, representing a unique and rare circumstance, also serving a revelatory purpose.

Forty-five students (28 male, 17 female) took part in this study, including this author, coming from 24 countries, as follows: United States (6), England (4), Hungary (4), Poland (4), France (3), Spain (3), Canada (2), Russia (2), Turkey (2), Argentina (1), Brazil (1), Georgia (1), Germany (1), India (1), Ireland (1), Italy (1), Lebanon (1), the Netherlands (1), Norway (1), Romania (1), Slovenia (1), Taiwan (1), Uzbekistan (1), and Venezuela (1). Out of 45 students, twenty-one (47%) were enrolled in summer courses (100 hours of instruction), fourteen (31%) enrolled in regular courses (330 hours of instruction) and ten (22%) were attending an Erasmus course[4] (70 hours of instruction), as the local institution is a partner in this EU lifelong learning programme.

Students were aged from 16 to 60+, 25 (56%) aged between 21 and 30, and 9 (20%) aged between 15 and 20. Over half of them (53%) were still pursuing their studies at different levels of formal education (i.e. from high-school to doctoral studies). As for their fields of study/work, they came from the following knowledge backgrounds: Business, Finance, Statistics, Economics, International Relations, Engineering, Linguistics, Literature, History, Philosophy, Psychology, Music, Arts, Food and Beverage Management, Hospitality and Service Industry, and Construction.

With regard to their knowledge of foreign languages, English, German, French and Spanish ranked topped the list. In contrast, learners pursuing studies in Linguistics and Philosophy had also learned languages such as Finnish, Icelandic, Latin, Old Slavic Church, and Swahili. Two students had learned their first foreign language informally (i.e. by not attending a course). No student had knowledge of Latvian, which belongs to the same branch of Lithuanian within the Indo-European language tree.

Finally, the main reason for learning Lithuanian was *mobility*, that is, presently working or living in the country and/or current or future study purposes, followed by having a *personal interest* (i.e. being of Lithuanian ancestry, for instance).

3.1.2 Methods

Four methods of gathering data were employed; however, for the purpose of this paper I will describe only the instruments which enabled me to obtain learners' causal attributions: *questionnaires* and *in-depth interviews*.

The two-page questionnaire comprised both closed/semi-closed and open questions (18 in total), based on Nunan (1992), in which learners' profile as well as past and present language learning experiences were investigated. The following open

---

English. Nowadays, it is spoken by over 3 million people in Lithuania, apart from the Lithuanian communities abroad, mainly in the United States, Argentina, Canada, Australia and Brazil, among others.

[4] This was not the usual Erasmus Intensive Language Courses (EILC) normally offered at the beginning of each semester but rather a different one organized into 70 academic hours. Nevertheless, the materials and tasks were the same as those used by students attending summer courses.

items were devised to gather the causal attributions for the perceived difficulties[5]: 18A. *I still have difficulties doing my homework*; 18B. *I still have some difficulties in the classroom*; 18C. *What I would like to learn/do next*; and 18D. *Comments*.

The interviews were based on Spradley's model (1979) of *ethnographic questions* (i.e. descriptive, structural and contrast questions), aiming at having learners describe, illustrate and explain their main perceptions. The aspects under investigation were motivation to learn Lithuanian, previous language experiences, their attempts to use the language outside the classroom, and finally the attributions for their difficulties. Interviewing was carried out in the middle or shortly before the end of the course of their studies.

The categories emerged from the data; in other words, no pre-determined categories were imposed on the participants. Therefore, following the example of Williams et al. (2004), the analysis was based on a grounded theory approach (Glaser and Strauss, 1967), aiming at identifying the semantic relationships between the terms and words used by the respondents (Casagrande and Hale, 1967; Spradley, 1979).

It is important to note that 2 participants out of 45 continued studying for another semester or year and agreed to take part once more, both by answering the same questions listed above and being interviewed one more time. Nevertheless, due to limitations of this paper, I will not highlight the main findings of the longitudinal data analysis.

3.1.3. Preliminary research findings

Six main categories emerged from the data, and a total number of 840 causal attributions were identified. These attributions were then grouped into two major domains: 1) LEF – Learning-environment factors (i.e. *sociocultural contexts)*; and 2) LF Learner factors (i.e. *individual differences)*, as shown below:

Table 2 – Attributions for the perceived learning difficulties

Domain	Category	Number of Occurrences	(%)	Dimension
1- LEF	1. Lack of appropriate educational resources	189	36%	External
1- LEF	2. Complex and different language system	139	27%	External
1- LEF	3. Lack of opportunity to practise beyond the classroom	109	21%	External
1- LEF	4. Inappropriate course design and instruction	85	16%	External
		522	62%	
2- LF	1. Lack of cognitive ability	305	96%	Internal
2- LF	2. Lack of confidence and effort	13	4%	Internal
		318	38%	
	Total:	840	100%	

---

[5] Considering the fact that no previous research was conducted in the context of Lithuanian as a foreign language, as well as the high frequency of failure in foreign language studies, along with the threats to achieving a plurilingual competence, I have chosen to focus solely on perceived failures (i.e. learning difficulties).

In addition, a few illustrations from the classroom can be seen in Annexes I and II (Tables 3 and 4), at the end of this paper.

Learning-environment factors domain: The sociocultural context
As can be clearly seen, **lack of appropriate educational resources**, such as materials, activities and tasks, accounted for 36% of the occurrences in this main category. Most of the attributions referred to the *activities and tasks* carried out in the classroom. The causes pointed mainly to the *lack of speaking and listening tasks* as well as *lack of motivating and more challenging tasks*. The level of *task difficulty* was also noted by a few participants in this study.

Furthermore, *lack of role-plays and games* was also mentioned. The *non-use of media resources* in the classroom, such as TV, radio, films and documentaries, as well as *non-use of authentic texts* were also cited as contributing to learning difficulties. The *absence of extra-mural activities*, such as going to the theatre, galleries and the like, also played a part. Finally, *lack of appropriate supplementary materials*, such as bilingual/pocket dictionaries and interactive software (e.g. CD ROMs), was a significant attribution made in this category.

Next, the particularities of the Lithuanian language in terms of being **a different and complex language system** accounted for 27% of the causal attributions under this domain. *No or few similarities with first/second/foreign languages*, along with having *a complex grammar and unfamiliar sentence structure*, being *old and difficult*, and its *unfamiliar vocabulary and spelling* were the main reasons supporting the perceived difficulties.

Lack of opportunity ranked third in the list in the sense that learners perceived having few chances to practise the language outside the classroom, by means of interacting with Lithuanian native speakers/citizens, apart from lack of opportunities in their own countries (e.g. *no language schools*). Local opportunity was cited through phrases such as *Lithuanians not being used to people learning their language*, being *intolerant to mistakes, impatient*, and *switching to other languages very quickly*, and *not mixing them*, and finally, *having to live/stay with foreigners* (i.e. at the students' hall of residence).

Inappropriate course design and instruction also played a role in their perceived learning difficulties. Statements related to the way the course was organized included wording such as having lesson presentations of a *lecture-type*, having *a boring structure* in which *you are sitting, learning the language through grammar, focusing too much on grammar*, having *a lot of grammar structure and vocabulary* and constructing *virtual knowledge* in the classroom (*without seeing, smelling or touching*). Lastly, student placement, mainly in terms of having *non-linguists learning in the same group of linguists*, was an important aspect of learner's perceived difficulties as well. As for instruction – the delivery of material, classroom management and teacher's characteristics – the most frequent attributions were made by the following expressions: presentation of *too many verbs and words* at a time, *lack of explanations in everyday life situations, thinking about Lithuanian in Russian, you cannot translate, shouldn't* *try to translate it all, it doesn't make sense in English sense,* and finally, *explanations* of new vocabulary items *only in Lithuanian* (at higher levels, *without any pictures*). With regard to teachers' characteristics, *speaking too fast* or *being too soft-spoken* were the main problems pointed out.

Learner Factors Domain: Individual differences
Lack of cognitive ability accounted for 96% of the causes in this domain and was expressed through terms such as *not remembering, not understanding, not knowing, not being able to speak, pronounce* or *spell, not being good at languages, being old to learn a language,* and *having a different learning style* or *needing more time to find answers* (i.e. having a different learning pace). **Lack of confidence** ranked second, and the following expressions were used: *if I am not sure that I speak correctly I don't speak; afraid to say something wrong; I don't have the courage; I feel more comfortable speaking English; I was kind of shy,* among others. Finally, **lack of effort** ranked last. Participants mentioned the following: *I didn't study so hard...it's true; it is probably my fault... not applying myself a little more;* and *that's my problem...I was a little bit lazy.*

Discussion of results
The findings showed that *internal attributions* accounted for 38% of the causes for the perceived difficulties, *lack of ability* being the most significant attribution made (305 occurrences). Therefore, as previous discussions have shown, teachers play a vital role in this sense and should help learners take more control of their learning outcomes while they are still constructing knowledge in the classroom. In addition, *external attributions* amounted to 522 occurrences (62%), and lack of educational resources was at the top at the list (i.e. 189 occurrences). Next, the particularities of the Lithuanian language (i.e. different and complex) in comparison to the languages learners knew are also significant as these factors are indeed uncontrollable and stable. This may pose a problem especially when it comes to achieving a plurilingual competence, by using the knowledge of previous languages while learning a new language. Also, the perceived lack of opportunity to practise outside the classroom also plays a part as learners perceived not having enough practice during the lessons, especially through communicative tasks. Finally, perceptions of the way the course is designed – having linguists and non-linguists in the same group – together with lesson delivery, by means of complex explanations (i.e. via direct translations, or only in Lithuanian/linguistic terms), among others, were perceived as causing difficulties.

Conclusions

Language plays a crucial role in our lives: not only does it mediate human interactions and help develop our higher mental skills but it also allows us to train our thoughts, to both negotiate and fix meanings. In the role of social agents, we also name things in the world; we create and re-create our own realities. Learning a foreign language can be a useful tool while communicating with other cultures, especially considering that rates of mobility continue to grow considerably worldwide. Consequently, education policies, such as those set by European Union, have lately emphasized the important role language learning plays in maintaining the Union's cultural heritage and helping its citizens satisfy their communicative needs while living, working and/or studying in another country.

There are, however, a few threats to such endeavours: some misconceptions about language learning, such as 'the need to be younger', 'or have a natural gift', along with the language being 'too difficult to learn' may work as an impediment to achieving plurilingual competence. As previously mentioned, learning never occurs in isolation; it is carried out via social interactions within classrooms (i.e. microsystems), which in turn are also inserted into higher systems, such as those in charge of establishing the educational goals of a given society (i.e. macrosystem). These may also work as vehicles that propagate the aforementioned threats. That is why attribution theory and its application to instructional settings play an important part.

In this study, the causes attributed to external dimensions – lack of appropriate educational resources, opportunity to practice, course design and instruction, along with the particularities of the subject (i.e. the Lithuanian language) – outnumbered the internal attributions of lack of ability, confidence or effort. Nevertheless, the number of such attributions is impressive (308), accounting for 38% of the total attributions made. If no interventions are made, learners may lose their initial motivation to attain their goals, which, in this case, will directly affect their participation in the Lithuanian society, in the role of students or workers, with their linguistic competence put at risk.

Finally, attribution plays an important part in instructional settings, and I believe the findings obtained via in-depth methods can be powerful indicators of quality in university teaching. However, identifying the main causes and grouping them into categories *only* does not help learners, teachers, course designers and curriculum developers to improve course design, instruction, materials and learning outcomes. Further analysis should be incorporated, so in this case, in particular, the educational resources – such as materials, activities and tasks – should also be investigated. The findings are expected to show significant information, considering these learning materials are a direct product of the local culture; thus, learners' perceptions in this study may have well been formed as a result of students' first-hand experience while living and/or studying in the country, through direct interactions within this particular context. Therefore, we may conclude by saying that, not only are motivation, perceptions and, especially, *ability* context bound, but they are also socially constructed within educational settings.

References

Baker, G., &Graham, S. (1987). Developmental study of praise and blame as attributional cues. *Journal of Educational Psychology, 79*(1), 62-66.

Beacco, J-C., & Byram, M. (2003). *Guide for the development of language education policies in Europe– from linguistic diversity to plurilingual education.* Strasbourg: Council of Europe.

Bempechat, J. (1999). Learning from poor and minority students who succeed in school. *Harvard Education Letter* May/June 1999 retrieved November 16, 2007 *from* http://education.calumet.purdue.edu/vockell/EdPsyBook/Edpsy5/Edpsy5_attribution.htm

Biddle, S. (1993). Attribution research and sport psychology. In R. N. Singer, M. Murphey and L. K. Tennant (eds.), *Handbook of research on sport psychology* (p. 437-464). New York: Macmillan.

Biggs, J. (2003). *Teaching for quality at university: What the student does.* 2nd edition. UK: SRHE/ PA: Open University Press.

Bronfenbrenner, U. (1942). *Social status, structure and development in the classroom group.* Unpublished doctoral dissertation. University of Michigan.

Bronfenbrenner, U. (1979). *The ecology of human development.* Cambridge: Harvard University Press.

Bronfenbrenner, U. (2004). *Making human beings human: bioecological perspectives on human development.* Thousand Oaks, CA: Sage Publications.

Casagrande, J. B., & Hale, K. L. (1967). Semantic relationships. In D. Hymes & W. E. Bittle (eds.), *Studies in Southwestern Ethnolinguistics* (p. 165-196). The Hague: Mouton.

Council of Europe (2006). *Plurilingual education in Europe – 50 years of international co-operation.* Strasbourg: Language Policy Division.

Dewey, J. (1910). *How we think.* New York: Dover Publications, Inc., 1997.

Dornyei, Z. (2005). *The psychology of the language learner: individual differences in second language acquisition.* Mahwah, NJ: Lawrence Erlbaum.

Eurydice in Brief (2005). *Foreign language learning: a European priority.* Brussels: Eurydice. Retrieved November 12, 2007, from http://www.eurydice.org/ressources/eurydice/pdf/0_integral/061EN.pdf

Franzoi, S. L. (2000). *Social psychology.* Second edition. Boston, MA: McGraw-Hill

Freire, P. (1970). *Pedagogy of the oppressed.* 30th Anniversary edition. Translated by Myra Bergman Ramos. London & New York: Continuum, 2007.

Glaser, B. G., & Strauss, A. L. (1967). *The discovery of grounded theory: Strategies for qualitative research.* Chicago: Aldine.

Heider, F. (1958). *The psychology of interpersonal relations.* New York: Wiley.

Jespersen, O. (1904). *How to teach a foreign language.* Translated from the Danish original by Sophia Yhlen-Olsen Bertelsen. London: George Allen & Unwin Ltd.

Kelly, M., Grenfell, M., Allan, R., Kriza, C., & McEvoy, W. (2004). *European profile for language teaching education. A frame of reference.* A report to the European Commission Directorate General for Education and Culture. September 2004. Southampton University, UK.

Kincheloe, J. (2008). *Critical Pedagogy Primer.* New York: Peter Lang Publishing, Inc.

Lippa, R. (1990). *Introduction to social psychology.* California State University. Fullerton.

Martini, M. L., & Boruchovitch, E. (1999). Causal attributions for academic success and failure of Brazilian children. In *VI European Congress of Psychology*, p. 284.

Martini, M. L., & Boruchovitch, E. (2004). *A teoria da atribuição de causalidade. Contribuições para a formação e atuação de educadores.* Campinas: Alínea Editora.

McQuillan, J. (2000). Attribution theory and second language acquisition: an empirical analysis. Paper presented at *AAAL Conference*, Vancouver.

Nunan, D. (1992). *Research methods in language learning.* Cambridge: Cambridge University Press.

Postman, N. (1995). *The end of education: Redefining the value of school.* New York: Vintage Books.

Rodrigues, A. (1996). *Psicologia social para principiantes – Estudo da interação humana.* 3 edição. Petrópolis: Vozes.

Schmalstieg, W. R. (1982). The Origin of the Lithuanian Language. Special Issue: The Lithuanian Language – Past and Present. *Lituanus, 28*(1). Ed. Antanas Klimas. ISSN 0024-5089. Retrieved March 28th, 2009, from http://www.lituanus.org/1982_1/82_1_01.htm

Spradley, J. P. (1979). *The ethnographic interview.* New York: Holt, Rinehart and Winston.

Tse, L. (2000). Student perceptions of foreign language study: a qualitative analysis of foreign language autobiographies. *The Modern Language Journal, 84,* 69-84.

Vygotsky, L. S. (1930-1935). *A Formação Social da Mente: o Desenvolvimento das Funções Psicológicas Superiores.* 6ª ed. 3ª tiragem. Tradução de José Cipolla Neto, Luis Silveira Menna Barreto e Solange Castro Afeche. São Paulo: Martins Fontes, 1999.

Weiner, B. (1979). A theory of motivation for some classroom experiences. *Journal of Educational Psychology, 71,* 3-25.

Weiner, B. (1980). *Human Motivation.* New York: Holt, Rinehart and Winston.

Weiner, B. (1986). *An attributional theory of motivation and emotion.* New York: Springer-Verlag.

Weiner, B. (1992). *Human motivation: Metaphors, themes and research.* Newbury Park, CA: Sage.

Weinert, F. E., & Schneider, W. (1993). The Munich longitudinal study on the genesis of individual competences (LOGIC). *Report 9, Max Planck-Institut fur Psychologische Forschung.*

Williams, M., & Burden, R. L. (1997). *Psychology for language teachers – A social constructivist approach.* Cambridge: Cambridge University Press.

Williams, M., & Burden, R. L. (1999). 'Students' developing conceptions of themselves as language learners'. *The Modern Language Journal, 83*(2), 193-201.

Williams, M., Burden, R. L , Poulet, G., & Maun, I. (2004). Learners' perceptions of their successes and failures in language learning. *Language Learning Journal, 30,* 19-39.

Zenzen, T. G. (2002). *Achievement theory.* A research paper. The University of Wisconsin-Stout. Retrieved December 9th, 2007, from http://www.uwstout.edu/lib/thesis/2002/2002zenzent.pdf

Annex I

Table 3 – Learning-environment factors (sociocultural contexts): Illustrations from the classroom

1. EDUCATIONAL RESOURCES (MATERIALS, ACTIVITIES, TASKS)
'We don't talk…speak…talk enough…we write…we do many exercises…but we… hum…we do not repeat enough…we don't speak enough about the same structure…in dialogue' (Regular Course)
'One day let's see a movie ….in Lithuanian language….we could do it….why not? We have four hours here' (Regular course)
'You have to write about your animals to your friends…and it is only writing…and you have to do it…if you would like to pass exams…you know…not so interesting' (Regular Course)
'Perhaps… songs… we need some games…you have to engage into it…that will bring out that learning…other than just text- filling…grammar exercise… I believe the learning material should focus on all learning methods: visual/audio etc… in Lithuanian… there is very little…good material…' (Summer Course)
'It is a dictionary that has got a grammar written by a professor of Slavonic languages in London…I mean…I am a linguist and I find it very hard to understand…and it wouldn't be very helpful to learners' (Summer Course)
'[the dictionary] It's not so good… because too small…it is difficult to learn…only translation' (Erasmus Course)
2. DIFFERENT AND COMPLEX LANGUAGE SYSTEM
'Because the grammar…as we discussed yesterday in the lecture…is very difficult for foreigners to understand …all these….genitives…datives… always 'kuo…ką…kam'… that makes it very difficult' (Regular Course)
'The language is old…the country is old… I was told it was the hardest language in Europe to learn' (Erasmus Course)
'It is very different from Norwegian…English and Spanish…' (Summer Course)

3. LACK OF OPPORTUNITY TO PRACTISE

'The few times I tried and was like a big stare…you know… total…they [Lithuanians] switched into another language….so that I found very frustrating … and they have very little tolerance of mistakes in the language' (Regular Course)

'It's a bad idea that I am learning Lithuanian here but I have to live with foreigners who can't speak Lithuanian' (Regular course)

'Our courses is only for Erasmus students… we don't study with Lithuanians' (Erasmus Course)

4. INAPPROPRIATE COURSE DESIGN AND INSTRUCTION

'Last year I was in the first group….and now I am studying with philologists but I think it is not correct … and until now… I don't understand…maybe if I hadn't been in the group with philologists…I wouldn't have had so many difficulties' (Regular Course)

'Lectures are very useful to get acquaintance how Lithuanian grammar is "organized" !!!'(Regular Course)

'Something that I found out very earlier on here…I shouldn't try to translate it at all…because it doesn't make sense…in English sense…. I should try to understand ….what is being said….and use the appropriate (forms) as opposed to translate each word' (Summer Course – English native speaker)

'We have only words…without explanations…only words …during our lessons our teacher tries to explain these words…in Lithuanian… I don't understand…why should I know so many and so special words?' (Regular Course)

'And you know…the teachers don't stop and say "let's reinforce this …because you cannot continue without this" …and they let you continue' (Regular Course)

Annex II

Table 4 – Learner factors (individual differences): Illustrations from the classroom

1. LACK OF COGNITIVE ABILITY
'It means that I still don't understand people talking Lithuanian…all I know… I feel is… that I know a lot of words but I don't understand them… and after so many months of studying I am a bit frustrated about that… I thought I would make faster progress in understanding Lithuanian' (Regular Course)
'When it comes to texts…writing and speaking…I all the time have to remember all the endings and this is the most difficult problem' (Erasmus Course)
'I just am not satisfied with learning by heart this ending is here…and this is here…you have to learn it and that's OK… I need to have different colours… you know… to underline…and all the things…this is the way I learn … most effectively…' (Erasmus Course)
'I am not a good learner…you are not a natural linguist…and English native speaker…' (Summer Course)
'I have never really been hugely good at learning languages…but I think that the English language system certainly at my school doesn't seem to be particularly good…' (Summer Course)
'I am finding it difficult…perhaps I can put it down to…my age' (Summer Course)
2. LACK OF CONFIDENCE AND EFFORT
'I don't have the courage to speak Lithuanian…If I start speaking Lithuanian and people don't understand…I feel…frustrated' (Regular Course)
'I kind wished I had learned more than I have…I think it is probably my fault…not applying myself a little more…but I haven't progressed as much as I thought…I hoped I would' (Summer Course)

The paper has been reviewed by external referees.

What makes the high-quality research experience of research postgraduates? Implications from Mainland Chinese research students' experiences at the University of Hong Kong

Zeng Min

Abstract

This paper discusses the indicators that account for the quality of research education at the postgraduate level from the perspectives of thirty Mainland Chinese research postgraduates (MCRPs) who were studying at the University of Hong Kong. On the basis of interviews with these students, we can conclude that the major elements that contributed to the high quality of students' research experiences were the availability of good supervisors, proper peer support, infrastructure, and research climate. A good supervisor was described by these students as a person who could provide high-quality supervision for their research tasks and thesis writing, a comfortable personal relationship, smooth communication, and help with students' professional development. The high-quality supervision has included such sub-elements as overseeing each stage of the research, keeping up students' motivation for research, being easily accessible, and providing prompt feedback and clear instruction and adhering to high standards. As the University of Hong Kong is an English medium university, some students considered the conducive language environment for English learning as an important contributor to their satisfaction with the educational experience. Although infrastructure, research climate, and peer support were almost always satisfying, some sub-elements of supervision and language learning environment were not. A model was derived after analysis of the interview data, which provided an explicit picture of what might have contributed to the quality of postgraduate education experiences of the MCRPs at the University of Hong Kong. Other findings and implications are also discussed in this paper.

Rankings as a measurement tool of the quality of higher education

There are diverse approaches to assess the performances of higher education institutions. Over the last twenty years, ranking with a league table has become a frequently used approach for the evaluation of higher education sectors around the world although the methodology and the use of the league table are quite controversial. In the 1920s the quality of graduate programs in the United States was evaluated through surveys, and the result was published in 1983 as "American's Best College Ranking". Now we have global ranking lists (e.g., World University Rankings by the *Times Higher Education Supplement*), regional lists (e.g., CHE (Centre for Higher Education Development) Ranking) and lists of universities in a specific field (e.g., Business School Rankings and MBA rankings from the *Financial Times*).

The research output of staff, students, or alumni is among one of the most frequently used indicators in these lists (e.g., Academic Ranking of World Universities by Shanghai Jiao Tong University, World University Rankings by the *Times Higher Education Supplement*, Leiden Ranking, *Newsweek* ranking and CHE Research Ranking). The research output is normally measured by the number of articles indexed in the Science Citation Index Expanded (SCIE) and the Social Science Citation Index (SSCI), citations received or funds obtained. In the Shanghai Jiao Tong ranking list, the staff and alumni's winning of Nobel Prizes and Field Medals is also an indicator of research output (Cheng & Liu, 2007). Through a series of studies on ranking lists, *The Times Good University Guides*, Yorke found that, in fact, most of the variance in institutional scores in the league table could be explained solely by variance in research (Yorke, 1998).

Another frequently used indicator in the ranking system is social assessment. In World University Rankings by the *Times Higher Education*, peer-reviewed international reputation and international reputation among recruiters were included, while in RatER assessment of higher education quality by employers, students, universities management, Russian Federation Ministry for Education and Science, experts were used (Artushina & Troyan, 2007). In CHE Ranking, subjective judgements of interested groups such as students, teachers and administrators are used (Centre for Higher EducationDevelopment, 2009). It is believed that such a ranking criteria could enhance the communication between the society and higher education institutions (Artushina & Troyan, 2007).

No ranking list could take into account all the recognized indicators. Nor can it include all universities all over the world, as reliable and comparable data may not be available. For example, Shanghai Jiao tong University ranked only the universities in five broad subject fields because no reliable and comparable indicators could be found in other fields.

While the public were using ranking lists as an information source for decision making or for understanding of higher education, researchers warned that it should not be used as a main method to assess what higher education is and does. First, it is believed that the ranking criteria reflect only the value judgements of the list compliers (Locke, 2007). The selection of indicators and the value given to them expressed the compliers' understanding of what higher education is. Therefore, one university was ranked dramatically differently in different lists. For example, when using academic effectiveness and efficiencies in teaching and widening participation as the criteria for ranking, post-1992 (teaching-oriented university) and Russell Group universities (research-oriented university) ranked completely opposite to their usual positions in ranking list compiled by *The Times Higher Education Supplement* (2004) (Pursglove & Simpson, 2007). Therefore, it may be inappropriate to force a comparison among higher education institutions across nations or cultures or universities regardless of their values and beliefs about what makes the quality of higher education (Higher Education Funding Council for England, 2008). It is also likely that the value of compilers would be passed to the readers through ranking lists. For example, the use of research performance as a major criterion for ranking may re-enforced the traditional view on the excellence of a university, which is in fact accurate only for traditional or older universities but gives very limited view of what newer universities are trying to achieve (Eccles, 2002). Such a tendency was criticized as being "biased toward research reputation and academic prestige rather than student learning" (Dill, 2006: p. 14).

Besides, most indicators used in the lists covered only the input and output of the higher education institutions (Higher Education Funding Council for England, 2008). When we consider carefully what is happening in higher education, there seems to be one thing missing from the evaluation system: the process. The input factors may suggest what universities have: the qualifications of entrants, student/staff ratios, expenditure per student, spending on libraries and information and communications technology, the qualifications of academic staff and research income. Output factors show the "products" of higher education: research output or employ rate. What process indicators may help to reveal could be whether or not student learning is happening, or whether students' knowledge is developed, and what helps the process and what hinders. With such information, a university would not only be able to compare with other universities, they would also be able to know which specific area they could work on to improve their education effectiveness. An evaluation of input and output could provide little evidence on this.

Measurement of students' experience for quality assurance

If the traditional standard of quality, related primarily to reputation and resources, is mainly relevant to old universities (Harvey, 2005), using students' evaluation of their educational experience as an indicator of the assessment may balance the bias. For example, a university which was regarded as not so remarkable in the traditional view received highest scores from their students in a 2006 NSS (University of Buckingham, 2006, cited in Ertl et al., 2008). The vice-chancellor of the top-ranked university said, "Our ethos is traditional teaching … I don't think all universities have this. Some places are obsessed with the research assessment exercise and rankings" (Ward & Jayanetti, 2006, cited in Ertl et al., 2008).

In the United States, Britain, and Australia and some other places as well, some surveys have been administered institutional or national wide to evaluate students' educational experience. The National Survey of Student Engagement (NSSE) was established in 1999 in the United States to measure undergraduate students' engagement in programmes and activities in higher education institutions. Each item of the survey was correlated to one of the five benchmarks of "good practices" empirically confirmed in undergraduate education: level of academic challenge, active and collaborative learning, student-faculty interaction, enriching educational experiences and supportive campus environment (Kuh, 2002). In the United Kingdom, the National Student Survey (NSS) was established in 2005 as part of the revised quality assurance framework (QAF) for higher education (Higher Education Funding Council for England, 2009). The aim of the survey is to gather students' feedback on the quality of courses in order to contribute to public accountability and to help inform the choices of future applicants to higher education (Higher Education Funding Council for England, 2009). It contains seven dimensions: teaching and learning, assessment and feedback, academic support, organization and management, learning resources, personal development, and overall satisfaction.

Developed from the Course Perceptions Questionnaire (Ramsden & Entwistle, 1981), the Course Experience Questionnaire was used in Australia nation-wide as a monitoring tool of accountability and the academic quality of degree programmes. It provides an instrument for the assessment of teaching effectiveness at the course or degree level. Students' responses give information about what they think about the quality of teaching, the degrees to which the educational goals and standards were expressed clearly, the appropriateness of workload and assessment, the perceived development in generic skills, the sense of belonging to a learning community and overall satisfaction (Institute for Teaching and Learning, 2009b). This study along with many others which used CEQ found a significant positive relationship between a graduate's final degree classification and their scores on the CEQ (Ertl et al., 2008). Based on Australian CEQ and its own educational context, the University of Hong Kong implemented surveys on undergraduate student experiences (Student Learning Experience Questionnaire (SLEQ)) in recent years to monitor academic quality for both curriculum reform and quality assurance purposes. It included most basic scales in CEQ such as good teaching, appropriate workload, appropriate assessment, clear standard and instructions and other issues specific to HKU's context such as medium of instruction and educational aims. By focusing on the exact experiences of the students, these surveys addressed the quality issues more directly and provided better evidence for enhancing and assuring the quality of higher education.

The study

In recent years, the evaluation of student experiences has been extended from undergraduate level to postgraduate levels (e.g., Postgraduate Research Experience Questionnaire (Institute for Teaching and Learning, 2009a) and Postgraduate Research Experience Survey (The Higher Education Academy, 2009)). The University of Hong Kong has been preparing for such surveys recently.

Before conducting such surveys, in-depth studies on the perceptions of related issues held by the "consumer" of higher education would help to find out what indicators should be included. As opinions of higher education quality may be shaped by culture, nation, and respondents' positions in the social structure or interest group, students from different backgrounds may have different experience of and request for education quality. Studies with students from different backgrounds are necessary. This study started from identifying to what extent research students were satisfied with the education they received and explored the important factors that contribute to students' satisfaction with the education they received. This study explored the indicators that might account for the quality of research postgraduate education from Mainland Chinese Research Postgraduates' (MCRP) perspective.

Method

Thirty MCRPs from eight faculties were invited to a focus group discussion to elaborate on these issues. The main questions used in the discussion were:

To what extent are you satisfied with your educational experiences at HKU? Can you point out the specific aspects that contribute to your satisfaction?

A discussion protocol was prepared to maintain consistency in the group discussion processes. The discussions were audio-recorded with participants' permission and transcribed verbatim. Given that the research experiences of research postgraduates have not been addressed sufficiently especially when the group characteristics were considered, the researcher employed the grounded theory approach to look at the new perspective that might help develop the theory to understand the phenomenon (Glaser & Strauss, 1968). This is particularly appropriate when comparatively less theory or knowledge has been developed and when in-depth understanding is sought (Corbin & Strauss, 1990). The process of theory building regarding MCRPs' research experiences follows the step from the concepts, categories, to propositions (Corbin & Strauss, 1990). In the data analysis, the researcher at first had planned to invite an independent colleague in a similar research field to crosscheck the categories the researcher had developed. However, as the MCRP community was rather close knit and small and most of the friends of the researcher also came from this community, the researcher did not invite an independent researcher to cross-validate in case they may identify specific informants from the descriptions of the informants' experiences. To ensure the confidentiality principle, the researcher checked back with the individual informants instead during data analysis to enhance credibility. In the following description of findings, "I" stands for the researcher in the quotation and the informants are named using "S" plus numbers from 1 to 30.

The context

Hong Kong is now a special administration region of China after being governed by the British government for more than 100 years. With its "hybrid" features influenced both by China and the West, Hong Kong has attracted more and more Mainland University students in recent years: increasing from virtually zero in 1990 to 6732 in the 2007/2008 academic year (University Grants Council, 2007). The higher education system of Hong Kong has followed the basic organization of US and/or British universities. About 90 per cent of all doctorate degrees of faculty members at Hong Kong universities were earned in foreign countries like Australia, Canada, the United Kingdom, or the United States (Postilgione & Tang, 1997). Second, English is widely used in most Hong Kong universities in classrooms, for academic learning and for communication with staff. The University of Hong Kong (HKU), where the informants were identified, is one of seven Hong Kong universities which recruit research students from all over the world. The research students admitted by this university receive scholarships giving a living allowance of the equivalent of US$ 1700 per month from the University Grants Council of Hong Kong. This is well above the salaries received by academics in most cities of Mainland China.

Findings

Five aspects of MCRPs' experience were identified as the indicators of quality educational experience through focus group discussions: academic interactions, social interactions, infrastructure, research climate, and intercultural experiences.

Academic interactions

Two types of academic interactions were categorized: academic interactions with supervisors and peers. In the discussion, the informants had spent a comparatively longer time in discussing their interaction with supervisors, which may either suggest that it was a very important indicator of quality of education or the informants had very impressive experiences in it. A high-quality academic interaction with supervisor was described as receiving good supervision on research, maintaining smooth communication on research issues, and obtaining supervisor's help for future professional development (see Table 1). Good supervision on research has included such sub-elements as overseeing research (e.g. topic selection, literature review, method selection, thesis writing, and time management), keeping up students' motivation for research, and providing easy access, prompt feedback, and clear standard and instruction.

The interactions among peers for academic purposes included activities such as seminars or group meetings conducted among students, personal communications about research, and practical help with one another's research. It was identified by the informants as a very important contributor to their satisfaction with research experiences. It helped a lot when their supervisor was not available.

> S1: In fact, the relationship between PhD students is very important too.
> S2: It is very important to hear from our peers about their experiences. They had gone through all those things. So, every time when they talked about their experiences, I took them as my teacher. I listened to them very carefully.
> S1: What you got from them could be more important than what you got from your supervisors some times.
> S3: Yes, we are of the same age and in the same situation.
> S4: What is more, you may soon be in where they were, about supervisors, about research, or other things. When our supervisor didn't give us feedback in time and I felt very anxious, I would try to talk with my peers first. If it was difficult to communicate with peers out of my field, I would talk with my academic sisters or brothers. Sometimes, they acted as my co-supervisors. I could get some more prompt advice from them.
> …
> S1: Now, there are three research students altogether in our faculty. We wrote papers very often. (When we finished one), we would communicate with each other and do peer-review for each other. It happened and it is good.
> S3: I think that is great too. But we don't have such a routine in our faculty. I may not use it very often, but it is good that the faculty could arrange or encourage such activities.

Social interactions

MCRPs' interactions with supervisors and peers also involved non-academic–related issues. Though they were not addressed directly as "research experience", they helped enhance research-related interactions greatly. Some MCRPs reported that their non-academic–interaction with supervisors had helped them establish a more comfortable personal relationship with their supervisors. They became emotionally closer to their supervisors since then and were more willing to communicate with supervisors and felt less intimidated by asking questions.

> S2: After we had communication about daily life, I could feel that he is amiable. I don't feel so intimidated by him and feel less scared of asking questions about academic research. It is less likely to happen that I would be afraid of asking silly questions and simple questions because he is my supervisor, who is professional and has authority in academic research. So I think, it is necessary for us to have some interactions in life because I felt more daring to ask questions after we ....
> I: You meant after you had that dinner together?
> S2: Not exactly. I just felt better. I remembered his photo on website and some meetings with him. He is so serious and ...
> S1: Very fierce.
> S2: Oh, yes. But after you had some more casual interaction. I feel he is not that fierce. I am not afraid of him so much as I was.

The social interactions with peers were regarded as not only helpful in building up support between fellow research postgraduates for better academic interaction but as also helpful in getting clues on how to cooperate better with supervisors. Besides, social interactions with peers helped establish friendship and emotional support, release pressure, and build academic partnerships too.

> I: Is it (the interaction among peers) really very important to you?
> S8: Of course. If you have a look at the research on research students, you will find that one of the biggest problems of them is battle against isolation.
> I: Does it refer to the emotional isolation or the isolation caused by restricted research fields?
> S5: Isolation caused by restricted research fields is one kind of emotional isolation. You can't communicate with others about what you are doing! ... As human being, we need a relaxed environment to live in. It is very important to have some people to be together. It is very important to have a supportive network.
> S8: By doing things together, we may feel we have companies.
> S7: By and by, you may become close to someone and she/he will become more willing to help you in many things including research. You could share the knowledge you gained, the perspective you have on a certain thing. Or like what he said review each other's paper.

S13: I prefer that type (of communication), in which we can share. It doesn't necessarily need to be about academic research. It could be about our experiences. As all of us have pressure, we could study hard together, develop fantasies for the future together, comfort each other, and encourage each other. We don't need to have very close research directions. We have already had the same experiences. We are actually in the same boat. Every one can understand the others. We have a lot in common. We are alike in many aspects such as our psychological status and so on. It is an advantageous thing for communication that we have so much in common.

Table 1 Dimensions of academic and social interactions with supervisors and peers

	Supervisor	Peer
Academic interaction	Research supervision	Helping with the ongoing research
	Overseeing each stage of the research	Discussing each other's project
	Providing easy access	Peer-reviewing
	Keeping up students' motivation for research	Exchanging research experience
	Providing prompt feedback	Learning strategies to manage supervisor
	Giving clear standard and instruction	Learning strategies to survive
	Maintaining smooth mutual communication on research issues	Exchanging resources (learning from each other's expertise)
	Helping with students' professional development	Learning from each other's research area
Social interaction	Establishing comfortable personal relationship	Providing emotional support and companionship

Infrastructure and intellectual climate

Infrastructure and research climate were mentioned as two of the factors that would contribute to satisfying educational experiences. In fact, infrastructure was mentioned almost all the time as one of the reasons why researchers were satisfied with their experiences at HKU. This is probably because the infrastructure at KU had generally met the expectations of most informants.

S11: Speaking about educational experience, I am quite satisfied. HKU provided me with a great platform. Whether or not I can give a great show would depend solely on me. I have got this platform I've longed for for a long time. If I can't perform well, it is me who should be blamed.
I: So you meant you are satisfied with the infrastructure of HKU?
S11: Yes, I am very satisfied with it. Or I could use the word: touched. For example, the library, I am really "touched" by the service it provided. If I can't achieve anything in these four years, I will feel guilty and will feel like owe something to it.

Good research climate was referred to as having an established mechanics for research students to communicate about research with each other within or even beyond faculties or university or with other academics in the faculty.

Intercultural experience

Whether or not intercultural experience could be included as one of the indicators of quality is a bit tricky. MCRPs were sojourning in a sibling culture. There were students who chose Hong Kong for their research studies because Hong Kong is close to Mainland China and its culture is similar to that of Mainland China. In contrast, there were also students who came to Hong Kong for research degrees because they thought Hong Kong is a place where west meets the east and they hoped to confront different cultures and enrich their cultural experiences. To the later, acquiring intercultural experience was probably one of their criteria for "high quality". Besides, HKU is an English medium university; English proficiency is a big concern of many MCRPs. Therefore, the language environment for English learning was mentioned as an indicator of "quality" by some informants as well.

The part each aspect played in students' overall satisfaction

In the discussion of their satisfaction with the educational experiences at HKU, the informants placed different values to the different aspects. As the ongoing progress in academic research was taken as the most important thing in their life as research students, the factors that were considered helpful in improving such progress become comparatively more important indicators. Academic interaction seemed to be more important than others as it directly influences the students' academic progresses.

Possible relationship between the indicators identified

According to what had been found from the discussions with the informants, a diagram of the relationship between indicators may be drawn (see Figure 1). First, it is very likely that infrastructure, research climate, academic interaction, and social interaction are four major attributes of satisfying research experiences. For some

MCRPs who have expectations of intercultural experiences, it might be a contributor too. The existing research climate in a given department may help enhance academic interactions among peers. Besides, social interaction may contribute to academic interaction as good social interaction with peers and supervisors was reported to have helped to enhance the academic interaction with respective groups.

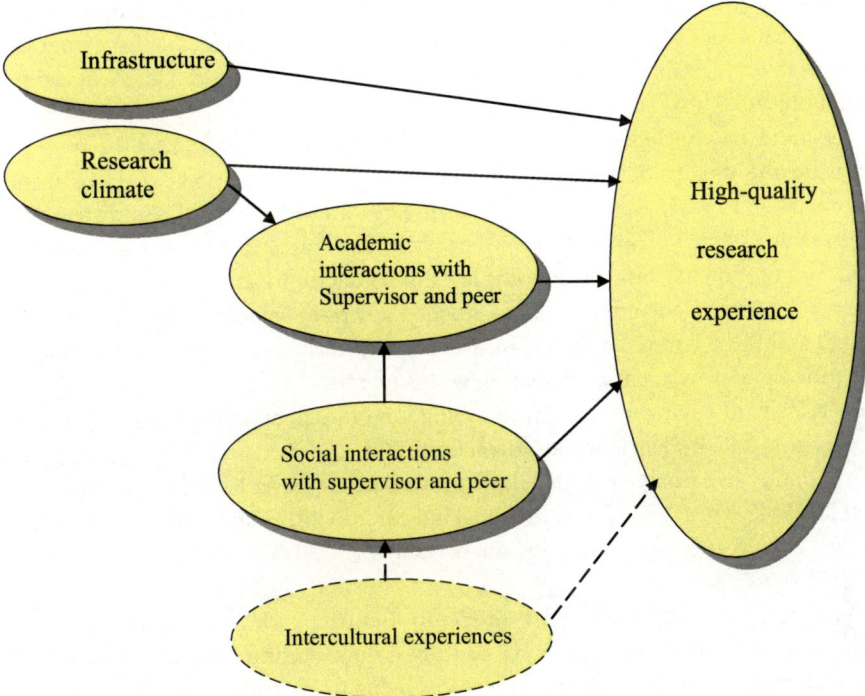

Figure 1 The diagram of possible relationships between the indicators of quality of research experiences

Discussion

While systematic and methodologically solid assessments of educational quality such as teaching quality assessment or research assessment were not usually accessible to and interpretable by the public, ranking lists provided the general public with references of the performance of higher education institutions. Institutions may also respond to such ranking league tables in order to improve their position in international rankings (Sadlak & Lui, 2007) by incorporating the outcomes into their strategic planning mechanisms, using them to identify weaknesses and resolve institutional problems, and develop better management information systems (Hazelkorn, 2007). However, the evidence about how the league table can actually help the quality assurance of higher education remains limited (Higher Education Funding Council for England, 2008).

Surveys on student experience may be a more effective way for quality assurance as they provide information to university administrators about what is happening in the process. The in-depth studies help to compile indicators for such assessment and reveal how the "consumer" of higher education thinks about the "service" they received. While it might not be practical to include students' evaluation of their educational experiences in the ranking system as subjective judgement may not be comparable, it certainly will help to find out the specific aspects of higher education that a university may need to improve.

As could be concluded from this study, five major indicators may be used to measure the quality of MCPRs' educational experiences at HKU. Two of them were similar to what were used in PREQ (2008) and PRES (2009): infrastructure and research climate. However, it is very likely that infrastructure was an essential indicator of "quality" but may become less influential to students' overall satisfaction once it meets students' needs or has reached a certain standard. "Supervision" in PREQ and PRES covered only one of the four dimensions of "research supervision" identified under "academic interaction with supervisor" in this study. This suggests the necessity of having more detailed evaluation of interaction experiences between supervisors and students. Social interactions and academic interactions with peers were another two newly identified dimensions that had never been assessed in PREQ and PRES. "Clear standard", an individual indicator in PREQ and PRES, was included as part of "research supervision" as the participants of this study regard it as a duty of their supervisors.

The fact that MRCPs weighted differently the part each aspect played in their overall satisfaction with the quality of education they received suggests that in future researchers may consider putting different weights to each dimension in the evaluation of student experience. The comparatively greater value the informants attached to academic interactions with supervisor suggests that they may contribute in a greater measure to MCRPs' overall satisfaction with their educational experience than other factors. The roles social interaction with peers served were very similar to what Ong and Ward (2005) found about the function of social interaction in acculturation research: emotional support, social companionship, tangible assistance, and informational support.

This study chose a special type of students, MCRPs, as the target from a larger group: research postgraduates at HKU. It helps to find out the indicators of the educational experience of MCRPs. More in-depth studies with other types of research students at HKU need to be conducted to obtain a fuller understanding of the whole picture.

References

Artushina, I., & Troyan, V. (2007). Methods of the quality of higher education social assessment. *Higher Education in Europe, 32*(1), 83-89.

Centre for Higher Education Development. (2009). *CHE ranking: Methodology*. Retrieved April 5, 2009, from http://www.che- ranking.de/cms/?getObject=619&getLang=en

Cheng, Y., & Liu, N. C. (2007). *Academic ranking of world universities by broad subject fields* (080 Journal Articles; 143 Reports: Research).

Corbin, J., & Strauss, A. (1990). Grounded theory research: procedures, cannons, and evaluative criteria. *Qualitative Sociology, 13*, 3-21.

Dill, D. (2006, 9 September). *Convergence and diversity: The role and influence of university rankings*. Paper presented at the Consortium of Higher Education Researchers (CHER) 19th Annual Research Conference, University of Kassel, Germany.

Eccles, C. (2002). The use of university rankings in the United Kingdom. *Higher Education in Europe, 27*(4), 423-432.

Ertl, H., Hayward, G., Wright, S., Edwards, A., Mills, D., & Yu, K. (2008). *The student learning experience in higher education: Literature review report for the Higher Education Academy*. Retrieved March 2, 2009, from http://www.heacademy.ac.uk/ourwork/research/litreviews

Glaser, B. G., & Strauss, A. L. (1968). *The discovery of grounded theory : strategies for qualitative research* London: Weidenfeld and Nicolson.

Harvey, L. (2005). A history and critique of quality evaluation in the UK. *Quality Assurance in Education, 13*(4), 263-276.

Hazelkorn, E. (2007). The impact of league tables and ranking systems on higher education decision-making. *Higher Education Management and Policy, 19*(2), 81-105.

Higher Education Funding Council for England. (2008). *Counting what is measured or measuring what counts? League tables and their impact on higher education institutions in England: Report to HEFCE by the Centre for Higher Education Research and Information (CHERI), Open University, and Hobsons Research*. Retrieved March 2, 2009, from www.hefce.ac.uk

Higher Education Funding Council for England. (2009). *National Student Survey*. Retrieved Feburary 5, 2009, from http://www.hefce.ac.uk/learning/nss/

Institute for Teaching and Learning. (2009a). *Postgraduate Research Experience Questionnaire (PREQ)*. Retrieved January 3, 2009, from http://www.itl.usyd.edu.au/preq/

Institute for Teaching and Learning. (2009b). *Student Course Experience Questionnaire (SCEQ)*. Retrieved March 2, 2009, from http://www.itl.usyd.edu.au/sceq/

Kuh, G. (2002). *The college student report*. Indiana University: Center for Postsecondary Research and Planning.

Locke, W. (2007). *Ranking Universities: Criteria and Consequences*. London: Centre for Higher Education Research and Information.

Ong, A. S. J., & Ward, C. (2005). The construction and validation of a social support measure for sojourners: The Index of Sojourner Social Support (ISSS) Scale. *Journal of Cross-cultural Psychology, 36*(6), 637-661.

Postilgione, G. A., & Tang, J. T. H. (1997). *Hong Kong's reunion with China : the global dimensions*. . Armonk, N.Y.: M.E. Sharpe.

Pring, R. (1992). *Academic respectability and professional relevance*. An inaugural lecture delivered before the University of Oxford 8th May. Oxford: Clarendon Press.

Pursglove, J., & Simpson, M. (2007). Benchmarking the performance of English universities. *Benchmarking: An International Journal, 14*(1), 102-112.

Ramsden, P., & Entwistle, N. (1981). Effects of academic departments on students' approaches to studying. *British Journal of Educational Psychology, 51*, 368-383.

Sadlak, J., & Lui, N. C. (eds.). (2007). *The world-class university and ranking: Aiming beyond status*. Bucharest: UNESCO-CEPES.

The-Higher-Education-Academy. (2009). *Postgraduate Research Experience Survey (PRES)*. Retrieved January 3, 2009, from http://www.heacademy.ac.uk/ourwork/research/surveys/pres

University Grants Council. (2007). *Non-local student enrolment (Headcount) of UGC-funded programmes by institution, level of study, place of origin and mode of study: 2006/07 to 2007/08*. Retrieved March 11, 2009, from http://www.ugc.edu.hk/eng/ugc/publication/report/figure2007/figures/13.pdf

University of Buckingham. (2006). *News: Buckingham's success in National Student Survey 2006*. Retrieved February 19, 2007, from http://www.buckingham.ac.uk/news/newsarchive2006/nss-results.html

Ward, P., & Jayanetti, C. (2006). *The measure of contentment.* Retrieved February 20, 2007, from http://www.thes.co.uk/story.aspx?story_id=2031982

Yorke, M. (1998). The Times' "league table" of universities, 1997: a statistical appraisal. *Quality Assurance in Education, 6*(1), 58-60.

The paper has been reviewed by external referees.

On the "Evaluation of undergraduate teaching work" in Chinese universities

Xie Surong

Abstract

Since 1999, in the course of the development of higher education massification in China, the teaching quality of higher education has become the focus of society along with the problem of over-recruitment in universities. It requires the construction of teaching quality assurance systems, which involves intensifying evaluation of higher education.

In order to guarantee the quality of teaching, starting from 2003, the government has been making efforts to "evaluate undergraduate teaching level" throughout universities in China. The first phase of the evaluation work was completed in 2008 and has brought out some positive effects and also received many criticisms. Therefore, it is important to think on the five years' practice and explore introspectively.

This paper is inspired by the questions that arise and the difficulties in the practice. It includes two parts: The first part introduces the "Evaluation of the undergraduate teaching level" in Chinese universities and explicates "why" and "how" we carry on the evaluation work. The second part is about the positive and negative effects of the practice; it examines some wrongdoings that should be avoided in the practice and points out the real reasons for the problems.

Through this paper we can gauge the general situation of the "evaluation of undergraduate teaching level" in Chinese universities and how to avoid the negative influential factors of the evaluation.

Keywords: Evaluation of undergraduate teaching level in universities, the Evaluation Program, multiple perspectives of teaching Quality of Higher Education, the standards of evaluation

Since 1999, in the course of the development of higher education massification in China, the teaching quality of higher education has become the focus of society along with the problem of over-recruitment in universities. It requires the construction of a teaching quality assurance system, which involves intensifying evaluation of higher education.

The evaluation of undergraduate teaching work in universities organized by the original National Education Council in 1993 can be divided into seven major categories of conduct. Each group designed their own evaluation indicators system. From 1994, we began to carry on qualified evaluation of undergraduate teaching in universities; in 1996 we assessed outstanding undergraduate teaching work; in 1998 we engaged in a random evaluation of undergraduate teaching level in universities.

Later, the Ministry of Education decided to unify the three kinds of evaluation for evaluation of undergraduate teaching level in universities. The evaluation program was researched approximately two years.

In 2002, the government used the program to evaluate 21 universities as an experiment. In order to guarantee the quality of teaching, starting from 2003, the Ministry of Education has been making efforts to aid the task of "Evaluation of undergraduate teaching level" throughout universities in China within five years. In 2003, 42 universities were evaluated; after that, the evaluation program underwent some adjustments, but there was very little change.

Then "why" do we carry on the evaluation work?

Because the vast majority of our graduates from undergraduate programs of study will begin their work, and the other part will be graduate students. This means that the quality of our graduates not only directly affects our country's economic development, social progress, and scientific and technological progress but also affects the quality of graduate students. Undergraduate education is in fact the subject and the foundation of higher education; good undergraduate teaching work is the key to raise the level of higher education in our country. So the Ministry of Education decided to evaluate 592 undergraduate colleges in every five years. 2003–2008 was the first turn, and the turns will continue.

What is the "evaluation program"?

The evaluation work is divided into three stages: self-assessment, the expert group inspection of the school, and the rectification period of one year. The inspection of the expert group in the school is not more than one week, so what the experts inspect is the result of the school's self-evaluation, that is to say the result of school self-evaluation is in fact the conclusions of the expert group. The purpose of assessment is to further promote the school director who is more concerned with the quality of teaching.

The effect of the evaluation work is displayed in two major aspects: One is satisfaction of the evaluation work, which includes school satisfaction, teacher satisfaction, student satisfaction and management satisfaction. The other is validity of the evaluation work, through the evaluation, to improve all aspects of the undergraduate teaching work. The evaluation program has seven indicators of the first level (and a feature item: If the university wants to be rated first in the evaluation, it needs the item to show its own features), 18 indicators of the second level and 38 assessing factors. The indicator system has A-class and C-class standards; between the ranges of A and C are the B-class; not up to C-class standard are D-class; and in fact D-class is not qualified.

1. The guidelines of the school
1.1 School positioning
    The main assessing factor is "School positioning and programming".
1.2 The ideas of the school
    It has two assessing factors: one is "education ideas", the other is "teaching centred".
2 Construction of teachers' team
2.1 Structure of teachers' team
    There are two assessing factors: one is "the overall structure and development trend of the team," including the following aspects: the condition of additional staff in the recent three years, such as the number and background; the condition of transfer and demission. It also requires well-developed academic leaders, academic team and appropriate number of teachers as the backbone of the team.
    The other assessing factors are "young teachers in the proportion of postgraduate degree". *Young teachers* refers to teachers younger than 35 years of age.
2.2 Instructors
    Instructors should have master's qualification and lecturer for professional and technical positions. New teachers should obtain certification through pre-job training. Professors and associate professors lecture to undergraduate students as much as possible, including basic and professional lessons.
3 Teaching conditions and the utilization of facilities
3.1 Basic teaching facilities
    They include the quality and utilization of facilities.
3.2 Teaching funding
4 Teaching development and teaching reform
4.1 Specialties
    It has two assessing factors: "new specialties" and "teaching programs".
4.2 Curriculum
    The most important assessing factor is "teaching content and curriculum reform", including the overall ideas of curriculum reform, concrete plans, measures, and results of implementation. The second assessing factor is "teaching books". The third one is "reform of teaching methods and means". A-class standard requires "the use of multimedia instruction". The fourth one is "bilingual education"; it is a target-oriented factor. A-class standards particularly emphasize the "teaching effect of bilingual education".
4.3 Practical teaching

It has three assessing factors; one is "the content and systems of practical teaching". At this point, A-class standard requires "attention to content update". It emphasizes the cultivation of students' innovation ability.

5 Teaching management

5.1 Management team

It has two assessing factors: one is "the structure and quality of the team", and the other is "the research and practical results of teaching management and its reform".

5.2 Quality control

It has three assessing factors: basic teaching documents such as educational programs and the necessary management systems. These documents and systems should reflect modern education ideas and actively implement modern management techniques.

"Quality standards of main teaching processes" mainly refers to the classroom teaching; the practical teaching includes experiments, internship, social practice, academic thesis, thesis (design) and so on. It examines the teaching quality, the specific arrangement of teaching procedure and the implementation of teaching plan.

"Self-evaluation and inspection of teaching": the school should set up a teaching quality assurance system and monitoring mechanism that has features for self-improvement and self-restraint.

6 Academic styles

6.1 Teachers' style

One assessing factor is "Teachers training and teachers' professionalism".

6.2 Style of study

It is mainly reflected in four aspects. (1) Campus atmosphere; (2) Management of students; (3) Social practice and other educational activities; (4) The school image.

7. Teaching effect

7.1 The basic theory and basic skills

Basic skills refer to the basic experimental skills, practical skills, self-learning ability, adaptability, communication skills, innovation skills and capabilities.

7.2 The thesis or graduation project

It mainly assesses the following aspects: (1) ability to solve practical problems; (2) ability to apply general knowledge; (3) ability to use various tools in the work, such as equipments, reference books, foreign languages and so on, (4) ability to write research reports and thesis (design); (5) teamwork capabilities, ability to deal with interpersonal relationships and so on.

7.3 Ideological and Moral Cultivation

It is mainly reflected in the performance of the students. "Ideological and political quality" is the most important quality.

7.4 Physical education

7.5 The reputation of the school

Feature indicator

If the university wants to be first rate in the evaluation, the feature indicator must be considered. It can be manifested in the following aspects: the overall strategy, the ideas of the university; educational characteristics; teaching characteristics, such as curriculum system, teaching methods; teaching management features, such as a set of scientific teaching management methods, a good operational mechanism and so on.

The "Evaluation of the undergraduate teaching level in universities" is an important means used by the Ministry of Education to supervise and macro-control universities. These seven first-level indicators of the evaluation program almost cover the management of undergraduate teaching in every aspect. In 2003, the Ministry of Education organized the evaluation of 42 universities, including Shanghai University and Capital Normal University, and the rate was near 50%. The results of the evaluation evoked a strong response. At present, our country has 750 undergraduate colleges and universities. According to the five-year plan of each turn, we should evaluate 150 universities each year. The continuous assessment system of many universities requires ensuring the quality of the evaluation work. The first turn of the evaluation work was completed in 2008, and it has brought us some positive results and also received many criticisms. Therefore, it becomes important to think on the five-year practice and explore the system introspectively.

As we know, the evaluation promotes the development of undergraduate teaching reform and improves the quality of education. It mainly manifests in the following aspects:

1) Increasing the input of undergraduate teaching

The evaluation program has explicitly demanded the indicators of teaching conditions. It improves the government and universities' initiative to increase the input of undergraduate teaching and has greatly improved the conditions for running schools. For example, in 2005, Dong Hua University organized education and teaching reform; it invests more than 300 million each year on the construction of teaching materials, curriculum reform and so on, and 15 million each year on experimental equipment.

2) Setting up teaching-oriented incentive mechanism

In order to improve teaching enthusiasm, the evaluation encourages schools to take positive incentive policies of teaching. Shanghai Jiao tong University has introduced reforms in teachers' incentive mechanism, and teachers' promotion is linked to the construction of state-level quality curriculums.

3) Promoting the reform of undergraduate teaching

In the teaching process, the student-centred concept continues to be strengthened. Shanghai Jiao tong University enhanced the study of inquiry-based learning methods and set up student-centred teaching evaluation system. The evaluation program lays emphasis on the combination of teaching and practice. It is conducive to improve student's practical skills. The Shanghai Applied Technology Institute has set up long-term internships and cooperative relations with 122 enterprises and invites entrepreneurs to give lectures in classrooms.

4) Exploring and forming the long-term assurance mechanism of teaching quality

An important objective of the evaluation is to promote the development of undergraduate teaching quality evaluation and long-term assurance mechanism of teaching quality. A number of colleges and universities form their own characteristic teaching quality assurance systems as the basis of the evaluation. Although the evaluation work has brought us some positive results, it couldn't conceal the existing questions, such as: use a single standard to evaluate all colleges and universities in our country; it engages in formalism and image project; it wastes a lot of valuable educational resources.

These criticisms reflect the specific problems and wrongdoings in the practice:

First of all, misunderstandings of the evaluation cause some wrongdoings. One is the utilitarian sense; the schools just prepare for passing the evaluation and lack a good self-restraint mechanism. All these features are not conducive to effective evaluation. In the actual evaluation process, some schools are concerned about the evaluation conclusions as they consider them as important factors in their own survival and development and therefore achieve good evaluations by resorting to fraud. In order to pass the evaluation, the school requests some teachers to work overtime; it disrupts the normal teaching, thus affecting the normal teaching order. A few education departments and colleges have not placed enough emphasis on the evaluation work. They are not aware of the formative and diagnosis functions of the evaluation and exaggerate the identification function of the evaluation. In fact, the real function of the evaluation is deepening of education reform and improving the quality of teaching.

In addition, a few of colleges and universities mistakenly believe that the evaluation is costly and superfluous. On the one hand, through scientific and reasonable evaluation, we can find the problems of teaching management and prevent redundant construction, extravagance and wasteful projects in time. It saves considerable costs. On the other hand, increasing the input of funds and facilities is beneficial to improving the teaching conditions, optimizing the teaching environment, improving the quality of teaching and cultivating more qualified students for the state as inputs gained from the evaluation are scientific and rational.

Second, some colleges haven't set up an assurance system. Although some colleges and universities actively take part in the evaluation, they haven't set up long-term management mechanisms. Judging from the results of the evaluation, most of us pay attention to the evaluation results and neglect learning how to diagnose the problem by evaluating and how to further develop the school. We consider the evaluation as a temporary mission And get back to the old way of functioning after completing the evaluation. This is contrary to the original purpose of the evaluation work.

The above wrongdoings indicate that we must carefully consider the following questions: Does the cooperative attitude of universities to the evaluation mean that they approve of and understand the concept and process of the evaluation? In the long term, does the "performance"-based funding system of higher education improve the performance of colleges and universities? Is it necessary to write exquisitely detailed evaluation reports? And to what extent does it increase the burden on universities? In order to obtain educational resources, is it possible for universities to give up the quality of higher education to meet the needs of the external evaluation standards?

Will colleges and universities compete for educational resources unfairly? What is the relationship between the evaluation and university autonomy? In order to answer these questions, we have to think about them introspectively to find out the real reasons for these problems. The negative influential factors of the evaluation include the following:

1) The unscientific evaluation methods affect the improvement of teaching quality

After years of research, evaluation experts set up the evaluation indicators of undergraduate teaching and applied them to practice, but they lack pertinence using the same indicators to measure different schools. The distinction between schools is not enough, and validity also cannot be assured. It is involved in more subjective factors, thus affecting the scientific and impartial conclusion of the evaluation. Especially for teaching evaluation, a single evaluation standard and a simple way of implementing make it difficult to develop a teaching style.

The evaluation must be standardization, but at different levels for different types of schools and faculties, based on the curriculum development and cultivation model, we must build a set of corresponding evaluation indicators of undergraduate teaching in universities, so that the evaluation can be more effective. Now, we have different levels and different types of colleges and universities with the development of higher education in our country, but the lack of diversity of the evaluation criteria makes it difficult to evaluate different schools with different styles and guidelines. Schools lost their features in the evaluation, making it difficult to improve the quality of teaching.

On specific evaluation methods, the various assessing factors of the indicator system have corresponding criteria, mainly using quantitative methods. There is a higher degree of accuracy and standardization in quantitative methods, logical reasoning is more precise, and the results of the evaluation are more scientific and objective. But if we use quantitative methods to evaluate the quality of teaching and scientific research, it will be difficult to obtain accurate conclusions. Undergraduate teaching process is dynamic; the evaluation should also be coordinated with the dynamic process. Detailed study is necessary to identify the educational activities accurately. The existing questions in the teaching evaluation system are not applicable to the actual situation. The existing problems are not adapting the evaluation indicators system for the actual teaching practice but adapting the teaching system for the evaluation.

2) The principal role of government in the evaluation affects the order of teaching management

The existing evaluation of undergraduate teaching level in our country is organized by the Ministry of Education; it is a typical administrative evaluation. The government is the educational administrator and educational evaluation executor, thus confusing the role of the government in educational activities. Because of the involvement of the government authority, the whole evaluation process is full of nervous feelings, prone to rigorous evaluation and the "disturbing" problem and so on. Driven by interests and pressure, the school will passively emphasize the importance of the evaluation, and it will cause formalism and fraud.

The method of implementing the evaluation is random, short term and administrative and lacks broad participation and multiple observations. Usually for achieving the standards and the requirements of the government, it will inevitably fall into a subjective one-sidedness. The government should commission social intermediary organizations to carry out the evaluation; this will be better than the evaluation directly organized by the government.

3) The results of the evaluation lack measurement of the process

The most serious problem of the evaluation is strong focus on the results, as it causes some wrongdoings. The first of which is the inconsistency between the results of the evaluation and the actual situation. After the first turn of Undergraduate Teaching Evaluation, it was concluded that most of the colleges and universities are good. Although the quality of colleges and universities has improved, the problem of quality still exists in undergraduate education, and we are far from reaching the conclusion that almost all institutions are good. Very few schools got a good rating without the solid foundation of teaching work; it is worthy of reflection. The second wrongdoing is that of being overly concerned with the results of the evaluation, which causes utilitarianism and formalism. Very few schools follow good practices and may fraudulently involve the participation of students. This runs counter to the integrity education.

In response, colleges and universities themselves must correctly handle some relations in the evaluation:

Relations between teaching work and the documents of teaching work. Teaching work is substantial and documents are a summary of teaching work. They are prepared for self-evaluation and as evidence for conclusions. The documents should have three features: pertinence, conciseness and clarity of levels. The documents should be categorized to form a directory, requiring clarity of levels and authenticity. They should emphasize the accumulation and collection of daily work and not ask teachers to prepare the document in a short time to meet the requirements of the evaluation, as this will result in human and financial waste and also easily lead to resentment of teachers.

Relations between the evaluation experts group and schools. The principal part of the evaluation should be schools, not the evaluation experts, nor the government. Since the purpose of the evaluation is to ensure the quality of teaching and school development needs, schools are the principal part of the evaluation. The evaluation work is part of the overall school's work; it directly influences the development of the school. The experts group helps the schools understand their own development status and existing problems. Therefore, we must establish school-centred concepts in evaluation.

4) The constitution of evaluation experts is simplified, and lack of social evaluation

The conclusions of the evaluation are worked out mainly by experts, so the quality of the evaluation experts is important. At present, the structure of the evaluation experts group is simple, with experts chosen mainly from higher education institutions. There is a lack of experts from the government management department and from the industry, including enterprise, and many colleges and universities abroad such as Germany's colleges and universities conduct the assessment as a business and have the experts take part in official assignments, so that a more objective and fair conclusion could be obtained. In addition, there is no reasonable incentive mechanism to assure the conclusions of the evaluation made by experts. The experts always face substantial preparatory work done by schools; it is difficult to make fair and objective evaluation conclusions under great pressure.

We should consider the evaluation of undergraduate teaching level in universities objectively; the evaluation will not necessarily improve the undergraduate teaching quality. We must pay more attention to the problems that emerge from the evaluation; we must strive to make the undergraduate teaching system adapt to the specific circumstances of the school, and in the evaluation program add a new evaluation indicator of the specific teaching and learning performance in schools and reduce the negative influential factors to a minimum. Higher education massification is the inevitable choice of social development; it challenges the quality of undergraduate teaching in our country. In order to improve the teaching quality of higher education, we must strengthen the teaching quality evaluation.

References

Feng Ailing, & Li Jianming (2006). The Practice of Building the Evaluation Centered Education Quality Assurance System. *Journal of Xi'an University of Arts and Science* (Social Sciences Edition), 9(4).

Lin Yao (2008). The Conflict and Coordinate Strategies of the Understanding of the Evaluation of Undergraduate Teaching Work in Chinese Universities. *Journal of Higher Education Management*, 2(3).

Zhang Bo (2008). The Problems Existing in the Evaluation of Undergraduate teaching work in Chinese Universities. *The Education Review*, 5.

Tong Huawe, & Peng Yan (2006). Higher Education Quality Safeguard and the University Teaching Quality Appraisal. *Journal of Architectural Education in Institutions of Higher Learning*, 15(2).

Wan Bingyun, & Zhu Shibo (2007). Evaluation of Teaching Work and Construction of Teaching Quality in Chinese Universities. *Journal of Chengdu University of Information Technology*, 22(4).

From Principles to Practice – or vice versa? The Value of Studying Consensus about Scholarship

Marit Allern & Lillian Vederhus

Abstract

According to Carolin Kreber, expert knowledge is important in the field of education, in conceptualizing scholarship and identifying unresolved issues, even though identifying experts can be problematic. We report from a small-scale investigation at the Faculty of Medicine at the University of Tromsø. Based on an external evaluation of the education of physicians, a revision of principles for this education has been approved, and a new curriculum is in progress. The new curriculum is to be implemented August 2010, and the learning outcomes are grouped into theoretical knowledge, social and practical skills and ethical attitude. This project will investigate how principles are concretized into curriculum, course plans, instruction and assessment and how and to what extent the roles of teachers and students change according to these new objectives. Following this process, we have applied a Delphi-technique similar to Kreber's study, to try and extract statements about the scholarship of teaching from faculty that teach first and second year for physicians to be, at the Faculty of Medicine (Phase I), and further come up with the extent of agreement to these statements (Phase II). We continue the paper with discussions of faculty as educational experts, the value of consensus in scholarship of teaching and specific ideas about scholarship from our particular study.

Introduction

Internationally there is increasing attention to education and a shift to pay more notice to the quality of teaching and what is called "The Scholarship of Teaching and Learning"(Boyer, 1990; Braxton, 2006). In higher education, investigating principles and developing frameworks in scholarship of teaching and learning (SoTL), as well as methods for benchmarking learning and teaching has become an expanding field of interest. As stated by Myers (2008), little effort has been spent on who actually practices the SoTL at faculties. Thus, identification of areas of importance, and listings of performance and quality indicators, has its origin in expert knowledge and literature validation, purportedly hampering implementations of SoTL in faculty. Insofar as change demands exchange, an approach where faculty is actively engaged in the process of informing ideals through realizable practice is to be preferred. This requires more research merging the "top-down-expertise" and the "bottom- up-expertise", since each will be restricted in the opportunity of forecasting emerging educational horizons. A quest for consensus is another implicit idea of SoTL, somewhat contrasting the perspectives of situated learning in the way of organizing general principles by sacrificing applicability. A focus comprising situated teaching could therefore be appropriate for a more comprehensive approach.

The Bologna process demands the development of a common qualification framework in higher education. In the Nordic countries there is a joint project to develop such framework. Royal Norwegian Ministry of Education and Research has agreed to a new qualification framework for Norwegian higher education in March 2009.[1] At the same time, many institutions in Norway have already started the work to revise study programs and modules. In an ongoing project at the University of Tromsø, Norway, we want to examine to what extent revising study plans and modules lead to substantial changes in teaching and assessment, particularly focusing on formative assessment. The theoretical perspective for this study is sociocultural theory as presented in the works of Lev Vygotskij, James Wertsch and Roger Säljö (Säljö, 2001; Vygotskij, 1978; Wertsch, 1998). This approach begins with the assumption "that action is mediated and that it cannot be separated from the milieu in which it is carried out" (Wertsch, 1991, p. 18). Faculty is supposed to engage in assessing their own work and document their teaching performance (Alexandersson, 1994; Braskamp & Ory, 1994; Seldin, 2004). The scholarship of assessment has also been introduced (cf. Rust, 2007).

There is need for more knowledge about how different ways of teaching and instruction function and how different types of assessment facilitate learning outcomes. Feedback from the teacher, peers or others can be powerful, but it is essential to know more about the effect of different kinds of feedback and how students act in accordance to the feedback they are given. The type of feedback

---

[1] Letter sent to Norwegian universities and colleges March 20th 2009, 200805673-/KEB

and good or bad timing make it differentially effective (cf. Gibbs, 2006; Hattie & Timperley, 2007; Havnes, 2008; Skjong, 2008).

The objective is integration of teaching methods and assessment to make students develop skills and tools in mediated action (cf. Wertsch, 1998). New roles for teachers appear as students take more responsibility in the learning process. One relevant question is to what extent teachers respond to this and enhance a holistic education for the students. Both the individual learning process and the social perspective are in this context understood as important. When a modified Delphi-technique was chosen as a method for our project, the advantages of extensive information within faculty, whereby informants remain anonymous to each other and mail-responses are free from fixed-time presence demands, were seen as outweighing disadvantages also known as challenging when using other methods, as for instance voluntariness of participation or withdrawal. The Delphi-method was originally applied to generate ideas and forecast developments, by expert opinions undergoing a progress of consensus formation when informants' ideas are revealed and rated individually.

Context

The Faculty of Medicine is working to revise the study plan for educating physicians'. That particular study was evaluated by an external committee in 2006. New principles for revising the curriculum for "tomorrow's physicians" were then approved in 2007. These principles have established strong claims to faculty teaching the students. Therefore, it seemed relevant to conduct a study about what these teachers think characterize "Scholarship of Teaching and Learning or outstanding teaching" (Boyer, 1990; Braxton, 2006; Kreber, 2001). This is carried out as a modified Delphi-study (Boyer, 1990; Kreber, 2001; Smith & Simpson, 1995). The first and partly the second year of medical education have joint courses for both physicians and dentists to be, each class with around 140–159 students. In this context the actual teachers are defined as the substituting experts, and we have initially included all persons teaching 1st and 2nd year and do not discriminate between professors, associate professors, assistant professors or fellow scholars. Neither is gender nor years of teaching experience an issue in this study. When concentrating on the first two years, it is likely that we will get a somewhat different result than if concentrating on the teachers of for example the fifth and sixth year. We could have defined head of departments, dean and vice deans as experts or even persons with an excellent reputation for their scholarly work on teaching and learning (cf. Kreber, 2001). The aim is mapping ideas of scholarship content and the attitudes of faculty teaching.

The first phase of a modified Delphi-study addressed 97 persons who teach these courses. On 16th June we sent a collective email asking the panel to formulate what characterize "Scholarship of teaching and learning". Some of the persons were no longer employed at the institution, and others had left for sabbatical and would not take part or said that they had no responsibility to answer this study. In the beginning we got little feedback and a reminder was sent to each person after approximately a month. This resulted in a few more answers, but we had to make phone calls to receive altogether 39 letters of feedback to our question.

In the second phase we made a questionnaire out of the statements from the teachers. This turned out to be complicated because many of the statements were confusingly alike but not identical. We wanted to be loyal to the idea of returning the statements made by the teachers, but mot utterances were also written in either an abbreviated style or in an extensive essay form, so most final statements have undergone a "sentence-completion". On 20th October the questionnaire was sent to the entire group of teachers/panel that got our first request. Altogether 117 statements were grouped by the authors under the following headings:

- Professional qualifications (17 items)
- Developing and organizing the curriculum (18 items)
- Skills to plan and lead different forms of teaching and learning activities (22 items)
- Skills to carry out different forms of teaching and learning activities (communication) (53 items)
- General social skills (7 items)

The instruction was to indicate the extents to which they agreed or disagreed by rating between 1, strongly disagree, and 7, strongly agree. By December we obtained responses from 36 informants in the final sample of ratings. A few persons wrote mails to support the enquiry and told us that they were especially engaged in the quality of medical education at the institution. A number of persons were really annoyed by the fact that many statements were alike, and this may have made answering the questionnaire complicated.

Preliminary tendencies and ideas from our particular study

Before the first phase, we did a literature review to try and establish a framework for the expected statements on scholarship of teaching and learning. We were asked to give some ideas about what this could be and came up with the following keywords as possible fields: professional level of teachers, the need for research-based knowledge, value of varied presentation and personal engagement, the value of using Information and Communication Technology (ICT), how to emphasize oral and written communication, the importance of motivation, preferred methodology, value of student cooperation, reflection on own teaching and the students' learning outcomes.

Statements from the panel far from filled the expected universe of characterization, so the total of 117 were, as mentioned earlier, disproportionately organized under five domains. Calculating the degree of agreement obtained from the second phase, and ranking the statements according to this, is not necessarily the same as identifying consensus. Agreement with statements is measured as mean or, often, median, but due to the amount of statements and refinement of ranking, we have chosen to analyse the mean as representing agreement with statements. Consensus around any degree of agreement is therefore measured in standard deviations, where small standard deviations represent stronger agreement within faculty. Also, some statements have larger dispersion (responses on the scale of seven possible agreements, or 1–6, or 2–7), even though only a few are at one end, and many statements are quite tight on the upper end, with all valid responses distributed in a variety of ways to 5, 6 and 7. Graphic plots and frequency tables show that there is some variation in response patterns, even though we found grand means for each of the five areas to be quite high, in the interval of 5.37 to 5.78.

In Table 1, we list the 19 statements that combine the property of entering the lowest-twenty-five means (lower agreement with statements), the largest twenty-five standard deviations (lower agreement within faculty), at the same time as they have dispersion over all seven, or six out of seven, values on the scale.

In Table 2, we list the 20 statements that combine the property of entering the twenty-five- highest means (higher agreement with statements), the twenty-five lowest standard deviations (larger agreement within faculty, that is, higher consensus) and also have a dispersion over only three or four values on the scale.

Discussion

Difficulties arise when trying to interpret results from the second phase in this unfinished project, where the next phase will reveal if there are any changes in individual responses when presented to group mean and standard deviation of each statement. It has been difficult to link the SoTL literature to the statements regarded important but obviously scattered across all levels of teaching practice. A more thorough theoretical analysis will be tracked as we enter the third phase.

Also, the value of considering faculty as educational experts is not obvious. We know that faculty in medicine as other faculty has many roles to fulfil. Most persons consider research their main activity, and in addition they might be teachers, committee members, curriculum developers, clinicians and so on. (Hand, 2006, p. 941). It is likely that when we ask all the teachers about defining "scholarship of teaching and learning", the answers are given rather spontaneously. They are in this context not asked to argue for their statements or to present a theoretical pedagogical perspective. Nevertheless, these persons are the ones teaching the students and we find it interesting to listen to their definitions. We are familiar with the fact that top-down decisions in Norwegian higher education often meet opposition and resistance. From research following the Quality Reform in Norwegian Higher Education in 2003, we know that it is hard to make shifts in teaching and instruction. What seems to result in changes is assessment. The implementation of portfolio assessment, for example, led to considerably more feedback on students' drafts, especially from teachers and less from peers.

Change of examination structure seemed to be the most widespread pedagogical consequence of the realization of the Quality Reform (Dysthe, Raaheim, Lima, & Bygstad, 2006, p.: 17). We know from the reports that teachers find the quantity of feedback burdensome and at the same time meaningful. At some departments at the University of Tromsø the tendency some years after the Quality Reform is to change back from portfolio assessment to traditional exams to reduce the work load for the teachers. Multiple choice tests may also have a "renaissance" at some faculties for the same reason. The motivation to implement peer assessment is rather weak because the teachers are convinced that they as expert will give better response than peers.

The intention of this study is to investigate how faculty teaching the students defines scholarship of teaching and learning. After phase III we will learn to what extent the attitudes are modified or changed and how this matches the revised study plan that is to be implemented in fall 2010. This study may also identify unresolved issues, especially through an analysis of matters absent and matters emphasized, thereby outlining areas for development that ought to be addressed among faculty members who both accept and plan for teaching responsibilities (cf. Smith & Simpson, 1995, pp. 231-233).

References

Alexandersson, M. (1994). *Metod och medvetande.* Göteborg: Acta Universitatis Gothoburgensis.

Boyer, E. L. (1990). *Scholarship Reconsidered* (1 ed.). San Francisco: Jossey-Bass Publishers.

Braskamp, L. A., & Ory, J. C. (1994). *Assessing Faculty Work Enhancing individual and institutional performance.* San Francisco: Jossey-Bass Publishers.

Braxton, J. M. (2006). Analyzing Faculty Work and Rewards: Using Boyer's Four Domains of Scholarship. In J. M. Braxton (ed.), *New Directions for Institutional Research, 129* (pp. 119). San Francisco: Jossey-Bass.

Dysthe, O., Raaheim, A., Lima, I., & Bygstad, A. (2006). Undervisnings- og vurderingsformer. Pedagogiske konsekvenser av Kvalitetsreformen. Bergen/Oslo.

Gibbs, G. (2006). How assessment frames student learning. In C. Bryan & K. Clegg (eds.), *Innovative assessment in higher Education* (pp. 23-36). Abingdon, Oxon, GB: Routledge.

Hand, J. S. (2006). Identification of Competencies for Effective Dental Faculty [ElectronicVersion]. *Journal of Dental Education, 70,* 937-947, from http://www.jdentaled.org/cgi/content/abstract/70/9/937

Hattie, J., & Timperley, H. (2007). The power of feedback. *Review of Educational Research, 77*(1), 81-112.

Havnes, A. (2008). Peer-mediated learning beyond the curriculum. *Studies in Higher Education, 33*(2), 193-204.

Kreber, C. (ed.) (2001). *Scholarship Revisited: Perspectives on the Scholarship of Teaching* (Vol. 86). San Francisco: Jossey Bass.

Myers, C. B. (2008). College faculty and the scholarship of teaching: Gender differences across four key activities [Electronic Version]. *Journal of the Scholarship of Teaching and Learning, 8,* 38-51.

Rust, C. (2007). Towards a scholarship of assessment [Electronic Version]. *Assessment & Evaluation in Higher Education, 32,* 229-237.

Seldin, P. (2004). *The Teaching Portfolio A Practical Guide to Improved Performance and Promotion/Tenure Decisions* (3. ed.). San Francisco: Jossey-Bass.

Skjong, S. (2008). "Å tvinge tanken til konsekvens". Digitale mapper i norskfaget i lærerutdanninga. In M. Allern & K. S. Engelsen (eds.), *Mapper i digitale læringskontekstar – erfaringar og perspektiv frå høgre utdanning* (Vol. 2). Tromsø: Norgesuniversitetet.

Smith, K. S., & Simpson, R. (1995). Validating Teaching Competencies for Faculty Members in higher Education: a National Study using the Delphi Method. *Innovative Higher Education, 19*(3), 223-234.

Säljö, R. (2001). *Læring i praksis: et sosiokulturelt perspektiv.* Oslo: Cappelen akademisk.

Vygotskij, L. S. (1978). *Mind in society: the development of higher psychological processes.* Cambridge, Mass.: Harvard University Press.

Wertsch, J. V. (1991). *Voices of the mind: a sociocultural approach to mediated action.* Cambridge, Mass.: Harvard University Press.

Wertsch, J. V. (1998). *Mind as action.* New York: Oxford University Press.

Table 1. Statements appearing with combinations of lowest agreement with statements (mean), lowest agreement within faculty (st.dev.), and largest dispersion (based on statement's set of actual responded values within scale of 1–7, but range is reported in table)

Statement:	Mean	St.dev.	Range
The teaching must be based on own and co-workers research to the extent possible *	2.94	1.608	5
You should emphasize teaching method rather than knowledge in itself ****	2.94	1.589	5
A lecture on Monday morning at 0800 hrs can use stories to make the students wake up ****	3.26	1.704	6
Teaching should if possible be framed as problem-based learning ***	3.28	1.750	5
Interactive Internet-based teaching can replace many of the traditional lectures **	3.44	1.443	5
The presentation must be ICT-based, adjusted to the needs of the students and motivating ****	4.09	1.837	6
Early in the first year of study the subject must be communicated in a simple way, not too detailed ****	4.51	1.442	6
The students must write papers to reflect and evaluate ***	4.53	1.581	6
The university should not make use of uncommitted lecturers who would rather devote all their time to research **	4.54	1.521	6
The teaching must be research based and in the front edge of the development of the medicine in the field ***	4.63	1.437	5
The students work harder with the subject matter if they have to submit a journal ***	4.79	1.533	5
Teaching should be given by lecturers with clinical experience as doctor/dentist *	4.81	1.721	6
At the beginning of a course it is vital to communicate that learning requires hard work ***	4.86	1.869	6
By correcting the students' obligatory laboratory journals one can learn if the learning outcome is as expected and one will be able to correct possible misunderstanding ***	4.88	1.493	6
Teaching should be research based, but the teacher needs not to be a researcher *	4.89	1.563	6
Lectures should be given by persons with research competence *	4.92	1.628	5
The university must let academic staff lecture in their research field; this is not always the case to day **	4.97	1.699	6
The presentation must be prepared thoroughly pedagogically and the use of IKT must be an important part of this planning ****	4.97	1.636	6
The students values teaching from the board that make them active by writing or drawing what is on the board ****	4.97	1.507	6

Note: * Statements in category Professional qualifications; ** Statements in category Developing and organizing the curriculum;
*** Statements in category Skills to plan and lead different forms of teaching and learning activities;
**** Statements in category Skills to carry out different forms of teaching and learning (communication). No statements in category General social skills.

Table 2. Statements appearing with combinations of highest agreement with statements (mean), highest agreement within faculty (st.dev.), least dispersion (based on statement's set of actual responded values within scale of 1–7, but range is reported in table)

Statement:	Mean	St.dev.	Range
The lecturer must have the capability to communicate knowledge to the students ****	6.56	0.607	2
The lecturer must be able to communicate the subject in a comprehensible way ****	6.44	0.746	2
The study must let the students take active part **	6.34	0.725	2
The study must result in students having good practical skills and tools when they leave to meet their patients **	6.31	0.668	2
A lecturer must show interest in students learning the topic ****	6.23	0.808	2
Students must be urged to develop their skills for co-operation and reflection ***	6.23	0.808	3
The education must be goal-oriented **	6.22	0.866	3
The students must be involved ***	6.21	0.845	3
The teacher must have good pedagogical skills (not necessarily formal) *	6.20	0.797	4
The lectures must be structured ****	6.19	0.822	3
The study must be on an adjusted professional level to meet the students **	6.17	0.737	2
The teacher must have the ability to simplify, explain in other ways, put things in connection ****	6.14	0.867	3
The teacher must be professionally confident and have a good overview in the field *	6.14	0.845	3
The teacher must have good pedagogical quality with easy-to-follow and systematic lecture, logical structure, breaks with summing up ****	6.11	0.718	2
Students must be called on to ask questions of their own and to use text books and Internet to answer these ***	6.09	0.742	3
Teaching and instruction must give examples relevant to the target group ****	6.03	0.785	2
The teaching must be open for dialogue ****	6.00	0.866	3
The teaching must be varied and activate the students to reading, practical learning and proficiency in addition to attitude ****	6.00	0.874	3
The teaching must be according to clear goals for learning outcomes so the students know what is expected of them **	6.00	0.840	3
The subject must be presented in a way that a large and relatively complex field can be simple, easy-to-follow and structured ****	5.97	0.834	3

Note: * Statements in category Professional qualifications; ** Statements in category Developing and organizing the curriculum;
*** Statements in category Skills to plan and lead different forms of teaching and learning activities;
**** Statements in category Skills to carry out different forms of teaching and learning (communication). No statements in category General social skills.

Impacts of Rankings on Internationalization of Higher Education Institutions in Hong Kong

Kwang Heung Lam

Abstract

Higher education institutions in Asia are proactively competing to attract international students in anticipation of global knowledge economy. International strategies are developed to build up the international profile of an institution as "world-class university" or a city as an "education hub" so as to increase its attractiveness to foreign students and external funding. These strategies include strategic partnerships with top-ranking institutions, recruitment of "star professors", changing focus from teaching to research through focused investment drives, as well as the change of immigration policies and government funding support measures.

Hong Kong aspires to become an "education hub" in Asia-Pacific region and therefore proactively works to shape "world-class universities" that are competitive internationally. International rankings are positively viewed as a measurement of achievement in this respect without much discussion of the flaws of these rankings and their implications in the whole higher education system. This study analysed the impacts of "World University Rankings" and their implications on the higher education system by reviewing internationalization policies at governmental level and international strategies at institutional level. The study applied qualitative research methods of discourse and textual analyses to analyse government policy papers, institutional strategic plans and media texts. It was found that "World University Rankings" have yet to benefit Hong Kong universities on international student recruitment due to their current focus on recruiting non-local students from mainland China. Nevertheless, "World University Rankings" are gaining influence in higher education policies and institutional strategic planning when the discourse of rankings takes root in public discussions and the city sets to promote Hong Kong's "world-class universities" for student recruitment in other parts of Asia. World university rankings have therefore become both the means and the end of internationalization strategies in Hong Kong universities, especially younger universities rising as challengers.

1. Introduction

Being the former colony of Britain, *internationality* is not a new term to Hong Kong people and Hong Kong's higher education institutions. Universities in Hong Kong are taught in English (except The Chinese University of Hong Kong, which maintains a tradition of bilingual education). Faculty members are recruited internationally. Academics have been publishing their work in international journals and collaborating with their counterparts abroad. Despite all these features of internationality, the student population of Hong Kong higher education institutions is predominantly Hong Kong Chinese since universities have been considered public goods serving local needs. International academic collaborations are sporadic based on individual faculty's networks and research interests. Until the recent two to three years, institutional "internationalization" efforts were very much limited to student exchange programs aiming to promote cross-cultural understanding and enhance students' employability.

In 2004, UGC identified higher education as the driving force for "economic and social development" of Hong Kong society in the document "Hong Kong Higher Education: To Make a Difference, To Move with the Times". Following that, all universities have developed strategic plans to position themselves for global competitions. Internationalization has now assumed a strategic role in institutional development covering a wide range of activities in addition to student exchange.

Many of the internationalization activities, such as strategic partnerships, international fellowship programs, and recruitment of star professors, aim to build up the international profile and reputation of individual universities. The flavour of image building and networking is strong since Hong Kong higher education system had been inward looking in the past decades and received little international attention. Institutions have taken for granted that brand building is an essential step for marketing Hong Kong, which is known as an "education hub" internationally. Such concepts of marketization and marketing of higher education have penetrated university management culture (Mok & Lo, 2002) armed with the discourse of "education hub" commonly shaped by UGC policies, Hong Kong Trade Development Council's involvement in promotion of Hong Kong higher education services overseas and the Hong Kong government's announcement of education (including tertiary education) as one of the six New Economic Pillars (FSO, 2009).

When branding and reputation are concerned, university rankings come into play as a convenient indicator of "international recognition". University rankings are not new to Hong Kong people because many Hong Kong students prefer to attend universities in English-speaking countries such as the US, UK and Australia. Rankings are often consulted by the students and their parents in the process of university selection. However, there is no official ranking of universities in Hong Kong. Before the introduction of Shanghai Jiao tong University's Academic Ranking of World Universities (ARWU) and the *Times Higher Education Supplement*'s World University Ranking (*THES*) in 2003 and 2004, respectively, the most widely discussed rankings were rankings of business programs offered by the three major universities in the city. There has been vertical stratification among the eight UGC-funded universities but no clear and visible ranking order as suggested by ARWU and *THES*. The two rankings have therefore ranked the universities in Hong Kong in a visible order and set the goal and benchmark for "improvement" of Hong Kong universities on annual basis (Appendix A).

In this study, I will look into internationalization strategies at both governmental and institutional levels in Hong Kong, with the role of university rankings being the means and end for these strategies. Government policy papers, institutional strategic plans and media texts are major data sources for discourse and textual analyses. A cultural perspective will also be introduced to briefly explain the impact of rankings in Chinese society where "foreign brands" are seen as equivalent to quality.

2. Literature Review

"World University Rankings" did not appear in the higher education scene until ARWU and *THES* were introduced in 2003 and 2004, respectively. Before that, U.S. News & World Report pioneered ranking of American colleges in 1983, aiming to provide consumer information (and opportunities for institutional marketing) as well as to impact the quality of education (Sanoff, Usher, Savino, Clarke, & Institute for Higher Education Policy, 2007) Subject-based rankings such as those for MBA and EMBA programs have also been in place to guide students' choices for "investment" and to be a convenient tool for institutions' program marketing.

According to Simon Marginson, the emergence of "World University Rankings" is associated closely with the global knowledge economy. Knowledge goods could, in principle, be disseminated at a zero cost in the global communicative environment nowadays. It is only when knowledge is assigned a status that it carries economic value. When higher education becomes a service for trade in the knowledge economy, university rankings come into play to produce university status and sustain an imperial global geo-politics of knowledge for economic purpose (Marginson, 2009).

While it may not be the aim of *THES* and ARWU to affect public policy and management of higher education systems around the world, their existence has intensified the "academic arms race" for building world-class universities in Europe and Asia in a Chinese '211 project' and

'985 project' manner (Mok & Wei, 2008). Following China's emerging global model (EGM) of research universities in '211 project' and '985 project', resources are concentrated on selected national universities to create "world-class universities" and boost their positions in global league tables. "Different forms of university research networks, university alliance or international research consortia have evolved to promote international collaboration aiming at higher ranking in the global university league" (Deem, Mok, & Lucas, 2008). Climbing up the World University Rankings tables becomes an impetus for reforms for institutions aspiring to be the best worldwide (Mohrman, 2008). Reforms hastened by rankings carry substantial influence on the long-term development of higher education systems, however. *THES* ranking is a reputational ranking; ARWU ranks only research output, and both of them are whole-of-institution rankings. They are affecting the heterogeneous and sustainable growth of higher education systems (Marginson, 2007).

In spite of mounted criticisms about the methodologies of ARWU and *THES*, their negative implications on public policy and sustainable growth of higher education systems around the world, universities worldwide are keen to promote the ranking of their universities in these rankings. Mok & Chan (2008) studied mainland China and Taiwan's attempts to restructure their university systems and search for new governance strategies in order to make their universities more competitive in the global world. Hazelkorn (2008) approached the phenomenon from an organizational perspective studying how rankings influence operational decision making and choices of institutional leaders and governments. Her paper shows that rankings do have impacts on key stakeholders of a university, affecting their decisions in areas such as funding, sponsorship and staff recruitment, and that governments also use rankings as a "policy instrument".

It is believed the World University Rankings are here to stay and gain increasing influence when more economies are ready to take part in the global trade of higher education services. Institutions with the most resources are the least inclined to reform existing rankings (Martin & Samels, 2007) despite the fact that some important public interests may not be reflected in such rankings (Dill & Soo, 2005).

It is against this backdrop that the case of Hong Kong higher education is analysed in this paper. Hong Kong embraces global knowledge economy, and higher education service is now identified as one of its New Economic Pillars. Reforms are hastened to "internationalize" Hong Kong's higher education, adopting the Emerging Global Model even though universities in Hong Kong are not included in China's "211" or "985" projects due to the city's autonomy in higher education policies under China's "One Country Two Systems" principle.

3. Hong Kong as an Education Hub

Hong Kong's higher education system was overtly assigned a new "economic" role in 2004 when the UGC document "Hong Kong Higher Education: To Make a Difference, To Move with the Times" was released. When introducing the new role of higher education, the Chairman of UGC said "the UGC firmly believes the higher education sector must play a key role in building Hong Kong as Asia's World City, driving forward the economic and social development of society and making Hong Kong the education hub in the region" (UGC, 2004a). Before that, higher education policies were also related to economics, but less direct, by emphasizing the need to produce quality manpower for Hong Kong's development (UGC, 1993).

To develop Hong Kong into an "education hub", the city must first prove itself an attractive destination for international students. International profile and recognition thus become essential in achieving the goal of turning Hong Kong into the "magnet" that attracts higher education seekers in Asia. However, given the short history of universities in Hong Kong, the city is disadvantaged in terms of reputation when compared with top universities in the US, UK and Australia. Handsome merit-based scholarships were therefore offered to undergraduate non-local students starting from the 1999–2000 academic year (UGC, 2002). Following that, fee-paying non-local undergraduate students were also accepted, and the number of non-local undergraduate reached 3,979 at 7% of total undergraduate students in 2007–2008. One must note that 93% of the non-local students were from mainland China (UGC, 2009a). It is not internationalization of the student body in a strict sense. World University Rankings therefore have relatively small effect since Hong Kong universities are still considered "foreign" by mainland Chinese students who believe that foreign universities promise higher quality of education than that in mainland China. Also, with the change of immigration policy in 2007 to allow non-local degree graduates to take up part-time jobs in the course of study and full-time employment after graduation (UGC, 2009b), a Hong Kong degree has become even more attractive to mainland students.

In 2007, the Hong Kong government increased the admission quota of non-local undergraduate students from 10% to 20% of approved student target numbers for UGC-funded institutions (UGC, 2009b) as a step further to establish Hong Kong as the education hub. However, without a "world recognized status", Hong Kong's universities have been viewed as a "stepping stone" to many mainland Chinese students who aspire to further their studies in overseas institutions. Talented local and non-local students tend to further their studies in overseas institutions. The "foreign" brand effect and Hong Kong advantage in attracting mainland students may also disappear with further integration of the city into China and the rise of other Chinese cities like Shanghai and Beijing in education standards and economic prosperity. Competition for world-class status and areas of excellence therefore intensified with discourses of "education hub", "excellence" and "international competitiveness" dominating higher education policies. These discourses are rarely questioned because Hong Kong has been an international city heavily reliant on capitalism and economics. The city embraces free trade and globalization, taking pride at being ranked the freest economy of the world (HKETO, 2009).

Staying "excellent" and "competitive" in the global competitions is believed to be the essential way for survival and prosperity in Hong Kong. The concept of "areas of excellence" with international competitiveness and admission of non-local students were found as early as 1993 in UGC's *Interim Report on the Review of the Development of Higher Education in Hong Kong* (UGC, 1993). It was further expanded in 1996 (UGC, 1996) and formally implemented in 2000. To compete for international status, resources are channelled into research with the establishment of the Areas of Excellence (AoE) Scheme, which aims to build "world-class institutions with distinct areas of excellence in order to retain its (Hong Kong's) leading economic position in the development of China and the Pacific Rim." (UGC, 2009c). When funding is awarded on competitive basis to research excellence at international level, the three major universities with the capacity to conduct basic research of international interests have an advantage over universities conducting applied research. Science and technology have also been the foci while humanities and social sciences (except business) are out of the scope. The following table shows the dominant institutions and academic fields awarded a total of HK$500m (€49m) under the AoE Scheme since its establishment in 2000:

Table 1. Projects and Institutions awarded Research Fund under AoE Scheme

Round	Project Title	Institution
First	Information Technology	The Hong Kong University of Science and Technology
	Center for Plant and Agricultural Biotechnology (previously known as "Plant and Fungal Biotechnology")	The Chinese University of Hong Kong
	Hong Kong Institute of Economics & Business Strategy	The University of Hong Kong
Second	Molecular Neuroscience: Basic Research & Drug Discovery	The Hong Kong University of Science and Technology

Round	Project Title	Institution
Third	Institute of Molecular Technology for Drug Discovery and Synthesis	The University of Hong Kong
	Chinese Medicine Research & Further Development	The Chinese University of Hong Kong
	Centre for Marine Environmental Research and Innovative Technology	The City University of Hong Kong
	Development Genomics & Skeletal Research	The University of Hong Kong
Fourth	Centre for Research into Circulating Fetal Nucleic Acids	The Chinese University of Hong Kong
	Control of Pandemic and Inter-Pandemic Influenza	The University of Hong Kong

Adapted from UGC Website (UGC 2009c):
http://www.ugc.edu.hk/eng/ugc/activity/aoes/aoes.htm

On one hand, UGC instigates competitions among universities by allocating funding on competitive basis like the above, and on the other hand, it assigns different roles to the UGC-funded institutions and encourages them to cooperate in order to achieve synergy (UGC, 2004b). It is hoped that Hong Kong's higher education system would be internationally attractive to scholars and students as a whole and contribute to the knowledge economy of the city. However, competition has overshadowed cooperation in Hong Kong's higher education scene given the small number of universities and academic circle in Hong Kong (Postiglione, 2007, p.67 and SCMP, 2009c). While the top three universities dominate the research funding allocation for projects of international excellence and gain "international recognition" through rankings such as ARWU and *THES*, universities upgraded from former polytechnics and colleges, such as City University of Hong Kong, are keen to "upgrade" themselves through research and knowledge transfer although they are assigned a major role in teaching according to the *Role Statements of UGC-funded Institutions* (UGC, 2007). Teaching activities are sidelined, even though the aim of building "world-class universities", to a large extent, is to attract international students and to be an "education hub".

The discourses of building "world-class universities" with "centres of excellence" to compete in the global knowledge economy are set to stay as the focus in Hong Kong higher education policies. With the "international recognition" indicated by ARWU and *THES* rankings, Hong Kong government has stepped up its plans to explore possibilities to recruit students from other parts of Asia (e.g. India) and establish university branch campus in mainland China to tap the market of the Pearl River Data (FSO, 2009). It is worth noting, however, that the first university to have set up a campus in China is Baptist University, which is a small university in Hong Kong with no "world-class" status and is not listed in the ARWU and *THES* rankings.

To conclude, it is doubtful whether a "world-class" status is a necessary first step to export Hong Kong's higher education service and whether the "centres of excellence" competitive at international level will contribute as much as applied research that could be capitalized through knowledge transfer. Higher education policies in Hong Kong have been formulated against the backdrop of the knowledge economy since 2004, assuming that higher education could contribute to Hong Kong's economy and society through export of higher education services and knowledge transfer. However, the Hong Kong government's allocation of resources seems to have encouraged dominant universities to compete for international status in academic research rather than developing teaching quality and applied research. While high-end research may ultimately yield high income and international fame of the institutions climbing up World University Rankings, over-emphasis on international competition and concentration of resources on research of international interests may create damaged feelings for universities dedicated to teaching and research of local interests. These universities may then draw their attention towards research at the expense of teaching quality, which will be discussed in detail in section 5.

4. Rankings as Indicators of International Recognition

Hong Kong's higher education system has been inward looking, serving local needs, because higher education institutions are largely funded by public money. Internationalization of student body was first started with the admission of the first cohort of sponsored non-local students from mainland China in 1999 (UGC, 2002). Although the discourse of "knowledge economy" has surfaced in government documents as early as mid-1990s, higher education as an "exportable service" caught public attention only in the recent few years and sparked off public discussions in 2009 when the Hong Kong government announced Education as one of the six New Economic Pillars to be studied for development (FSO, 2009). Being a late-coming higher education service exporter aiming at the China market, ARWU and *THES* rankings are not yet used as "marketing tools" for student recruitment as one may have expected. The two rankings, however, have boosted Hong Kong higher education institutions' ambition and confidence to compete internationally and attracted few criticisms since Hong Kong institutions took encouraging positions.

After analysing the news coverage of university rankings returned by a search using a Hong Kong news database www.wisers.com (Appendix A), it is noted that news coverage of university rankings spiked in 2007 when the University of Hong Kong hit No. 18 in the *THES* ranking (Figure 1). Before that, the media held lukewarm attitude to the two rankings. When ARWU was first released in 2003, only the pro-China newspaper Ta Kung Pao picked up the news lauding that Hong Kong had four universities ranking top ten in China (TKP, 2003). Between 2003 and 2007, news coverage about university rankings was dominated by the rankings of MBA/EMBA programs offered by the three major universities in Hong Kong. Many of the articles were sponsored articles which were more for publicity and marketing purposes.

Figure 1. News Coverage of University Rankings in Hong Kong 2003–2009

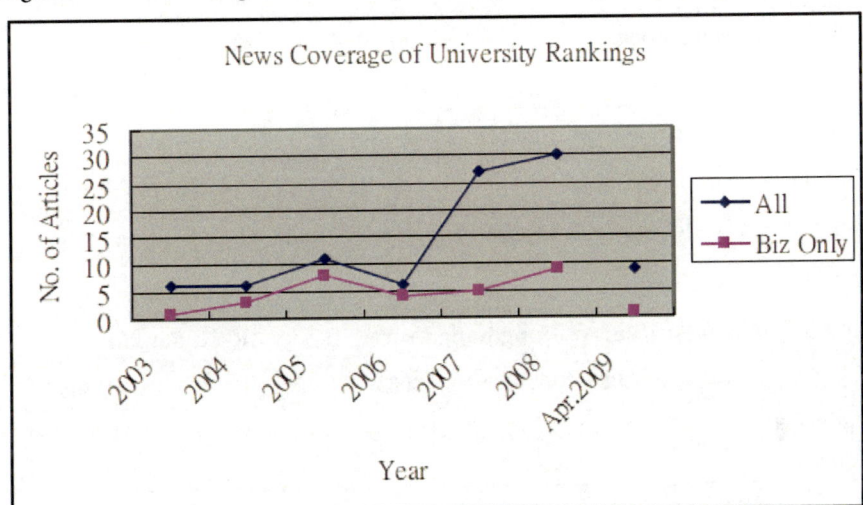

Before ARWU and *THES* rankings caught public attention in Hong Kong, there was no official ranking among the eight UGC-funded institutions. The University of Hong Kong and the Chinese University of Hong Kong had been competing for the top position comparing the entry qualification of annual student intake and the employability of their graduates. Hong Kong University of Science and Technology was commonly viewed as No. 3 given its short history and specialization in Science and Technology. City University of Hong Kong, Hong Kong Polytechnic University, which were upgraded from polytechnics, and Baptist University and Lingnan University, which were upgraded from colleges, were commonly known as second or third tier universities. There was some degree of vertical stratification but not as clear and visible as that being nailed down on paper by ARWU and *THES*.

While ARWU seems to be objective counting world recognized publications and *THES* seems authoritative given its association with a reputable British newspaper specialized in education, the ranking order of universities in Hong Kong (Tables 2 & 3) and the exclusion of smaller universities not engaged in Science and Technology research have given a misleading impression of the universities' quality in the city. The University of Hong Kong seems to have won over The Chinese University of Hong Kong given its leading position in the *THES* ranking over the years. The City University of Hong Kong may see itself better than the Hong Kong Polytechnic University given its inclusion in *THES* and a higher position in ARWU. It is hoping to upgrade itself to the top 100 league and has reportedly announced it as its goal (CDHK, 2008 and SCMP, 2009b).

Table 2. Ranking Positions of Hong Kong Universities by *THES* Ranking

	2004	2005	2006	2007	2008
University of Hong Kong	39	41	33	*18*	26
The Chinese University of Hong Kong	*84*	*51*	50	38	*42*
Hong Kong University of Science and Tech.	*42*	*43*	58	53	*39*
City University of Hong Kong	198	178	154	149	147

Source: *THES* World Top 200 Universities http://www.timeshighereducation.co.uk

Table 3. Ranking Positions of Hong Kong Universities by ARWU Ranking

	2003	2004	2005	2006	2007	2008
University of Hong Kong	251-300	202-301	203-300	*151-200*	203-304	201-302
The Chinese University of Hong Kong	301-350	202-301	203-300	201-300	203-304	201-302
Hong Kong University of Science and Technology	251-300	202-301	203-300	201-300	203-304	201-302
City University of Hong Kong	301-350	302-403	301-400	301-400	*203-304*	303-401
Hong Kong Polytechnic University	401-450	302-403	301-400	301-400	403-510	303-401

Source: SJTU Academic Ranking of World Universities http://www.arwu.org/

Despite the common belief of being the top university in Hong Kong constantly competing with the University of Hong Kong, The Chinese University of Hong Kong appears to be a "loser" with the top position being confirmed to have gone to Hong Kong University and the second position being challenged by the Hong Kong University of Science and Technology, according to the THES ranking. Little attention was given to the fact that The Chinese University of Hong Kong has a bilingual tradition, respecting both English and Chinese as the languages for teaching and research. The University has been "disadvantaged" in this sense, thus calling into question the medium of instruction for the university (CUHK, 2006a). It was with the adamant resistance of the alumni and students that bilingualism continues to be respected by the university, which was established with a mission to allow students with Chinese language background access to quality higher education in Hong Kong.

As one may expect, the University of Hong Kong was the focus of news coverage when it hit No. 18 in *THES* in 2007 (SCMP, 2007a-c). The university was reported to have outperformed "Stanford University" (CDHK, 2007) and gained its position through "hard work and dedication" (SCMP, 2007a). The news coverage portrayed it as an achievement of Hong Kong to have a university ranked among top 20 universities in the world and four universities staying on the chart over the years. It was reported as "international recognition" and "rising standards" of Hong Kong higher education system (SCMP, 2009a&d). The City University of Hong Kong, which has been one of the many second tier universities, edges its way to one of the four *THES*-ranked universities. It has boosted its confidence and ambition to strive for the world's top 100. Both the University of Hong Kong and the City University of Hong Kong therefore enjoyed the publicity and reacted to the rankings positively while other universities remained more or less silent because they were not ranked or ranked unfavorably.

While the Hong Kong media presented the rankings in a positive light as "international recognition" and improvement of Hong Kong higher education system, Hong Kong University was asked to explain its drop in the ranking in 2008 to 26th. The University blamed it on the lack of research funding and took the chance to press for more (SCMP, 2008a). In late 2008 and 2009, the media began to bring in alternative views of world university rankings including one for European universities (SCMP, 2009e) and one for developing countries in South East Asia (SCMP, 2008b&c). Nevertheless, before the new rating systems in Europe and South East Asia are launched, it is likely that Hong Kong media will continue to refer to *THES* and ARWU as world standards of higher education. Universities unfavourably ranked or not ranked by the two rankings will continue to find their ways to climb up the ladders. This will be discussed in the following section.

5. Internationalization as a Strategy of Institutional Brand Building

With an analysis of the strategic plans of UGC-funded institutions (Appendix B), we can find common strategic research areas identified by the four universities ranked by *THES* (Table 4). The four universities all aspire to be "world-class", "internationally recognized", while the others aspire to be a "premier" or "preferred" institution or a "liberal arts" college.

Internationalization strategies stated by smaller universities such as Lingnan University and Baptist University mainly concern student learning experiences such as exchange programs, overseas internships, international curriculum or recruitment of non-local students to create an international mix of student body.

Hong Kong Polytechnic University, which has the largest student population in Hong Kong taking into account also part-time students, is not ranked by *THES* but ARWU following City University of Hong Kong. Its strategic plan has the most overt expressions in pursuit of international recognition through "strategic partnerships with top-ranking institutions" and the establishment of an International Advisory Committee (IAC). Under the section "Branding, Marketing and Internationalisation", it states the following:

To further enhance the brand image and recognition of PolyU and to market our core activities to local, national and international target audiences....we shall develop and implement a focused international campaign....We shall establish an International Advisory Committee to provide guidance and direction to the University...To develop and implement a plan to enhance networking with top ranking universities in the world through collaboration in education, research and student exchange, and by organizing major international conferences. (PolyU, 2008)

The message of ranking-driven partnerships for the purpose of brand-building is clearly exposed. Even though other universities in Hong Kong do not express on paper their strategies to partner with top-ranking institutions, we can see similar network-building activities expressed in other forms. City University invited Robert Armstrong, Director of the Massachusetts Institute of Technology Energy Initiative, to advise on establishment of a cross-departmental energy and environment school (SCMP, 2008d). Hong Kong University of Science and Technology set up an Institute for Advanced Study modelled on the internationally renowned Institute for Advanced Study at Princeton. The Institute "will target the recruitment of a small number of genuine "stars" – people whose names are instantly recognized by the international academic community and whose presence at HKUST would bring immediate visibility"(HKUST, 2007).

From the above examples, we can see that recruitment of "star professors" and networking with top-ranking institutions are common strategies for building up an international profile. These are particularly important for new universities because they are not mature enough to have nurtured home-grown academics with international status due to their short history.

The University of Hong Kong outlined a more comprehensive strategy for "raising global presence and visibility" including international recruitments of students and staff, introducing international curricula and benchmarking against high-quality international institutions. On top of that, it plans to "review the University's existing international network and alliances in order to develop those that will strengthen the global presence and visibility of the University" and to "Take a more active role in strategic international alliances e.g., Universitas 21; develop meaningful bilateral alliances; make use of the strengths and achievements of our partner universities" (HKU, 2003). The idea that partnerships have to be "strategic", "meaningful" and adding "strength" to enhance the global visibility of the university implies that the partners should be of equal standing or higher than the university itself. Rankings are not mentioned up front, but one may assume that they play a role as referential instruments if the concern is reputation and positive visibility through partnerships.

Hong Kong's higher education managers are heavily influenced by American and British lines of thought. They are well aware of the idea that "You are increasingly known by the company you keep" as University of Exeter Vice-chancellor Steve Smith said it (SCMP, 2009d). The "elitist" ideology and discourse inherited from the British tradition are still deep-rooted in higher education management culture despite Hong Kong now having a massified higher education sector.

The Chinese University of Hong Kong has a grass-root origin, granting access to students with Chinese language background to university education during the colonial era. In the past four decades, it has developed into a challenger of the University of Hong Kong's top position but maintains its tradition of bilingual and bicultural education. The University is aware of its unique heritage of Chinese and Western learnings and possible advantage in serving rising China with its strong connections with Chinese culture, language and network. However, the University has been ranked much lower than the University of Hong Kong by *THES*, giving an impression that it is not as internationally "reputable" as the University of Hong Kong.

Similar to the other *THES*-ranked universities, The Chinese University describes itself as follows:

Uniquely characterized by a bilingual and bicultural intellectual environment and endowed with a profound humanitarian concern for Chinese culture, CUHK is committed to the advancement of society not only through economic progress powered by science, technology and commerce but also through spiritual enrichment inspired by the humanities, creative arts and social sciences. (CUHK, 2006b)

Nevertheless, in the strategic plan, it announces that to achieve the level of excellence as one of Asia or the world's best university "requires selection and focus". Five Focused Areas of Research were identified. They are: *Chinese Studies, Biomedical Sciences, Information Sciences, Economics and Finance,* and *Geoinformation and Earth Sciences.* Under Chinese Studies, it supports all projects related to China open to Humanities, Social Sciences but is not exclusive to these two disciplines meaning science and medical issues in China could also be considered. To justify its additional support to science and technology instead of the humanities and social sciences, the University stressed that "quality in other areas will be sustained and improved as well, and in fact world-class excellence in one area will help to set benchmarks that elevate standards in other areas of scholarship as well". Moreover, the University has established a Committee to "examine, reflect, refine and rearticulate the University's language policy", questioning the bilingual tradition, which has implications for the university's internationalization plan and quest for world-class status since English is the dominant language for these two purposes. Rankings are not explicitly mentioned as the reasons for these departures from the University's mission, but one may assume that the changes in research focus and medium of instruction will have a positive impact on the university's ranking.

THES and ARWU's tilted interests in English-published journals and subjects in science and technology coincides with Hong Kong government's focused investments in Areas of Excellence Scheme, which in turn become the institutions' foci. The four *THES*-ranked institutions are found to have shared common research foci dominated by Science and Technology as shown in Table 4 below. Areas of research which may be of social and cultural importance to Hong Kong are nearly invisible even though China studies are included as one of the research foci of the two major universities.

Table 4. Focused Areas of Research in Hong Kong's *THES*-ranked institutions:

	Focused Areas of Research
University of Hong Kong	Biomedicine China Community (Public Health; Law, Policy and Development; Science of Learning) Environment Frontier Technology (Genomics, Drug, Nano-biotechnology, Computational Sciences, Information Technology)
The Chinese University of Hong Kong	Biomedical Sciences Chinese Studies Economics and Finance Geoinformation and Earth Sciences Information Sciences
Hong Kong University of Science and Tech.	Biological Science and Biotechnology Electronics, Wireless & Information Technology Environmental & Sustainable Development Management Education & Research Nano-Science & Technology
City University of Hong Kong	"CityU can challenge the best", including: Applied mathematics

Chinese	linguistics and language information sciences
	Environmental sciences
	Nanostructured materials
	Optoelectronics
	Wireless communications

In short, except Hong Kong Polytechnic University, which clearly stated "ranking" as a reference for its internationalization and branding strategy, the word *ranking* is not explicitly mentioned in the strategic plans of other institutions. However, its variations "leading institutions", "strategic partner", "university of international reputation" do shed some light on the universities' plans to partner high and be ranked top. In order to do that, selective and strategic partnerships together with concentration of research in science and technology are common practices.

6. Conclusion

Post-colonial Hong Kong has retained its British traditions in upholding elitism and the use of English as the predominant medium of instruction in its higher education system. Before ARWU and *THES* were released, vertical stratification of universities was an accepted norm even though there was no official ranking of the city's eight UGC-funded institutions. The notion of research excellence and admission of non-local students were also mentioned as early as 1993 (UGC, 1993) although they were only implemented some six or seven years later. With such a background, the release of ARWU and *THES* did not seem to have disrupted Hong Kong higher education system as much as that in Europe or South East Asia. They did not benefit Hong Kong universities much as marketing tool either because the demand of mainland Chinese students eager to study in Hong Kong has far exceeded available quota for non-local students, which is capped by the Hong Kong government. Nevertheless, both ARWU and *THES* rankings were well received by government officials and media as recognition of Hong Kong's higher education quality and rising standards. Pride was associated with Hong Kong University and City University of Hong Kong, which were ranked higher than expected. Other universities in Hong Kong responded to the rankings with mixed feelings. On one hand, *THES* ranking of four universities in Hong Kong among the world's top 50 universities has anchored Hong Kong's universities favourably as a whole on global level, and ARWU ranking on national level. On the other hand, these rankings have nailed down a clear and measurable order among universities in Hong Kong. They have therefore intensified competitions among universities in Hong Kong despite Hong Kong government assigning a specific role to each university and encouraging cross-institution collaboration for synergy. Universities anxious to make a significant climb in the ranking may steer their focus from teaching activities to research of international interests or derived strategic plans departing from their tradition or existing strengths if they are in humanities or social sciences. Such a trend in shrinking disciplinary diversity and research of local interests may carry long-term implications on the academic as well as socio-cultural development of Hong Kong.

Moreover, university rankings appear to be a means to build up international profile and status. Younger universities openly seek strategic partnerships with "top-ranking institutions" to enhance their strength and international visibility. Older universities with established international networks have planned to "review" their partners so as to strengthen their international standing. Such a trend of selective partnership has been aided by World University Rankings, which are convenient referential tools with their global comparisons on a single list. Such use of rankings may limit upward mobility of lower ranked universities as well as the sustainable development of Hong Kong's higher education system. When the "foreign brand" effect of Hong Kong universities loses its appeal to mainland Chinese students and universities, Hong Kong may find itself isolated by universities in South East Asia's developing countries, which may have built up partnerships with mainland China directly.

All in all, World University Rankings are both the means and end of internationalization strategies adopted by universities in Hong Kong. Their impacts on government policies and institutional strategic planning are detected although no causal relationship could be proved in this study. The impacts on younger universities are believed to be stronger as seen in their explicit attempts to rise through partnerships with top-ranking universities. Older universities are more subtle in the use of rankings, but traces of ranking-driven plans are evident in research foci and partnership review.

References

ARWU Academic Ranking of World Universities. (2009). *The Story of Academic Rankings*. Retrieved April 26, 2009 from http://www.bc.edu/bc_org/avp/soe/cihe/newsletter/Number54/p2_Liu.htm

Baptist University. (2006). *Strategic Plan 2006*. Retrieved April 26, 2009 from http://www.hkbu.edu.hk/strategicplan/2005-10/focus_1.htm

CDHK. *China Daily Hong Kong Edition*. (2007). HKU Outperforms Stanford. Teddy Ng. November 9, 2007.

CDHK *China Daily Hong Kong Edition*. (2008). CityU Aims To Be World's Top 100 Universities. Teddy Ng. May 27, 2008.

City University of Hong Kong. (2003). *Strategic Plan 2003-08 – Meeting the Challenge of Change*. Retrieved April 26, 2009 from http://www.cityu.edu.hk/op/plan/plan_2003-2008.htm

CUHK The Chinese University of Hong Kong. (2006a). *CUHK Upholds Bilingual Education*. Retrieved April 26, 2009 from http://www.cuhk.edu.hk/ipro/pressrelease/060907e2.htm

CUHK The Chinese University of Hong Kong. (2006b). *Strategic Plan*. Retrieved April 26, 2009 from http://www.cuhk.edu.hk/v6/en/cuhk/strategicplan/images/strat_plan_eng2.pdf

Deem, R. R., Mok, K.H., & Lucas, L. L. (2008). Transforming higher education in whose image? Exploring the concept of the 'world-class' university in Europe and Asia. *Higher Education Policy, 21*(1), 83-97.

Dill, D., & Soo, M. (2005). Academic quality, league tables, and public policy: Across-national analysis of university ranking systems. *Higher Education, 49*(4), 495-533.

Financial Secretary Office (FSO) of HKSAR. (2009). *Developing New Economic Pillars*. Retrieved April 26, 2009 from http://www.fso.gov.hk/tfec/eng/doc/New%20Economic%20Pillars%20_TFEC-D03_%20Eng.pdf

Hazelkorn, E. (2008). Learning to live with league tables and ranking: The experience of institutional leaders. *Higher Education Policy, 21*(2), 193-215.

Hong Kong Economic and Trade Office. (2009). *Reports*. Retrieved April 26, 2009 from http://www.hketowashington.gov.hk/dc/reports.htm

HKU University of Hong Kong. (2003). *Strategic Plan 2003-2008*. Retrieved April 26, 2009 from http://www.hku.hk/strategic-booklet/

HKUST Hong Kong University of Science and Technology. (2007). *Strategic Plan 2005-2020*. Retrieved April 26, 2009 from http://www.ust.hk/strategy/brochure.pdf

Lingnan University (2009). *Strategic Plan for 2009-1016*. Retrieved April 26, 2009 from http://www.ln.edu.hk/reg/info/plan.pdf

Marginson S. (2007) Global university rankings: implications in general and for Australia. *Journal of Higher Education Policy and Management, 29*(2), 131–142

Marginson, S. (2009). Open source knowledge and university rankings. *Thesis Eleven, 96*(1), 9-39.

Martin, J., & Samels, J. E. (2007). New rules for playing the rankings game. *University Business, 10*(4), 37-38.

Mohrman K. (2008). The emerging global model with Chinese characteristics *Higher Education Policy, 21*, 29-48.

Mok, K. H., & Chan, Y. Y. (2008). International benchmarking with the best universities: policy and practice in mainland China and Taiwan. *Higher Education Policy, 21*(4), 469-486.

Mok, K. H., & Lo, H. C. (2002). Marketization and the changing governance in higher education: A comparative study. *Higher Education Management and Policy, 14*(1), 51-82.

Mok, K. H., & Wei, P. (2008). Contested concepts, similar practices: The quest for global university, *Higher Education Policy, 21*, 429-438

POLYU Hong Kong Polytechnic University. (2008). *Strategic Plan 2008/09 –2011/12 – Achieving Excellence in an Era of Challenge*. Retrieved April 26, 2009 from http://www.polyu.edu.hk/cpa/polyu/the_university/strategic_e.php

Postiglione, G. A. (2007). Hong Kong: expansion, reunion with China and the transformation of academic culture. *The Changing Conditions for Academic Work and Careers in Selected Countries*, Werkstattberichte 66, 67

Sanoff, A. P., Usher, A., Savino, M., Clarke, M., & Institute for Higher, E. P. (2007). *College and university ranking systems: global perspectives and American challenges*. Institute for Higher Education Policy.

SCMP *South China Morning Post, Young Post* (2007a). HKU's High Ranking Due To Hard Work And Dedication. Germaine Sng. November 19, 2007.

SCMP *South China Morning Post*. (2007b). Global HKU Is On Top Of The World. Mimi Lau. November 10, 2007.

SCMP *South China Morning Post*. (2007c). HKU In World's Top 20, Chinese University 50th. Liz Heron. November 09, 2007.

SCMP *South China Morning Post*. (2008a). HKU Blames Lack Of Cash For Rankings Slip. University Calls For More Funding After Falling Eight Places On Elite List. Mimi Lau & Yojana Sharma. October 9, 2008.

SCMP *South China Morning Post*. (2008b). A New Order. December 6, 2008.

SCMP *South China Morning Post.* (2008c). New Rating System Proposed For Universities In Southeast Asia. Liz Gooch. December 6, 2008.

SCMP *South China Morning Post.* (2008d). The American Way. September 6, 2008. SCMP *South China Morning Post.* (2009a). Grooming Talent. Editorial. April 20, 2009.

SCMP *South China Morning Post.* (2009b). Major Push To Attain Global Prominence. Susie Gyopos. March 21, 2009.

SCMP *South China Morning Post.* (2009c). Higher Thinking. Editorial. February 16, 2009.

SCMP *South China Morning Post.* (2009d). Rising Standards Lure Overseas Interest. February 7, 2009.

SCMP *South China Morning Post.* (2009e). Europe Piloting Wide-Ranging Ranking System. Liz Heron. March 21, 2009.

STD *Sing Tao Daily.* (2009). Universities Leap In World Rankings. Fang Bin. November 16, 2007.

THES *Times Higher Education Supplement.* (2008). *World University Rankings.* Retrieved April 26, 2009 from http://www.timeshighereducation.co.uk/hybrid.asp?typeCode=243&pubCode=1

TKP *Ta Kung Pao.* (2003). 科大城大 港大中大 踞中國大學榜前十名 台大清華 科大列三甲科研社科成就獲世界認同. July 31, 2003.

University Grants Committee (UGC) of HKSAR. (1993). *Higher Education 1991-2001" – An Interim Report.* Retrieved April 26, 2009 from http://www.ugc.edu.hk/eng/ugc/publication/report/interim/interim.htm

University Grants Committee (UGC) of HKSAR. (1996). *Higher Education in Hong Kong – A Report by the University Grants Committee.* Retrieved April 26, 2009 from http://www.ugc.edu.hk/eng/ugc/publication/report/hervw/ugcreport.htm

University Grants Committee (UGC) of HKSAR. (2002). *Report on the 1998-2001 Triennium.* Retrieved April 26, 2009 from http://www.ugc.edu.hk/english/documents/triennium98 01/ENGLISH.HTM

University Grants Committee (UGC) of HKSAR. (2004a). *Hong Kong Higher Education – To Make a Difference, To Move with the Times.* Retrieved April 26, 2009 from http://www.ugc.edu.hk/eng/ugc/publication/press/2004/pr300104e.htm

University Grants Committee (UGC) of HKSAR. (2004b). *Hong Kong Higher Education-Integration Matters.* Retrieved from April 26, 2009 http://www.ugc.edu.hk/eng/doc/ugc/publication/report/report_integration_matters_e.pdf

University Grants Committee (UGC) of HKSAR. (2007). *Role Statements of UGC-Funded Institutions.* Retrieved April 26, 2009 from http://www.ugc.edu.hk/eng/ugc/publication/report/figure2007/annex/09.pdf

University Grants Committee (UGC) of HKSAR. (2009a). *Where do the non-local students come from? Is the student composition diverse enough?* Retrieved April 26, 2009 from http://www.ugc.edu.hk/eng/ugc/faq/q603.htm

University Grants Committee (UGC) of HKSAR. (2009b). *What are the UGC's plans or strategies for facilitating Hong Kong to be an education hub for the region and beyond?* Retrieved April 30, 2009 from http://www.ugc.edu.hk/eng/ugc/faq/q601.htm

University Grants Committee (UGC) of HKSAR. (2009c). *UGC Areas of Excellence Scheme.* Retrieved April 26, 2009 from http://www.ugc.edu.hk/eng/ugc/activity/aoes/aoes.htm

Appendix A

Hong Kong News Coverage of University Rankings during Jan 2003–April 2009

1. Grooming talent [South China Morning Post] 2009-04-20 EDT12 EDT
2. Sponsorships taint universities [China Daily Hong Kong Edition] 2009-03-30 P05 Comment
3. More funds urged for research, development [South China Morning Post] 2009-03-24 EDT2 EDT Liz Heron
4. Major push to attain global prominence [South China Morning Post] 2009-03-21 S16 Classified Post Public Sector Career Susie Gyopos
5. Europe piloting wide-ranging ranking system [South China Morning Post] 2009-03-21 EDU2 EDU Liz Heron
6. Higher thinking [South China Morning Post] 2009-02-16 EDT11 EDT
7. HKU could teach Yale a thing or two [The Standard] 2009-02-12 P21 City Talk FAME AND FORTUNE Siu Sai-wo
8. Rising standards lure overseas interest [South China Morning Post] 2009-02-07 EDU4 EDU
9. (M) Cultural mix gives course the edge [South China Morning Post] 2009-01-19 BIZ8 Sponsored Supplement

1. A new order [South China Morning Post] 2008-12-06 EDU5 EDU
2. New rating system proposed for universities in Southeast Asia [South China Morning Post] 2008-12-06 EDU2 EDU Liz Gooch
3. Australia, Britain and Denmark top tables [South China Morning Post] 2008-11-22 EDU2 EDU Yojana Sharma
4. (M) University's MBA course knocked off top spot [South China Morning Post] 2008-10-28 CITY3 CITY Will Clem
5. HK 16th best for higher education [South China Morning Post] 2008-10-25 EDU3 EDU Liz Heron
6. (M) MBAs bag No1 ranking [South China Morning Post] 2008-10-25 EDU3 EDU Liz Heron
7. Foreign professors need right ambience [China Daily Hong Kong Edition] 2008-10-17 P09 Opinion
8. (M) HKUST MBA is Asia's finest [The Standard] 2008-10-14 P23 Education Joyce Kam

9. HKU blames lack of cash for rankings slip. University calls for more funding after falling eight places on elite list [South China Morning Post] 2008-10-09 CITY1 CITY Mimi Lau in Hong Kong and Yojana Sharma in London
10. French call for broader university rankings [South China Morning Post] 2008-10-04
EDU2 EDU Yojana Sharma
11. Asia competes with the best [South China Morning Post] 2008-09-27 EDU6 Special Report: Premium Universities
12. (M) HKUST's business programme climbs world rankings [South China Morning Post] 2008-09-27 CITY4 CITY Elaine Yau
13. (M) Best of the best [China Daily Hong Kong Edition] 2008-09-08 B07 Companies/Industry
14. The American Way [South China Morning Post] 2008-09-06 EDU5 EDU
15. (M) Students must think out of the box [South China Morning Post] 2008-08-16
I03 Investing in an MBA
16. Better by degrees [South China Morning Post] 2008-07-10 CITY16 LIFE
17. In search of excellence [South China Morning Post] 2008-06-23 EDT11 EDT Regina Ip
18. Stop random college ranking [China Daily Hong Kong Edition] 2008-06-14 P04 Comment
19. CityU aims to be world's top 100 universities [China Daily Hong Kong Edition] 2008-05-27 HK1 HK & Delta Teddy Ng
20. CityU alumni face US-style donation drive [South China Morning Post] 2008-05-27 CITY4 CITY Lai Ying-kit
21. Students pressured to praise universities [South China Morning Post] 2008-05-17 EDU2 EDU Yojana Sharma
22. Passion vs perseverance [China Daily Hong Kong Edition] 2008-05-03 P08 Beijing Weekend Guide Chen nan
23. University rankings' reliability in doubt [South China Morning Post] 2008-04-12 EDU1
EDU Liz Gooch and Will Clem
24. 'Universities in Asia make big progress' [China Daily Hong Kong Edition] 2008-04-05 P03 Hong Kong/Delta Teddy Ng
25. Appointments to Hong Kong University of Science and Technology Council [IS Department, Hong Kong SAR Government (English)] 2008-03-31 Press Release
26. (M) Alumni help Hong Kong MBA program hit high spots [The Standard] 2008-01-29 P12 Local Timothy Chui
27. (M) Top ranking programme in a class of its own [South China Morning Post] 2008-01-28 BIZ8 Kellogg-HKUST EMBA program
28. (M) Cross-cultural benefits [South China Morning Post] 2008-01-28 BIZ8 Kellogg-HKUST EMBA program

29. High-ranking faculty draws top students [South China Morning Post] 2008-01-12
    S19. Postgraduate Degrees Research
30. Chinese students flock to Harvard [China Daily Hong Kong Edition] 2008-01-04
    P11. International Li Xiaokun

1. Students subsidizing British universities [China Daily Hong Kong Edition] 2007-12-13
    P11 Opinion Victoria Adam
2. (M) Profile rising as reputation for quality gains global reach [South China Morning Post] 2007-12-01 CITY11 Polyu Graduate School of Business Graduation
3. University rankings a source of pride, but not complacency [South China Morning Post]
    2007-11-24 EDU4 EDU You Say Cheng Kai-ming You Say
4. Oxford University seeks stronger ties with China, India [China Daily Hong Kong Edition] 2007-11-24 P03 Hong Kong/Delta
5. HKU's high ranking due to hard work and dedication [SCMP-Young Post] 2007-11-19
    Y4 Young Post Germaine Sng
6. UNIVERSITIES LEAP IN WORLD RANKINGS 世界排行榜公布本港四大學躍進 [Sing Tao Daily] 2007-11-16 F09 英文版 新聞英語 范斌
7. HKU wants more cash to help lure staff [South China Morning Post] 2007-11-12 EDT2
    EDT Scarlett Chiang
8. University rankings no cause for complacency [South China Morning Post] 2007-11-12
    EDT12 EDT editorial
9. Tongue-tied schools set for shake-up [The Standard] 2007-11-12 P01,P03 Front Page headline Winnie Chong
10. Global HKU is on top of the world [South China Morning Post] 2007-11-10 EDU1
    EDU Mimi Lau
11. HKU in world's top 20, Chinese University 50th [South China Morning Post] 2007-11-09 EDT3 EDT Liz Heron
12. HKU outperforms Stanford [China Daily Hong Kong Edition] 2007-11-09 P06 Hong kong/Delta Teddy Ng
13. HK & Delta [South China Morning Post] 2007-11-09 EDT1 EDT
14. (M) Varsity tops world MBA chart [The Standard] 2007-10-23 P14 Local Katherine Friedman
15. (M) EMBA course on top of the world [South China Morning Post] 2007-10-23 CITY1 CITY Mimi Lau

16. 'University collaboration a global trend' [China Daily Hong Kong Edition] 2007-10-16
    P04 Hong Kong/Delta Teddy Ng
17. (M) HKUST biz school ranks No 1 in Asia [The Standard] 2007-10-03 P23 Education
18. (M) HKUST is top MBA school in Asia for second year [South China Morning Post] 2007-09-29 CITY4 CITY Dennis Chong
19. 上海交大世界大學排名衝擊「法國例外」[Hong Kong Economic Journal] 2007-08-21. P15
    時事評論 劉志俠
20. 世界級一流大學？ [Hong Kong Economic Journal] 2007-07-20. P12
    時事評論 教育 評論 程介明
21. Universities bill foreigners 'as much as they can' [South China Morning Post] 2007-06-30 EDU2 EDU Yojana Sharma
22. Forget ranking universities [China Daily Hong Kong Edition] 2007-04-12 P09 Comment
23. City U needs excellence [South China Morning Post] 2007-04-10 EDT14 EDT Letters
24. 博雅教育烏托邦M [Hong Kong Economic Journal] 2007-04-04 P41
    副刊 面對面 鄭天儀
25. Japan needs to improve English education system [China Daily Hong Kong Edition]
    2007-03-30 P15 Opinion Shinichiro Noriguchi
26. Global university with Asian heritage [China Daily Hong Kong Edition] 2007-03-12
    SP1 Special Supplement, Singapore
27. 唸書一動不如一靜[Oriental Daily News] 2007-02-06 E06 副刊

1. (M) Global rankings put reputations on the line [South China Morning Post] 2006-12-09 S04 MBA Careers
2. (M) Local programme grows its international credibility [South China Morning Post] 2006-12-01 CITY9 Sponsored Supplement
3. (M) HKUST falls to third in FT's EMBA rankings [South China Morning Post] 2006-10-28 EDU3 EDU Liz Gooch
4. Focus should be on quality, not quantity, of patents, expert says [South China Morning Post] 2006-10-17 EDT5 EDT KEVIN HUANG
5. (M) HKUST tops HKU as best for business [South China Morning Post] 2006-10-13 CITY4 CITY LIZ GOOCH
6. Liberal dose of arts rounds out new graduates [South China Morning Post] 2006-05-06
   EDU6 EDU Katherine Forestier

1. (M) Rankings don't equal research. Lists of top universities are more arbitrary than accurate, critics tell Linda Yeung [South China Morning Post] 2005-12-10 EDU10 SPONSORED FEATURE
2. (M) Top business schools part of MBA tour [China Daily Hong Kong Edition] 2005-11-15 P05 nation Xu Jitao
3. (M) Recognition for faculty as course makes it to top 50 [South China Morning Post] 2005-11-02 EDT17 SPONSORED FEATURE
4. (M) Course rated global second [South China Morning Post] 2005-11-01 Y3 Young Post
5. (M) MBA course rated world's second best [South China Morning Post] 2005-10-25 EDT4 EDT LINDA YEUNG
6. Shanghai university sets global standard on research [South China Morning Post] 2005-10-22 EDU2 EDU Geoffrey Maslen
7. Mainland's first foreign-managed university opens [South China Morning Post] 2005-09-17 EDU3 EDU3 Liz Heron
8. HKU wears crown as top university [China Daily Hong Kong Edition] 2005-07-23 P02
HONG KONG/delta Jennifer Ho
9. (M) HKUST's business school earns top recognition in international survey [South China Morning Post] 2005-05-20 Y3 Young Post LILIAN GOH
10. (M) 3 大商學院 入全球一百 [Hong Kong Economic Times] 2005-02-24 A29 教育
11. (M) Reputation ranks highly with graduate [South China Morning Post] 2005-01-15 S06 Postgraduate Degrees

1. (M) MBA the ticket to rapid promotion [South China Morning Post] 2004-10-21 CITY10 CITY
2. 大學排名指標有玄機 [Wen Wei Po] 2004-10-11 C06 副刊視野
3. HKU marks out its global standing strategy [South China Morning Post] 2004-09-18
EDU3 EDU Linda Yeung
4. (M) University boycotts MBA survey [South China Morning Post] 2004-09-04 EDU1 EDU Linda Yeung
5. Five find place in top global university rankings [South China Morning Post] 2004-08-28 EDU3 EDU Geoffrey Maslen
6. (M) Universities aim for top business school [The Standard] 2004-05-26 B05 Matthew Lee

1. Making great universities [South China Morning Post] 2003-11-27 12 EDT
2. 澳洲大學龍虎榜 聲譽排名 [Ming Pao Daily News] 2003-11-14 D10 學府無涯 熱門 學府
3. (M) Three regional executive MBA programmes in world's top 50, survey finds [South China Morning Post] 2003-10-21 EDT2 EDT LINDA YEUNG

4. 科大城大 港大中大 躋中國大學榜前十名 台大清華科大列三甲科研社科成就獲世界認同 [Ta Kung Pao]
   2003-07-31 B04 大公教育
5. Educators cautious over pupils' world ranking [South China Morning Post]
   2003-07-03
   EDT3 EDT POLLY HUI
6. Don't blame us for City University's lowered ranking [South China Morning Post]
   2003-06-25 12 EDT

Note: (M) Ranking news concerning MBA, EMBA programs

Appendix B

The Chinese University of HK	University of Hong Kong	HK University of Sc. and Tech	
1. Advancement of Scholarship 2. Quality of Education 3. Four-Year Curriculum 4. Student Experience 5. Development of Resources 6. Campus Development 7. Administrative Measures	1. Enhancing academic excellence 2. Raising global presence and visibility 3. Developing and supporting "The University Family" 4. Partnering with society and serving the community	1. Five High-Impact Areas 2. Institute for Advanced Study 3. Undergraduate Education 4. School of Inter-Disciplinary Studies 5. Campus Development	
Lingnan University	**Baptist University**	**Hong Kong Polytechnic University**	**City University of Hong Kong**
1. Research 2. Academic Development 3. Student Development 4. Institutional Advancement 5. Campus Development	1. Research and Scholarship 2. Academic Programs 3. Teaching and Learning 4. Institutional Advancement 5. Community and Professional Service 6. Internationalization 7. Resource Management	1. Academic Strength and Research Development 2. Positioning and Core Business 3. Education 4. Student Development 5. Knowledge Transfer, Entrepreneurship, Partnership and Service to Community 6. Branding, Marketing and Internationalization 7. Management 8. Campus Development	1. Building on Research Excellence 2. Priorities for Education 3. An Infrastructure for Research and Education 4. A Partnership with the Community

Quality development through the graduates' perceptions and experiences

Ana Paula Cabral

Abstract

In the current *marketization* of Higher Education systems and the growing competition, institutions increasingly acknowledge the importance of assessing the graduates' satisfaction in achieving their career goals, work-relevant competencies and employer satisfaction as the starting point for the assessment of the institutional quality indicators settled in the teaching and learning process.

This paper presents a study about the graduates' perceptions and opinions of a Portuguese institution (ISPGaya – Gaya Superior Polytechnic Institute – Superior School of Social and Communitarian Development) aiming to determine the relationship between current work performance and the quality of their learning experiences in higher education. In a more specific way, we intend to characterize the academic/professional profile of the graduates; identify the main reasons for the enrolment in higher education, in the course and institution; assess the quality of the graduation course/institution according to the graduates' experience; identify the skills and abilities acquired; characterize the current professional situation; analyse the strategies and difficulties of job search; determine the association between the graduation and the employment field and identify needs of instruction.

The data were collected using a questionnaire composed of four sections: characterization; course/institution satisfaction; professional insertion and instruction needs. The outcomes allow us to emphasize some quality indicators such as quick professional (re)insertion, mainly in the area of instruction with high levels of employability, stability and professional fulfilment. On the other hand, the level of satisfaction with the quality of the course/institution may indicate the possibility of returning for attending post-graduation courses in a lifelong learning perspective.

Introduction

A major trend in Higher Education over the past decades has been the concern about institutional performance measurement based on an increasingly high governmental and societal pressure. Therefore, one outcome has been an attempt by institutions to apply industrial concepts, formulae and techniques to their management contexts. In fact, by following this industrial emphasis, institutions have been measuring their performance on the notion of quality. However, this concept is very ambiguous even in the commercial world where its synonyms range from luxury and merit to excellence and value: it can mean how well the product fits patterns of consumer preferences', the degree to which a specific product conforms to a design or specification or the level of excellence at an acceptable price and the control of variability at an acceptable cost' (Pounder, 2000).

In the commercial world, it seems that quality means different things and similarly, in the educational context, the notion is open to several interpretations depending on the perspective of the interested parties and is likely to vary with different political cultures, national traditions and education systems. In this scope, many authors oppose the idea of taking Higher Education as an example of a service industry. According to Gilroy et al (1999) there appear to be many similarities: Higher Education does offer a service to its 'customers' – the service of Education. According to Morley (2003, p. 129) "in a market economy, students are no longer perceived as recipients of welfare, but purchasers of an expensive product". On the other hand, as stated by Green (1994, p.13) "many of those currently working in higher education and grappling with the increasing pressures to demonstrate that the "product" they offer is at least as good as that offered by their competitors". However, in a climate dominated by all these managerialist tone and market discourse one important difference between service industries and Higher Education has to be made. Without, in any way, putting in question the student autonomy or their right to comment on the kind of 'service' they receive, it has to be accepted that students lack the overall understanding of their course, both its content and its underlying rationale. Moreover, students do not have a clear idea of what they are about to 'purchase' as a result of graduating from that course.

In addition, besides the gap between what a customer expects and what they are actually provided with, Parsuraman et al. (1985) identified a gap in the service provider's section of the model between what the service managers believe are their customers' expectations and what in fact those expectations actually happen to be.

According to Scriven (1996) evaluation should require some understanding of the nature and concepts of the core discipline, some analytical (not merely practical) work in more than one of the applied fields, including some competence in performing the evaluation-specific tasks, concepts and components (e.g. pedagogical skills). In fact, traditional forms of course evaluation feedback cannot support valid and effective judgements about a course if you don't join the several perspectives of the same "service", nor can they be used as a basis for planning future developments of that course. According to Gilroy et al (1999) if students' evaluation is the only criterion for evaluating the course then, in the same way as if only the course providers' views of a course were to be considered, the resulting evaluation is hopelessly biased and misinformed.

In an important sense, the service that the 'customer' seeks in higher education is prepared and developed by a whole system involved in the educational system: the administration/state, the curricula and the academics. However, we must point out the fact that students' perspective may be one of the references especially when it comes to evaluating the results of learning and teaching. Moreover, student participation in quality assurance has become widely recognized in the European Higher Education Area (EHEA) as Ministers declared in 2001 in Prague that students are important stakeholders on all levels and reaffirmed the importance of student participation in the 'European standards and guidelines on quality assurance' (EUA, 2007).

As stated by Hans-Uwe Erichsen (2003) quality assessment and assurance are or should be an essential part of the self-understanding of Higher Education not only based on concepts associated with how well financial support is being invested but also to guarantee the standards regarding students' expectations and their mobility, the expectations of the labour market and also of the "academic world." Therefore, embedding graduate evaluation into internal quality assurance systems can be a starting point for 'understanding the market and performance in key dimensions (to) enhance planning and promote development although taking into account the complexity and multidimensionality of the graduate's transition to employment'.

In this scope, the UK's Quality Assurance Agency (QAA) for Higher Education's mission is to safeguard the public interest in sound standards of higher education qualifications and to inform and encourage continuous improvement in the management of the quality of higher education. In particular, the Integrated Quality and Enhancement Review focused on a college's management of the student learning experience for its higher education provision also based on the need to identify students' views about their experiences as learners and to draw on these views in considering colleges' higher education provision (QAA, 2008)

According to the European Association for Quality Assurance in Higher Education standards (ENQA, 2005), an institution's information systems are expected to include, amongst other things, figures on graduate employability and student satisfaction with study programmes. In addition, graduate surveys provide valuable information on the monitoring of study programmes such as feedback from graduates, programme labour market relevance, achievement of intended learning outcomes as well as the assessment of the learning resources and student support, especially those referring to transition processes. Prades & Rodrigues (2007) state that this information is valuable for the academic institutions themselves, is key to employment services and turns to be essential to inform and guide students and graduates.

In this scope, many national level surveys have included sections such as the paid employment status, time use, adult education, barriers to adult education, helpfulness of formal education, learning skills, employment-related informal learning, learning and work relations, labour process issues, job changes, household/family status, incomes and benefits but also dynamics of the labour market experience, school-to-work transition in terms of percentage of sample members employed and in school, number of jobs held and age at entrance into first job (Klerman & Karoly, 1995).

At the European level, the project *Careers after Higher Education: a European research study* studied the professional trajectories of graduates including some essential topics such as the proportion of unemployed, the average period for getting the first job, the average annual remuneration, the professional experience in a foreign country, the required skills (computer science, information/data collection and research, decision taking and ability to assume responsibilities), the satisfaction level with the trajectory and the current job, the personal development, the taste for knowledge and internationalization (Teichler, 2000).

In 2002, also in the European context, under the fourth European Program of the Target Socio-economical and Educational Research, the so-called Education Expansion and Labour Market developed a multidisciplinary comparative research between six European countries and the United States about students' trajectories and their relation with the development of the labour world.

In a wider approach, the *Comparative Analysis of Transitions from Education to Work in Europe Project* (Smyth, 2001) supported by the EU Educational Research Board developed a more comprehensive conceptual framework of school to work transitions in different national contexts and applied it to the empirical analysis of the transition processes across European countries.

In this scope, Wilson, Lizzio & Ramsden (1997) based on the *Course Experience Questionnaire* (a development of work originally carried out at Lancaster University in the 1980s) demonstrated positive correlations with students' approaches to learning, perceived course satisfaction, academic achievement and reported generic ("enterprise") skills development. Also based on CEQ, Richardson & Kabanoff (2003) developed the *Workplace Relevance Scale* to measure course satisfaction based on five scales pertaining to Good Teaching Practices, Clear Course Goals and Standards, Appropriate Workload, Appropriate Assessment and Generic Skill. According to the collected results the graduates' judgement of the quality of their undergraduate study hinges upon the utility value of the knowledge and skills developed during their study to their current workplace.

More recently, Prades and Rodrigues (2007) developed a study in Catalunya (Spain) based on a survey to assess the graduate transition to the labour market focusing on the following key evaluation items: employment/unemployment rate, quality of employment, job functions, satisfaction with the training received, competences required, scope of practical work in the curriculum, career services, job functions and competences required.

In a general way, research suggests that the extent to which graduates attribute the success of this transition can be gauged from feedback they give regarding their experience and their employment outcomes (Richardson & Kabanoff, 2003). Overall, and according to the study developed by Menon (2002), evidence suggests that the satisfaction is likely to depend, to a great extent, on the perceived adequacy of his/her preparation for the labour market. In fact, Chadwick & Ward (1987) reported that the degree to which the university performed in the labour market was the strongest predictor of the student's willingness to recommend the institution to others.

Therefore, the need for changes in the professional preparation of the graduates brings the challenge of adopting new conceptions of knowledge in a more lifelong learning perspective and draws attention to the importance of developing more work-based learning programmes (Boud & Solomon, 2001), increasing vocational training (Abbott, 1999) and embedding employability into the curriculum (Yorke & Knight, 2006). On the other hand, the satisfaction ratings and the collected perceptions concerning the aims and character of their institutions provide valuable information that can be used as an alternative criterion in evaluating the effectiveness of higher education institutions (The Quality Assurance Agency for Higher Education, 2008).

The institutional context

Gaya Superior Polytechnic Institute is a private polytechnic institute in the north of Portugal with approximately 900 students, mainly community student-workers. It was founded in 1990 to create and convey the latest science and engineering knowledge in ways that would be most useful to the society. The institution is structured into two superior schools: Social and Community Development Superior School and Science and Technology Superior School and the following graduation courses, fully adapted to the *Bologna System*.

The *curricula* have been continuously reshaped and adapted to satisfy the evolution of both students and the labour market but has remained true to its original mission of fusing academic inquiry with social needs and linking new knowledge to applications. The institution aims to promote the development of the personality of the students through a technical-scientific, socio-cultural integrated instruction.

As a higher education institution, its mission is to be fully adapted to the needs of the modern society and to the labour market, combining theory and practice. One of the institutional policies is centred on the dialogue among all the members of the educational community based on the continuous evaluation of its services.

Being aware of the urge for answers to these questions, the *Graduate Trajectories Observatory (GTO)* intends to collect and analyse information about graduates in the process of transition to active life by studying the contexts and difficulties of professional insertion, identifying the instruction gaps in order to develop support strategies.

This mission is based on the belief that a higher education institution must know the students and that this meeting must take place in the pedagogical relation and academic environment. To achieve this goal it is essential to collect data to characterize the students before, during and after their graduation and, at the same time, develop the professional skills that satisfy the work world demands.

Based on experience, the background and profile of the students (mainly student-workers from the community) tend to indicate that the students usually perceive higher education as a step for accessing different work tasks/positions, career progression and professional fulfilment.

These experiences and perceptions informally collected throughout the years is now the starting point for an institutional research line associated with quality and excellence.

Aims

The capacity to evaluate the inputs from the higher education system based on the graduate experience of the outcomes of study is the primary focus of this research with the testing of a measure of graduate perception of the relevance of their study experiences. Therefore, this study was designed to focus on the relationship between current graduate' work performance and their learning experiences in higher education. In a more specific way, the present study intends to

- characterize the academic profile of the graduates;
- point out the main reasons for enrolling and choosing the course and institution;
- assess the quality of the graduation course/institution;
- identify the abilities acquired with the perspective of preparation for the active life;
- analyse the needs for the acquisition of skills and instruction.

Methodology

The research design is based on the *Academic and Professional Trajectories Questionnaire* using closed answers so that the responses were standardized and the satisfaction with each of the issues could be assessed (Table 1).

Quality Assessment	Main reason for choosing that course	Acquisition of knowledge/personal interest; professional exits; experience in the area; professional fulfillment; useful career; payment; prestige; influence of family/friends; required average to enter; vocational tests; other
	Main reason for choosing the institution	Prestige of the institution; institution with the chosen course; schedules night/after-labour classes; location; recommendation of friends/family, other
	Course/ institution Quality Assessment	Scientific/pedagogical quality; administrative and academic services and resources, infrastructures and equipment.
	Level of competence	General/cultural knowledge, ability to work in a team, leadership/innovation, communication and critical skills
	Level of preparation for the professional life (five levels in the *Likert* scale)	
	Current Professional Situation	

Table 1: Course Assessment items

The target population of the study are the graduates from the academic years from 2001 to 2006 ($N = 428$), and the sample is formed by 142 subjects/valid answers, what constitutes a return outcome of 33.1%.

Results

The collected data prove the fact that usually more than 70% of the students are student-workers attending after-labour classes. Therefore, this is the reason why issues associated with the expectations, perceptions and impact/changes in the workplace due to graduation are vital for the development of the institution as a learning reference and a professional partner for many of the region's companies and community institutions (Table 1).

Identification	
Gender and Age	The majority of the subjects are female (73.2%), with ages mainly between 25 and 29 years (54.9%).
Class Attendance Regimen and Student status	71.4% are student-workers and 75.6% attended the course in after-labour/night periods.

Table 2: Graduates' identification

2. Reasons for choosing the course and institution

Based on informally collected perceptions and experiences the first step was to determine the motivations for choosing the course and institution based on personal and professional items (Table 3).

Reasons for choosing the course and institution	
Reasons for choosing the course	Although disperse, the data indicated that 27.7% considered the possibility of getting a well-paid job, followed by the fact of having worked in the area (21.9%) or the possibility of acquiring knowledge of personal interest (15.3%), getting professional fulfilment (11.7%) or a useful job (10.2%). At the end, we find the influence of family/friends or teachers (5.8%), the professional exits (5.1%), the prestige of the course (1.5%) and other reasons (0.7%).
2. Reasons for choosing the institution	Data indicated that having the desired course and the location are the most determinant factors for the choice of this institution (both with 31.9%) followed by the schedules and attendance regimens (18.5%), the recommendation of family and friends (11.1%) and, finally, for the prestige of the institution (1.5%) and other reasons (5.2%).

Table 3: Level of Satisfaction with the course/ institution

It is easily understandable how the financial factor appears as the most important for the subjects mainly considering the current socio-economical situation and not factors as the acquisition of knowledge of personal interest or professional fulfilment. On the other hand, we have to take into consideration the fact that most of the subjects are student-workers. In fact, we can infer how a degree can represent the possibility of enjoying a different professional status and be a step towards professional fulfilment.

Moreover, this new professional opportunity is very frequently associated with a deep personal commitment towards the development of a new set of skills and opportunities and, in some cases, a new life project.

Regarding the private nature of the institution, the question of the reasons for being chosen is seen as vital for the assessment of the factors that constitute its main advantages. At this level it is relevant to point out the extent to which student-workers really need to attend mostly night/after-labour classes, close to their home and/or workplace. On the other hand, as the enrolment contexts are usually characterized by uncertainty and limited information, the role of the recommendation of family or friends or even some fellow workers, some of them attending the same institution or course, is understandable. In fact, the institutional marketing relies mainly on the informal relations/contacts that legitimize its quality and emphasize its regional strategic position.

3. Quality of the course/institution

This item assumes a central role in the assessment process as it is the epitome of the academic experience, which moves from the scientific to the administrative scopes (Table 4).

Quality of the course/institution Five-point scale (1 = Very low and 5 = Very high quality)
The mean values indicate that the scientific and pedagogical quality has the highest scores (3.76) followed by the academic services (3.60), facilities and equipment (3.01), the Library (2.93) and, finally, the level of the global quality of the institution (3.56).

Table 4: Quality of the course/institution

The results emphasize the satisfaction of the graduates with the scientific-pedagogical quality of the course and institution and its academic services, which, from the institutional point of view, is relevant as these are the two major pillars of the institution. The other factors were assessed with a medium level of satisfaction, which may be associated with the fact that in the institution, during their graduation process, the facilities were still limited and the infrastructures inefficient, although the situation has considerably improved since then.

4. Level of Competence and professional life preparation

The professional abilities and level of preparation for active life are a consequence of the new complexities and uncertainties of an economic and social environment marked by competitiveness, permanent need of innovation and where abilities and potential skills are always in demand.

Taking into consideration their experience and knowledge about the necessary skills for their personal and professional development, the graduates evaluated their instruction concerning specific content, general knowledge/culture, teamwork abilities, leadership and innovation, communication and critical abilities as the starting point for measuring their own perception of preparation for their professional life (Table 5).

Level of Competence Five-point scale (1 = Very low competence and 5 = Very high Competence)
The mean values indicate that teamwork ability is the strongest ability (3.79) followed by the development of critical abilities (3.71), communication skills (3.67), general knowledge/culture (3.62), leadership and innovation (3.59) and finally the specific content (3.57). When trying to evaluate the global level of ability a 3.74 level was achieved.
Professional Life Preparation Five-point scale (1 = Very low and 5 = Very high preparation)
The level of preparation for professional life is 3.54.

Table 5: Level of Competence and professional life preparation

The data indicate that the abilities associated with the professional activity in its relational component, namely the capacity to work in teams, is the most developed one, in fact, one of the most demanded and valued abilities in business. Afterwards, we find a set of abilities associated with personal/professional enrichment such as the development of critical spirit, communication skills, general culture and leadership and innovation that tend to have higher levels of competence than the specific content itself. What will have to be worked out is the evaluation of the course bearing in mind the adequateness of the contents/syllabuses and the effectiveness of the teaching/learning processes together with the acknowledgement of the set of skills and professional profile/experience of the students as soon as they start their academic experience.

Based on the previous analysis, we aimed to evaluate if there was an adjustment between the abilities considered to be essential for the achievement of the course objectives and for the instruction of competent, competitive, innovative and flexible professionals with a recognized professional performance and assured employability.

Therefore, according to the results the level of preparation for professional life is 3.54. Although being a very subjective indicator and changeable according to the professional area and experience, it allows us to point out the satisfying adequacy of the course to the requirements/contingencies of the work market.

5. Current Professional Situation

Employability is one of the major concerns nowadays and a decisive indicator of the quality of instruction and professional insertion effectiveness (Table 6).

Current Professional Situation
The data indicate that the great majority of the subjects are employed (87.5%), while only 4.4% are looking for the first job or unemployed and 3.7% are student-workers.

Table 6: Current Professional Situation

The analysis of the process of insertion of graduates reveals quite positive results, although we cannot forget that most of the subjects were already working during their graduation course and belong to different graduation years.

Conclusions

This study by using graduate surveys tried to assess graduates' academic experience and transition to the labour market providing clues for ways to improve the embedding of these indicators in processes involving the internal quality assurance of programmes and institutions.

One of the most relevant results relies on the meeting between the subjects' motivations and expectations towards the institution/course. In fact, the outcome of their academic experience tends to be achieved as the majority of the graduates are employed. This quality effort has come to frame a global picture of efficiency and prove the accomplishment of the objectives and educational project of the institution itself.

The graduates' perceptions concerning the quality of the institution can also provide valuable information and help to point out the potential areas of improvement, namely in the field of envisioning learning and instruction as privileged sources for personal and professional outcomes concerning the access to knowledge, the widening of perspectives and interests and self-positioning in the global market.

In order to increase the quality of the "educational service" we emphasize the need to fully integrate the three key elements involved in the process of graduate transition to the labour market: defining and reviewing programme specifications in order to bring the graduates' work expertise into the class environment, practical work in the curriculum as a source of experience exchange and designing and evaluating actions that promote the transition from higher education to the labour market, specially strengthening the ties and setting bridges.

Moreover, a set of regulation and intervention strategies has to be undertaken combining the outcomes of these assessment initiatives with the institutional projects, always meeting the different perspectives and contexts. In fact, a great investment has still to be done on the development of other assessment tools and methodologies that involve not only the students but also the administration, the community and employers.

References

Abbott, I. (1999). Why Do We have to Do Key Skills? Student Views about General National Vocational Qualifications, *Journal of Vocational Education and Training*, 49, pp. 617-630.

Boud, D. & Solomon, N. (2001) (Eds). *Work-Based Learning: a new Higher Education*. Buckingham: Open University Press.

Center for Human Resource Research (1988). *National Longitudinal Survey-Youth (NLS-Y)*.

Counsell, D. (1996). Graduate careers in the UK: an examination of undergraduates' perceptions. *Career Development International*, 1(7), pp. 44 – 51.

Erichsen, H. (2003). *Quality Assurance by Accreditation*. Paper presented at the 12th annual Meeting of EDEN, Rhodes.

European University Association (2007). *Embedding quality culture in Higher Education- a selection of papers from the 1st European Forum*. Brussels: European University Association.

European Association for Quality Assurance in Higher Education (2005). *Standards and Guidelines for Quality Assurance in the European Higher Education Area*. Helsinki: European Association for Quality Assurance in Higher Education.

Gilroy, P., Long, P., Rangecroft, M. & Tricker, T. (1999). The Evaluation of Course Quality through a Service Template, *Evaluation*, 5(1), pp.80–91.

Green, D. (1994). *What is quality in Higher Education?* The Society for Research into Higher Education, Taylor and Francis.

Institute for Social Research (2004). *National Survey of Learning and Work Wall Survey*.

Klerman, J. & Karoly, L. (1995). *Transition to Stable Employment: The Experience of U.S. Youth in Their Early Labor Market Career*. RAND – U.S. Government.

Martin, A., Milne-Home, J., Barrett, J., Spalding, E. & Jones, G. (2000). Graduate Satisfaction with University and Perceived Employment Preparation. *Journal of Education and Work*, 13 (2), pp.199-213.

Menon, M. (2002). The mission of universities and the vocational paradigm: an investigation of students' perceptions'. *Journal of Vocational Education & Training*, 54(4), pp. 515-532.

Miller, B. (2006). *Assessing Organizational Performance in Higher Education* San Francisco: Jossey-Bass

Morley, L. (2003). *Quality and Power in Higher Education*. The Society for Research into Higher Education. Open University Press, MacGraw-Hill Education.

Nusche, D. (2008). Assessment of learning outcomes in higher education: a comparative review of selected practices. OECD Education Working Paper No. 15.

Parsuraman, A., Zeitheml, V. A. & Berry, L. L. (1985). A Conceptual Model of Service Quality and its Implications for Future Research, *Journal of Marketing*, 49, pp. 41–50.

Pounder, J. (2000). Evaluating the Relevance of Quality to Institutional Performance Assessment in Higher Education, *Evaluation*, 6(1), pp. 66–78.

Prades, A. & Rodríguez, S. (2007). Embedding graduate survey indicators into internal quality assurance systems – What can institutions learn from graduate surveys? In European University Association, *Embedding quality culture in Higher Education- a selection of papers from the 1st European Forum*. Brussels: European University Association.

Roberts, V. (2001). Global Trends in Tertiary Education – Quality Assurance. *Implications for the Anglophone Caribbean, Educational Management & Administration*, 29(4), pp. 425-440.

Scriven, M. (1996). The Theory behind Practical Evaluation, *Evaluation*, 2(4), pp.393-404.

The Quality Assurance Agency for Higher Education (2008). *The Handbook for Integrated Quality and Enhancement Review*. Gloucester (UK): The Quality Assurance Agency for Higher Education.

Parasuraman, A., Zeithaml, V., and Berry, L.L. (1985). A Conceptual Model of Service Quality and Its Implications for Future Research, *Journal of Marketing*, 49 (Fall), pp. 41-50.

Richardson, A. & Kabanoff, B. (2003). Graduates' Perceptions of University Study and it's Contribution toward the Development of Workplace Competence. 2003 Conference of *The Australian Association for Research in Education/* New Zealand Association for Research in Education, Auckland.

Smyth, E. (2001). *A Comparative Analysis of Transitions from Education To Work in Europe – Final Report*. EU-supported educational research 1995-2005 – new perspectives for learning.

Stephenson, J. & Yorke, M. (Eds) (1998). *Capability and Quality in Higher Education*. London: Kogan Page.

Teichler, U. (2000). *Careers after higher education: a European research survey – CHEERS, 2000*, available at http://www.uni-kassel.de/wz1/tseregs.htm

Wilson, K; Lizzio, A. & Ramsden, P. (1997). The development, validation and application of the Course Experience Questionnaire. *Studies in Higher Education*, 22 (1), pp. 33 – 53.

Yorke, M & Knight, P. (2006). *Embedding employability into the curriculum*. Learning and Employability Series 1. York: The Higher Education Academy.

What is in between from teacher-centred to student-centred teaching? A comparison of Western European and Chinese research-intensive university teachers' beliefs

Wu Wei

Abstract

The purpose of this study was to improve our understanding of educational beliefs both in Western and Chinese research-intensive university teachers. We investigated differences and similarities between Western European and Chinese university teachers' beliefs with respect to knowledge, teaching, learning and teacher–student relationships by using semi-structured interviews. Twenty research-intensive university teachers from a Dutch and a Chinese university were selected for interview because they had cross-cultural university teaching experience. A qualitative analysis of interviews resulted in a "mapping-plane" with five themes, each containing up to five categories of description of the variation within each theme. A model was constructed to locate these five categories of university teachers' beliefs. The results of this study might help both Western European and Chinese research university teachers to become aware of their own beliefs and improve understanding of cultural differences in university teachers' beliefs.

Keywords: educational beliefs; research-intensive university, university teachers; cross-culture

1. Introduction

1.1. University teachers' beliefs

Since the late 80s, there has been a growing literature on teachers' beliefs (Fang, 1996), including beliefs about education, beliefs about teaching and learning, and so forth. Although there has been considerable research into beliefs about teaching among school teachers, many university lecturers consider themselves quite different from school teachers. Indeed many university academics hardly consider themselves "teachers" at all, instead visualizing themselves more as a member of their discipline (Becher, 1989). Universities also operate under different value systems and traditions from schools. While some elements of the school-based research were likely to be applicable to university beliefs, it was probable that there would be dimensions which would not be apparent in school teachers.

A large number of teacher beliefs have been identified by many researchers (Fox 1983, Biggs 1989, Dall'Alba 1990, Dunkin 1990, Martin and Balla 1990, Dunkin and Precian 1992, Martin and Ramsden 1992, Pratt 1992, Samuelowicz and Bain 1992, Gow and Kember 1993, Kember and Gow 1994, Prosser, et al. 1994, Trigwell, et al. 1994, Christensen et al. 1995). These beliefs were arrayed from the most teacher-centred extreme to the most student-centred extreme by most of the researchers (Gao 1999). After reviewing the above studies, Kember (1997) recognized five dimensions on which university teachers constructed their beliefs about teaching and learning: the essence of learning and teaching; the roles of student and teacher; the aims and expected outcome of teaching; the content of teaching; and the preferred styles and approaches to teaching. Teachers' views in each dimension were found to range from the most teacher-central to the most student-central. Further review of the descriptions of the conceptions identified by the above researchers showed that, in spite of the differences in the labels and descriptions of teaching beliefs made by different researchers, there was a high degree of commonality in the research findings. The 'teacher-centred/content-orientated' orientation covered the 'imparting information' and 'transmitting structured knowledge' conceptions. The 'student-centred/learning orientated' orientation covered the 'facilitating understanding' and 'conceptual change/intellectual development' conceptions. The 'student–teacher interaction/apprenticeship' concept acted as a bridge concept between the two opposite orientations.

1.2 Teaching as a cultural activity

With the development of higher education internalization, many universities are trying to attract more and more international students, which places new demands on university lecturers and teachers. Due to their different cultural backgrounds and traditions, students and teachers from abroad can be very different from students and teachers at the "host university" with respect to their ideas about essential aspects of learning, teaching, teacher-student interaction, and so on. These differences in ideas may go unnoticed and, as we have seen in the past, may lead to mutual adaptation problems and even dropout of students from the program. A first step in solving this problem might be to get a better view of what exactly these differences are both among students and university teachers. As we know, differences certainly exist between Western-European universities and universities from East Asia.

Beside this, more and more comparative educational studies have also begun to explore the culture and value orientation behind educational phenomenon with the aim of better understanding. A cross-cultural investigation of teachers' beliefs can be valuable because the comparison of two distinct culturally embedded belief systems can make implicit beliefs and assumptions more transparent (Correa & Perry et al, 2008). There have been many studies on international students' cultural adaptation and acculturation, and there have been several comparative studies about Western and Chinese teachers' beliefs. Most of these researches have emerged only from Western perspectives to explain Asian students or education in the Chinese context. So it would be worthwhile to compare and analyze teacher beliefs both from the Western and Chinese perspective, especially filling a gap in these comparisons.

1.3. Why compare Chinese and Western European university teachers who had cross- cultural university teaching experience?

Previous research has established a close link between students' and international students' conceptions of learning and teaching. Until recently, there have been few studies of university teachers' beliefs about teaching and teaching in different culture for improving cultural awareness among university teachers. Therefore, the aim of this study is to promote cross-cultural and mutual understanding and adjustment both between university teachers and international students, which would foster inclusiveness and improve interactions between teachers and students from different cultures.

This paper reports outcomes of a study that considers different ways Western European (especially Dutch) and Chinese university teachers view knowledge, teaching, learning and teacher–student relation in higher education. Although Chinese and Western European educational systems and teachers at secondary schools have been contrasted, our study fills a gap in these comparisons by examining university teachers' beliefs, and all teachers who were invited to this interview study are those who had cross-cultural university teaching experience, which means Chinese university teachers who had university teaching experience in Western European universities, and vice verse. These teachers might know more about differences in teaching, university and culture aspects.

The following research question was addressed in this study: What are the differences and similarities between Western European and Chinese research-intensive university teachers' beliefs about teaching, learning and teacher–student relations?

2. Method

2.1. Context of the study

All interviews were conducted both at Leiden University and Xiamen University. These two research-intensive universities are highly comparable in terms of their education program purposes and fairly representative of research universities in each country.

2.2. Participants

Twenty interviews (9 Dutch, 8 Chinese, 2 British and 1 French) were conducted from June to September 2008. The interviewees were volunteer teachers (male = 13, female = 7) who had cross-cultural teaching experience at Leiden or Xiamen University. Their academic experiences range from 5 years to 30 years. All of these teachers represent a range of characteristics such as gender, subjects and student level they have.

Prior to the main discussion, the use of terms *East Asian* and the *West* need to be clarified. In line with many cross-cultural scholars (e.g., Kim, 2002; Trompennaars, 1993; Woodward, 2002), the term *West* is used throughout the thesis to include Europe, North America, Australia, and New Zealand, as referring to traditions of thought and practice and an historical trajectory. In this paper, the terms *Western Europe* (Western European) in the West and *China* (Chinese) in *East Asian* are used as umbrella terms for the two targeted cultures in the research study.

This is not to suggest that these cultures are not very different from each other in many ways—social, religious, historical, and educational. However, there does seem to exist a sufficiently identifiable core of rhetorical traditions, which will allow for grouping of them together for the purpose of contrasting them. Furthermore, supported by substantive literatures (e.g. Cortazzi & Jin, 1997; Hall, 1976; Hofstede, 2001; Tanaka, 2002; Ting- Toomey, 1999; Tormpenars, 1993), it could be assumed that teachers coming from China may have common views and experience common challenges in adapting to Western European academic environment and vice versa.

2.3. Instrument

With the aim of teachers to explain their stories and perceptions of this cross-cultural journey through in-depth interviews, five commonly recognized dimensions proposed by Kember (1997) were referred to, and 20 open-ended interview questions under five themes about (1) purpose of higher education; (2) qualities of a good university teacher; (3) qualities of a good learner, (4) teaching content (relationship between teaching content and teachers' research); (5) teacher-students relationship were constructed for teachers to express what they think before and after cross-cultural teaching experiences. Therefore, these questions focused on three different aspects: the 'belief questions' eliciting teachers' responses about their opinions and values relating to teaching, learning and teacher–student relations; the 'practical questions' eliciting teachers' responses about their cross-cultural teaching experiences and behaviours in another culture and the 'analysis questions' trying to encourage teachers to outline the reasons for their beliefs and changes.

2.4. Procedures

A brief introduction to this research and the interview questions were sent before interviews. The duration of the interviews ranged from 1 hour to 1.5 hours. To facilitate the subsequent data analysis, all interviews were recorded.

2.5. Analysis

The purpose of analyzing interview data is to "understand the meaning of the communication" and to "look for meaningful relationships in the data" (Mostyn, 1985). Data were analyzed by using an open coding framework 'mapping-plane' for identifying teachers' beliefs designed by Gao Lingbiao and David Watkins (2001) in an inductive and iterative process (Lincoln & Guba, 1985), which involves three major stages.

Stage A. Data selection: quoting key word and phrases for five themes

The first stage focused on understanding what teachers said during the interview and then on quoting key words and phrases from the data for the question in this study: teachers' beliefs. The systematic analysis started after all the interviews were done. The researcher re-listened to the interview record and the quoted key words and phrases related to five themes, which were based on Kember's 'bipolar' nature of the dimensions. These served as a framework for further coding.

Stage B. Data display: coding and identifying teachers' beliefs

This stage refers to the efficient means of organizing and displaying information involving the use of charts, graphs, matrices, and networks, but they also have a part to play in the data collection phase (Robson, 2002). And the focus in the second stage was to seek "if any regularities occur in terms of single words, themes, or concepts" (Mostyn, 1985), so that the data could be organized systematically for the identification of teacher beliefs based on the five themes found in the first stage.

Under each theme, synonymic words and phrases with similar meaning were put together as a group. A single word or phrase was then selected as the representative of the group. For example, when responding to the question about the aims of university teaching, teachers used the following words and phrases: "to help students to understand themselves and find their own interests", "to let student to know what they really want" and "to cultivate students' curiosity". All these implied or emphasized finding interest during the teaching process, so the word *interest-based* was used as a representative of this kind of belief.

Then a combination of Kember's 'bipolar' nature of the dimensions and the 'mapping- plane' for identifying teachers' beliefs designed by Gao Lingbiao and David Watkins (2001) was used. The strategies used in this stage included the following:

(1) Coding teachers' beliefs according to the dimensions identified
Teachers' beliefs were coded to each of the dimensions and arranged in order from the most teacher-centred to the most student-centred based on the "bipolar" nature of the dimensions.

(2) Identifying categories of teachers' beliefs
A "mapping-plane" (see the following figure) was formed for identifying teachers' beliefs.

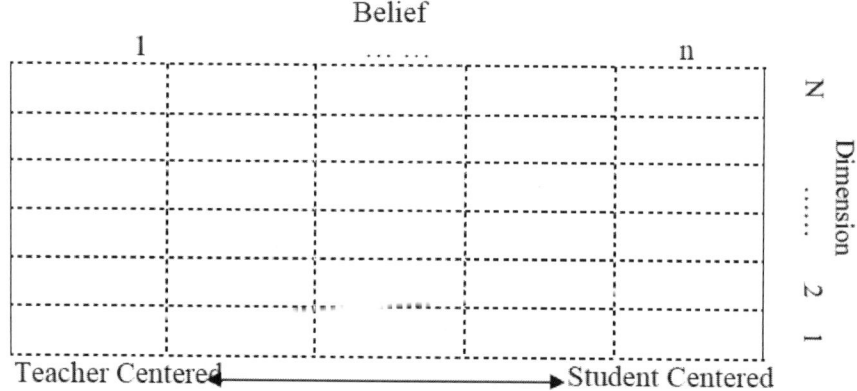

Figure 1. "Mapping-plane"

Teachers' beliefs of the same dimension arrayed in the same row and from the most teacher-centred extreme to the most student-centred extreme. Those ideas that overlapped in the same "block" were combined as one. Thus, ideas expressing the most teacher-centred views formed a column as the far-left side in the "mapping-plane". This implied one category of teacher belief. The number of columns that emerged in the "mapping-plane" implied the number of categories of teachers' beliefs, that is, the number of teacher beliefs held by university teachers both in China and the Netherlands.

Stage C. Conclusion drawing and verification
Actually, this stage has been paid attention to from 'the start of data collection, noting patterns and regularities, positing possible structures and mechanisms'. Mile and Huberman (1994) stress that this should be accompanied throughout by a verification process: that is, testing validity and reliability, for example, is an explanation

plausible? Can you find evidence confirming it? Can a finding be replicated in another data set?'

(1) To minimize possible biases, another consultant was invited to take part in the analysis.

Considering that almost half the interviews were conducted in Chinese, another researcher was invited to do his own interview analysis by following the above procedure. Subsequently, they discussed their analysis with a view to developing consensus. When two researchers discussed the interview analysis, they thought that it would be most worthwhile to have an analysis discussion on those points where disagreement or confusion arises, both for the categories and the dimensions. The following methods were applied: a. quotes from the interviews were used to discuss these issues; b. while discussing the issues of confusion/disagreements, rules for assigning a certain code to a quote can be phrased more clearly, and eventually, categories can be refined, slightly changed, and so on; c. the same holds for the description of the dimensions.

(2) Discussions on disagreements

Discussions on key words and phrases

All the key words and phrases were put together. Those quoted by both persons were kept together. Those quoted by one person were discussed to decide whether they should be dropped or kept. When identifying the meaning of the key words and phrases, two researchers then discussed the meaning of representative words and phrases. When a conflict in understanding was found, the related conversation was re-listened to to arrive at a common understanding.

Discussions on categories

Both researchers agreed on five dimensions through analysis. While comparing these categories from different researchers, they focused on 'the final goal (what does this teacher or these teachers really want/how do they evaluate whether they have achieved their teaching goal?)' to title these dimensions. For example, the first research defined one dimension as "attitude promotion" and the second found a related one and called it "interest oriented". After discussions, they reached an agreement that this dimension focused more on "students' needs" and "a process of internal pursuit". Attitude promotion was accompanied by the process. So they defined it as "interest oriented".

3. Findings

Five qualitatively different categories were identified: knowledge oriented, outcome oriented, process oriented, interest oriented and holistic-life oriented. Western European teachers tended to be more learner-centred and Chinese teachers more teacher-centred.

3.1 General overview
Table I. Snapshots of university teachers' beliefs

	Knowledge-oriented	Outcome-oriented	Ability-oriented	Interest-oriented	Holistic-life oriented
Purpose of higher education	Delivery, accumulation of knowledge; increasing information	students get good results and find good jobs; what is taught could be applied in real life; development of individual's social adaption	Improve students' ability in the process of learning and research; forming the scientific way of thinking; group working together to examine existing knowledge	Help students to find their interest; a process of internal pursue ;	Both teacher and students are trying to become all-round people; cultivation; Enjoy life; collective knowledge construction
Teaching and teacher	"Have a bottle of water before give students half bottle of water"; knowledgeable in subject; controller; responsible	Trainer; Combining university teaching with social needs	Facilitator; Motivator; reformer; Guider; International view (know the cutting edge) in his research	Patient; observer; Open view; Challenger; inspirer	Knowledgeable; enthusiastic towards life; passionate
Relation between teacher and students	Little interaction; passive students; export and import; Teacher is an expert; learner is passive	"Boss" In an education factory; Setting tasks with defined parameters	Colleagues; cooperation; feedback in learning; bridge between students and unknown field;	Friends; Listener ; teacher is a facilitator; learner active in the development of finding own interest	Both director and friends; friendly and interactive, implicit manner; teacher and learners have joint responsibility for learning
Learning and Learner	Following; study hard; learn as much as possible; passive receiver; acquire;	competitive ; capable in finding job;	Critical; explorer; Active and independent in learning and research; Know what is unknown and how to know; Active builder; Flexible	Following interest; flexible; Independent; creative; Ambitious;	knowledgeable but also have ethic and good behavior; good relations with others; give contribution to society; Appreciation to the world and life; Self-reflection; learning through co-constructive dialogue
relation between teaching and research	pre-determined by syllabus and textbooks (teachers do not have freedom to choose);	Both pure and applied knowledge; related jobs requirement; requirement from qualification examination; skills that required by society	teachers' recent research/ project; new filed According to students' level and needs;	Combination with student-interest related and demanded-knowledge ; meet the needs of students;	Related what is required to teach to society problems; care about life and the world

194

Table II. Profiles of 20 interviewees (B=British; C=Chinese; D=Dutch; F=French)

Categories of teacher belief	Teacher	Gender	Country of origin	Subject	From teacher-centered to student-centered		
					T-centered	T-S interaction	S-centered
Knowledge-Oriented (2C+1F)	C1	F	China	History	×		
	C2	M	China	Chinese	×		
	F1	F	France	Law	×		
Outcome-Oriented (2 C+1 D)	C3	M	China	French	×		
	C4	M	China	Mathematics	×		
	D1	M	The Netherlands	Dutch Literature	×		
Ability-Oriented (2 C+4D+1B)	C5	F	China	English		×	
	C6	M	China	International relation		×	
	D2	M	The Netherlands	Public Administration		×	
	D3	F	The Netherlands	Physics		×	
	D4	M	The Netherlands	Sinology		×	
	D5	M	The Netherlands	Computer science			
	B1	M	Britain	English		×	
Interest-Oriented (1C+2 D+1B)	C7	M	China	Art			×
	D6	M	The Netherlands	Chemistry			×
	D7	M	The Netherlands	Biology			×
	B2	M	Britain	English			×
Holistic-life Oriented (1 C+2 D)	C8	F	Chinese	Education			×
	D8	F	The Netherlands	Dutch literature			×
	D9	M	The Netherlands	Sinology			×

3.1 Specific examples

(1) Knowledge-oriented

There was a sense of higher education as an environment in which students were inducted into field-specific practices, which the teachers modelled to their students, and in which knowledge transfer played a significant role in teaching and learning. (Pickering, 2006)

Some interviewees saw the university teachers as having a deep obligation to help students to learn and become knowledgeable. Three teachers (2 Chinese and 1 French) felt that their identity as an authority and expert took precedence over that as a teacher. For example, one Chinese teacher said:

> I think university teacher is a bank of knowledge. When you want to give students half bottle of water, you must have a bottle of water before. I also believe that good learner should learn and remember as much as possible. And I also I like those students who know the knowledge learnt accurately and in detail. Students should treat teachers with respect both inside and outside class. ...(C2)

> ...En...I would try to teach as much as possible to let my students know more information. Sometimes when you are talking they [Dutch students] often stop you in the middle with disagreement, which I seldom expected before. That makes you very embarrassed and scared. They had better listen to me first, at least until people have finished talking. (C1)

And from a Dutch teacher's experience, we could also find some clue to this knowledge-oriented belief that exists in the Chinese context:

> Teachers in China have absolute authority and are treated with quite high deference. In fact, the word teacher in Chinese can be literally translated as "born early," implying that teachers (because they were born earlier and had much more experience) deserve respect and deference. In exchange, teachers are expected to demonstrate wisdom and knowledge of his subject. (D5)

Actually, it is typically in East Asia, for example in China, that maintaining respect to the elders, especially teachers, and avoiding offence or confrontation appear to be of greater value and importance than the search for absolute truth (Hofstede & Bond, 1984).

(2) Outcome-oriented

This belief is more concerned with fulfilling the expectations of society and other stakeholders. These teachers believe that interaction with the outside world is the most important way for students to learn or is the most important purpose of university teaching. Teachers in the outcome-oriented category relied mostly upon external motivators such as the examinations or the final qualification for students' career and whatever benefits that might bring.

> You know, comparing to English, French is not so popular. So I should encourage my students to join in the qualification examination also French test to be more qualified for career pursuit. (C3)

> ...nowadays the competence is becoming more and more intense for students to find a job....they are complaining that what they have learnt at university is not enough or useless...so I tried to collect and organize materials that will be interesting to students and help them to develop insight into business and connect those to real business issues. (C4)

> I would pay attention to the new development of real society situation and new requirements from marketplace to prepare my students to more operational competent in the future. (D1)

(3) Ability-oriented

Teachers, who share this ability-oriented belief have the desire to create a space for learning and encourage students to be independent, especially students' critical and creative thinking, which is more related to academic ability.

> ...according the level of my students, I combine some parts of my research into my lectures and have some of my students involved in. (D2)

> It is not enough to know what the things are. As a teacher or supervisor, you need to help students to think about the reasons behind things and to find a scientific approach to find their relations. (D3)

> I am trying to help students to be more critical, innovative, challenging with the subject matters and things that they learn and receive. (C5)

> Everything is uncertain. Teacher's obligation is to help student to question both familiar and unfamiliar things and encourage their independent thinking, critical thinking and creative problem solving. (B1)

> The best learning comes from working alongside improving different abilities. (C6)

The spirit of critical thinking is that people take nothing for granted or as being beyond question. In academic debate, arguments are analysed to find inconsistencies, logical flaws or evidence to the contrary (Walkner & Finney, 1999).

People's innovative spirit and comprehensive development are required in the 21st century. Research-oriented higher education, responding to this requirement, which aims at cultivating students' innovative spirit and promoting their comprehensive development, has been turning into an important part of many Western European Universities' focus. Research-oriented education means both teaching and learning activities that students choose and confirm subject from the nature, society and life to study and obtain and apply knowledge during the research process to solve problems under the teachers' guidance (Brenda & Janet, 2006). Leiden University is aiming for an internationally recognized position as a top-ranking research-intensive university, and the three guiding principles of the University are an international orientation; the research-intensive character of the University; and maintaining the quality of education and research.

In China, critical and creative thinking abilities are and emphasized more in university teaching. One Chinese teacher mentioned that

> Compared to Western relationship between teachers and students, I find that Asian culture believes that a higher level of communication is communication without language. In Chinese, things and feelings are more implicit. You need get the message behind the language. So this means that as a teacher, you should behave well, students will look into every aspect of your way and learn from you. However, the situation is changing now, both teachers and students have known the importance of critical and independent thinking. And students are encouraged to speak out their ideas and questions, no matter right or wrong. Students will benefit from this ability in learning and in future.

(4) Interest-oriented

There is a shared belief among both Chinese and Western European teachers that university teaching must be actively committed to make students' learning interesting. Teachers in the interest-oriented category relied mostly upon students' internal motivators such as students' questions and potentials.

> Nowadays teaching is less about the content and knowledge, but more about the way, the appropriate strategies to facilitate and challenge your students to be more creative and cooperative. (C7)

> Most of all, learning depends on individuals' interest in his or her life. I normally pay attention to provide an atmosphere where all my students could think freely and grow their abilities. I think it is important to make a distinction between different groups of students. (D7)

These teachers saw higher education as a place for learners who will be to a significant degree self-motivated. That is the nature of the support which teachers felt should be provided to students for their learning was interest motivated.

> The students I enjoy having in groups are the ones which are fundamentally interested in the subject. ... The students that I have the least time ... are those which simply want a qualification and have very little commitment to the particular field of study. They never come to me for the further discussion or information share. (B2)

(5) Holistic-life oriented

How to become a "whole person" is the most important concern among teachers with this holistic-life oriented belief.

> It might be a good way of transmitting essential information to large groups, but I do believe that students could learn better by following their own heart and interest to find whatever they like and I would support them. (C8)

> ...Trust students and show my respect of students and support them to find what they really want in their heart. I am trying to make a progress with my students with a hope that we are all in the process of becoming a nice person with appreciation to this world and enthusiasm towards life. (D8)

> Teachers need to be mindful of each student's characteristics and their needs. The goal of teaching is helping both teachers and students to become all-round person. Student learning means knowing how to mature gradually. (D9)

4. Conclusion and discussion

The results of this small study need to be viewed cautiously. The study does not claim to be comprehensive, but connections with themes in other research suggest that findings are interesting and relevant. We also emphasize that we are not advocating the adoption of Western European culture and university teachers' beliefs in China. We are addressing a situation that is already in place.

To answer our central research question, what are the differences and similarities between Western European and Chinese research university teachers' beliefs about teaching, learning and teacher-student relations? We identified, as a result of interview analysis, five categories: knowledge-oriented, outcome-oriented, ability-oriented, interested- oriented and holistic-life oriented. It is remarkable that university teachers from both Chinese universities and Western European universities were found in each category. Another finding was that compared with Western university teachers, more Chinese university teachers are in the left columns.

Inspired by Carnell's model (2007) "A two-way continuum of teaching", a model of university teachers' beliefs is formed using a two-way continuum from collective to individual and from objective to knowledge to subjective knowledge. According to Carnell, the collective-individual continuum is to do with the dynamics of teaching and learning. The objective-subjective continuum is to do with how knowledge is seen, that is, knowledge is either given or constructed. By considering teaching along two axes, the above-mentioned five categories of teachers' beliefs' are identified (Figure 2).

The construction of this model provides a framework within which to set out different teachers' beliefs both in Western European and Chinese university settings, rather than providing a rigid categorization to handle complexity. The continua are about educational beliefs and how knowledge is seen. The teacher collective-individual continuum is to do with the educational beliefs. The objective-subjective continuum is to do with how knowledge is seen, that is, knowledge is either given or constructed. In creating this model we do not wish to over-simplify. (Carnell, 2007) Actually, in practice, beliefs may overlap and teaching may not 'fit' into any one quadrant. It is important to point out that we do not believe that one kind of belief is necessarily more valuable than another, per se. However, the analysis of the data suggests that teachers' beliefs about teaching in higher education sit squarely in the teacher-centred and student-centred quadrant (community). Each kind of beliefs implies a different emphasis in purpose.

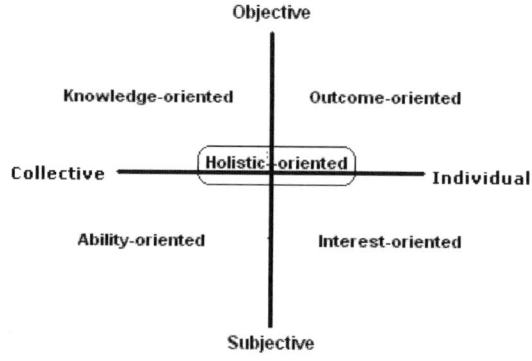

Figure 2. A two-way continuum of university teacher's beliefs

On the basis of the results of this study, it is not possible to make a generalization about the whole population of Chinese and Western European, especially Dutch, university teachers, because our sample consisted of a small number of universities and teachers. A large-scale study is needed to investigate whether these five categories can be found in the larger population. Other aspects worth investigating are the way or direction in which these teachers' beliefs changed and what cultural influences facilitate or hinder the understanding of university teaching in another culture.

References

Becher, T. (1989) Academic tribes and territories: Intellectual enquiry and the cultures of disciplines. Milton Keynes: SRHE and Open University Press.

Biggs, J. B. (1989) Approaches to the Enhancement of Tertiary Teaching. Higher Education Research and Development, 8, 7-26.

Brenda Rush & Janet H. Barke. (2006). Involving mental health service users in nurse education through enquiry-based learning. Nurse Education in Practice, 6(5): 254-260.

Christensen, C. A., Massey, D. R., Isaacs, P. J. and Synott, J. (1995) Beginning teacher education students' conceptions of teaching and approaches to learning. Australia Journal of Teacher Education, 20 (1), 19-29.

Carnell, E. (2007) Conceptions of effective teaching in higher education: extending the boundaries, Teaching in Higher Education, 12:1,25-40.

Correa, Christopher A. & Perry, Michelle et al. (2008). Connected and culturally embedded beliefs: Chinese and US teachers talk about how their students best learn mathematics. Teaching and Teacher Education, 24(2008), 140-153.

Cortazzi, M., & Jin, L. (1997). Communication for learning across cultures. In D. McNamara & R. Harris (Eds.), Overseas students in higher education: Issues in teaching and learning (pp. 76-90). London & New York: Routledge.

Dall'Alba, G. (1990) Foreshadowing conceptions of teaching. Research and Development in Higher Education, 13, 291-297.

Dunkin, M. J. and Precian, R. P. (1992) Award-winning university teachers' concepts of teaching. Higher Education, 24, 483-501.

Fang, Z. (1996). A review of research on teacher beliefs and practices. Educational Research, 38(1), 47–65.

Fox, D. (1983). Personal theories of teaching. Stud. Higher Educ. 8: 151–163. Gao, L. & Watkins, David A. (2001). Toward a model of teaching conceptions of Chinese secondary school teachers of physics. In D. A. Watkins & J. B. Biggs (Eds.), Teaching the Chinese learner: Psychological and pedagogical perspectives (pp.27-45). Hong Kong: Comparative Education Research Centre, The University of Hong Kong.

Gao, L.B. (2004) A study of Chinese Teachers' Conceptions of teaching. Wuhan: Hubei Education Press. 116.

Gow, L. and Kember, D. (1993) Conceptions of teaching and their relationship to student learning. British Journal of Educational Psychology, 63, 20-33.

Hall, E. T. (1976). Beyond culture. New York: Doubleday.

Hofstede, G., & Bond, M. H. (1984). Hofstede's culture dimensions: An independent validation using Rokeach's Value Survey. Journal of Cross-Cultural Psychology, 15(4), 417-433.

Hofstede, G. (2001). Culture's consequences: comparing values, behaviors, institutions and organizations across nations (2nd ed.). Thousand Oaks, CA; London: Sage.

Kember, D. & Gow, L. (1994) Orientations to teaching and their effect on the quality of student learning, Journal of Higher Education, 65, 58-74.

Kember, D. (1997). A reconceptualisation of the research into university academics' conceptions of teaching. Learning and Instruction, 7(3), 255-275.

Kim, Y. Y. (2002). Adapting to an unfamiliar culture. In W. B. Gudykunst & B. Mody (Eds.), Handbook of international and intercultural communication (2nd ed., pp. 259-274). Thousand Oaks, CA: Sage.

Lincoln, Y. S. & Guba, H. G. (1985) Naturalistic inquiry (Beverly Hills, CA, Sage). Martin, E. and Balla, M. (1990) Conceptions of teaching and implications for learning. Research and Development in Higher Education, 13, 298-304.

Martin, E. and Ramsden, P. (1992) An expanding awareness: How lecturers change their understanding of teaching; Conference Paper; Paper presented at the 1992 HERDSA Conference, Gippsland.

Miles, M. B. & Huberman, A. M. (1994). Qualitative data analysis (2nd ed.). Thousand Oaks, CA: Sage.

Mostyn, B. (1985). The Content Analysis of Qualitative Research Data: A Dynamic Approach. In M. Brenner et al (eds.) The Research Interview: Uses and Approaches. London: Academic Press.

Pickering, A.M. (2006). Learning about university teaching: reflections on a research study investigating influences for change. Teaching in Higher education, vol.11, (3), 319-335.

Pratt, D.D. (1992) Conceptions of teaching. Adult Education Quarterly, 42, 203-220.

Prosser, M., Trigwell, K. and Taylor, P. (1994) A phenomenographic study of academics' conceptions of science learning and teaching. Learning and Instruction, 4, 217-231.

Robson, C. (2002) Real World Research: A resource for social-scientists and practitioner researchers. 2 nd Edn. Oxford: Blackwell.

Samuelowicz, K. and Bain, J. D. (1992) Conceptions of teaching held by academic teachers. Higher Education, 24, 93-111.

Tanaka, J. (2002). Academic difficulties among East Asian international graduates: Influences of perceived English language proficiency and native educational/ socio-cultural background. Unpublished doctoral dissertation, Indiana University, Bloomington.

Ting-Toomey, S. (1999). Communicating across cultures. New York: Guilford. Trompenaars, F. (1993). Riding the waves of culture. London: Nicholas Brealey. Van Oudenhoven, J., & Eisses, A. (1988). Integration and assimilation of Moroccan immigrants in Israel and the Netherlands. International Journal of Intercultural Relations, 22, 293-307.

Trigwell, K., Prosser, M. and Taylor, P. (1994) Qualitative difference in approaches to teaching first year university science. Higher Education, 27, 75-84.

Walkner, P., & Finney, N. (1999). Skill development and critical thinking in higher education. Teaching in Higher Education, 4(4), 531-544.

Woodward, K. (2002). Understanding identity. London: Arnold.